FIRTHLANDS
OF
ROSS AND SUTHERLAND

Edited by

John R. Baldwin

Published in Scotland by:

The Scottish Society for Northern Studies
c/o School of Scottish Studies
University of Edinburgh
27 George Square
Edinburgh EH8 9LD

ISBN 0 9505994 4 1

The Scottish Society for Northern Studies gratefully acknowledges
financial assistance in the publication of this volume from

CALEDONIAN TOWAGE AND MARINE SERVICES LTD
HIGHLAND FABRICATORS LTD
HIGHLAND REGIONAL COUNCIL
T. D. HUNTER LTD (SUTHERLAND WOOL MILLS)
ROYAL COMMISSION ON THE ANCIENT AND HISTORICAL
MONUMENTS OF SCOTLAND
SUTHERLAND DISTRICT COUNCIL
and from its major commercial sponsor

BRITOIL plc

Text set throughout in 10 on 11 Sabon

Printed by W. S. Maney and Son Ltd Leeds England

CONTENTS

Cast-iron fountain, Portmahomack.

ACKNOWLEDGEMENT

We are indebted to all the contributors for giving so freely of their time and expertise, both at the Conference at Bonar Bridge in 1983 and to the present volume.

The Scottish Society for Northern Studies is also particularly grateful for photographs, plans and other illustrations to the Royal Commission on the Ancient and Historical Monuments of Scotland, the Royal Museum of Scotland, the Historic Buildings and Monuments Directorate of the Scottish Development Department, the National Galleries of Scotland, the National Library of Scotland, the Scottish Record Office, the Scottish Tourist Board, the Earl of Cromartie, Mr B. Urquhart of Craigston, Mrs H. Ross of Lochslin, Dr J. C. Close-Brookes, Mr J. Forsyth and Miss H. Hoare. Jane Davidson, formerly of the School of Scottish Studies, University of Edinburgh, very kindly re-typed several sections of the manuscript, and a number of illustrations were skilfully drawn or re-drawn by Douglas Lawson temporarily with the Scottish Wildlife Trust.

The Society is delighted to record financial assistance towards publication from Britoil plc, Highland Regional Council, Caledonian Towage and Marine Services Ltd (J. P. Knight Ltd), T. D. Hunter Ltd (Sutherland Wool Mills), Sutherland District Council, Highlands Fabricators Ltd. In addition, the Royal Commission on the Ancient and Historical Monuments of Scotland has most generously grant-aided the chapter by Mr G. Stell. To the Commission also, therefore, our most sincere thanks.

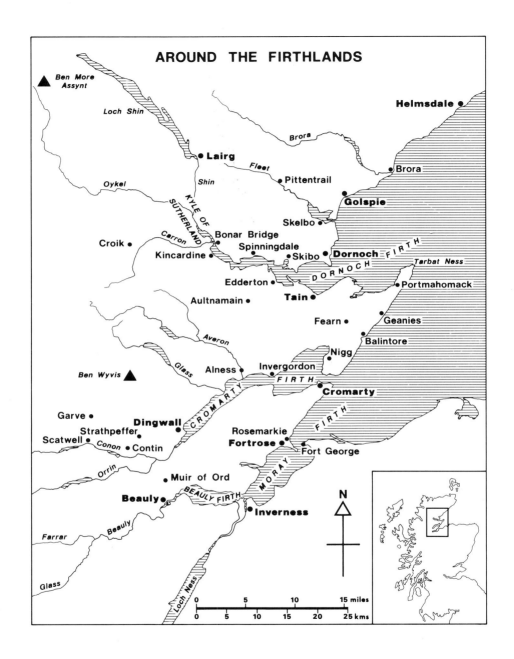

AROUND THE FIRTHLANDS

EDITOR'S PREFACE

'Firthlands' embraces those eastern lowlands clustered around the Dornoch, Cromarty, Beauly and Inner Moray Firths. *Firthlands of Ross and Sutherland* focuses more particularly on the gentle and fertile country around the Dornoch and Cromarty Firths — from Golspie and Loch Fleet in the north, to Bonar Bridge, Tain and the Easter Ross peninsula, across to Cromarty and the Black Isle, and up-firth to Dingwall and Muir of Ord.

Of the twelve contrasting chapters, one provides a broad geological background to the area and highlights landscape features as they have evolved through time — the Great Glen and Helmsdale Faults, glacially-deepened and drowned river valleys, raised beaches, wave-formed shingle barriers. And it is the underlying geology that gave rise to the shape of early habitational and communications networks, to the Brora coal-mines and to the spa waters of Strathpeffer, to stone and sand and gravel and peat for extraction, to the nature and balance of agricultural practice, to the oil and gas fields off the coast.

Such economic activity is most apparent for relatively recent times, so that six chapters concentrate on the seventeenth to early twentieth centuries. Some explore trade and family links across to Moray and the Baltic, as well as with other parts of Scotland and beyond; others concentrate on changes in settlement patterns, agriculture and stock-rearing, both in the firthlands and their highland hinterland; yet others are more concerned with a particularly rich architectural heritage. In each case, there is a weave between Highlander and Lowlander, spiced with the ever-increasing exposure of the north to southern influences and pressures. For the firthlands have long faced in multiple directions. Historically the Black Isle, for instance, and in particular its eastern edge, has been lowland and non-Gaelic in character; whilst the extended Easter Ross peninsula, in spite of a gentrified veneer of lowland ways, remained largely Gaelic in culture, reinforced by continuing immigration from the west. 'Lowland Highlanders', its inhabitants have been termed; 'Gaelickers' in Cromarty parlance, who saw their neighbours south of the Firth as 'no more than Lowland Bodies'. The most evident turn-about, however, is Inverness — a fully east coast and lowland burgh transformed through massive and sustained immigration into the undisputed capital of the Highlands.

The firthlands, then, are hardly 'highland' either geographically or, to some considerable degree, historically or culturally. But whilst so many influences would seem to have come from the south, this was not invariably so. Pictish sculptured stones and place-names are earlier instances of links across the Moray Firth certainly, but Norse place-names and traditions identify the area most distinctly as a 'southern outlier of Scandinavian Scotland'. Thus five chapters, in part or in whole, are concerned with the Norse and with their more identifiable influences on political and administrative structures, on ecclesiastical organization, on land-holding and place-naming.

From the ninth to the twelfth centuries, these low-lying peninsulas and waterways of the firthlands accommodated an intermingling of Picts and Norsemen increasingly infiltrated by Gaelic speakers from the west. They appear to have provided a zone of contact unique in Scotland, both culturally and politically; for although the traditional southern boundary of the Norse world came to be identified with the Dornoch Firth and *Ekkialsbakki*, Scandinavians settled successfully over the Easter Ross peninsula, along the northern edge at least of the Black Isle, and into Strath Conan beyond Dingwall — their place of legal assembly. Given the fertility of the firthlands, this need cause little surprise; strategically also, it was most attractive.

Yet if the Great Glen were of major importance for Norse communications with the southern Hebrides and beyond, there were equally good, more northerly routes direct to the west from Easter Ross. Perhaps the Conan River once provided a second, more shadowy frontier, following westwards by Strath Bran and giving access to evident Scandinavian interests around Gairloch, Loch Maree, Torridon and Loch Carron, with Raasay, Rona and Skye just beyond. It also gave direct access by Strath Garve to Loch Broom, that fjord-like sea loch opening westwards across the Minch to Lewis and Harris, and linked closely to the Kyle of Sutherland by Glen Achall and Strath Kanaird, Strath Oykell and Strath Carron. Place-name evidence suggests a marked Scandinavian presence along both the Oykell and the Carron (as rather more modestly along the Conan); such a presence is also evident beside Loch Broom, with its fine natural harbours and rare north-west mainland Norse settlement site (Ullapool). Other 'land use' names reinforce the impact of the Scandinavians here (Ristol, Calascaig, Langwell), together with a fairly plentiful scatter of topographical elements (Lael, Reiff, Kanaird, Raa, Oscaig, Sionascaig). And then there are the enigmatic Summer Isles in outer Loch Broom — of which Tanera, harbour island, is but one.

Here, on the north shore of the loch, the lands of Coigach for long lay apart from those to the south; they went with Assynt and the northern Hebrides rather than with geographical 'North Argyll' or the Lay Abbacy of Applecross, which embraced only the southern part of Lochbroom parish. Whilst there is no apparent evidence to suggest a cognate of Norwegian *Sunnmøre* as an origin for the name nowadays applied to the archipelago, nor is there any to deny the possible survival of a Norse geographical name or a Norse regional or territorial name subsequently attached to islands marking the southern limit. By contrast, the usual explanation — *na h-Eileanan Samhraidh* — runs counter to their traditional use for out-wintering stock at least as much for summer grazing. In an area where winter grazing was scarce, why emphasize so strongly their summer role? Is the Gaelic, therefore, a rationalization of what had become a meaningless earlier name? Did Loch Broom have a political and territorial significance for the Norse that we have not yet fully appreciated? What might its relationship have been with that east coast territorial marker, *Ekkialsbakki*?

What such links, actual and speculative, help confirm is that the eastern firthlands, distinctive and lowland though they are in many respects, cannot be divorced from the true Highlands. The two areas are inter-dependent. So it was that, in the east, Scandinavian settlers had their main farms and settlements in the fertile lowlands (Skibo, Torrobol, Arboll, Cadboll), exploiting shielings and other resources inland and upland (Linside, Bossett, Rossal, Soyal, Langwell, Alladale, Diebidale, Amat, Rusdale). So also, presumably, did the Picts before them; so also the indigenous farmers of later times; so also, to a degree, their east-coast improver successors who out-summered beef herds both inland and in the west. And by contrast, just as some improvers brought stocks back from the west for the winter, west-coast crofters have also sent their sheep to winter-grazing in Easter Ross.

Circumstances had changed, however. As economic revolution over-took the north from the eighteenth century, part of that wider Industrial Revolution affecting the whole of Britain, the land itself and its diverse resources came to be seen less as an 'item of assumed common inherit-ance', rather as an 'economic asset in terms of monetary rent'. Responsible and balanced exploitation of natural resources linked to local control was lost; wealth generated amongst the inhospitable hills and moorlands was all-too-often diverted to good living and investment elsewhere. Ironically this wealth helped create that fine architectural heritage that we value today — in Edinburgh and London, as well as in Easter Ross and East Sutherland; but the manner of much of its generation led to impoverish-ment of the land through over-grazing and over-burning, and impoverish-ment of the indigenous human resource through clearances and changes in the social order.

However wild today's highland 'wilderness', these moors and moun-tains are in so many respects as degraded and desolate as derelict industrial wasteland. Whether massed sheep, deer or conifers, such an approach to land-use was ever ecologically unsound; and it is rather to less intensive, diversified yet integrated and locally controlled patterns of land-use, blending the experience of tradition with the benefits of technology, that many are now looking to reverse the trends of two hundred and more years — to reverse the outward flow of resources, human or otherwise, and to improve the quality of life and environment in the north.

A far cry perhaps from the general tenor of this collection of essays? But may not *Firthlands of Ross and Sutherland* have more than an historical fascination and value? A balanced appreciation of past patterns of life and experience can contribute to a clearer evaluation of change and to socially and environmentally progressive policies for post-industrial man.

John R Baldwin
Edinburgh 1986

Fig. 1.1 Hugh Miller, from a D. O. Hill calotype *c.*1843.

GEOLOGY AND LANDSCAPE OF EASTER ROSS AND SUTHERLAND

Con Gillen

GEOLOGY AND PHYSICAL LANDSCAPE

A look at the geological map [Fig. 1.2] shows that the firthlands are surrounded by a great V-shaped swathe of Old Red Sandstone rocks. Only the Dornoch Firth breaks through and penetrates into the older underlying harder Moine schists. The Old Red Sandstone, well-known in the east coast towns from Inverness to Dornoch as a useful and distinctive building stone, was made famous by the researches of Hugh Miller [Fig. 1.1], the Cromarty stonemason whose birthplace is preserved by the National Trust for Scotland. He was a meticulous worker who accurately described, catalogued and figured his remarkable finds of fossil fish from the Black Isle [Fig. 1.3].

Moine Schist and Lewisian Gneiss

The oldest rocks of the area, the Moine schists, occur in the hinterland of the firths. These rocks represent shallow-water sandstones and shales which were folded and altered by high pressures and temperatures deep within the Earth's crust during the Caledonian mountain-building period, some 500 million years ago. The resulting crystalline metamorphic rocks are granular feldspar-bearing quartzites and mica schists, which often break into slab-like flagstones at the surface. Ben Wyvis which dominates the scenery north-west of the Cromarty Firth is made of Moine schist of high metamorphic grade; the main rock type is coarse-grained garnet-mica schist or gneiss.

Along the Moray Firth shore of the Black Isle and at the south-east end of the Tarbat Ness peninsula, outcrops of Moine schists occur that contain narrow slivers of older Lewisian Gneiss which have been deformed with the Moine rocks (Harris 1977) [Fig. 1.2]. The main outcrop of Lewisian Gneiss is in north-west Scotland and the Outer Hebrides. This rock probably forms the basement underlying the entire Scottish highlands, and it has been brought up as slices along the Great Glen Fault and interleaved with the Moine schist during the Caledonian mountain building event. Similar slices of banded quartz–feldspar–hornblende gneiss occur elsewhere along the Great Glen, notably on the shore of Loch Ness opposite the Abriachan granite (NH 585365). The North and South Sutors are made of hard flaggy Moine schist, which is rather crushed and invaded by granite veins and sheets which in turn have also been milled down and recrystallized. Behind these bosses of metamorphic rocks occur the softer

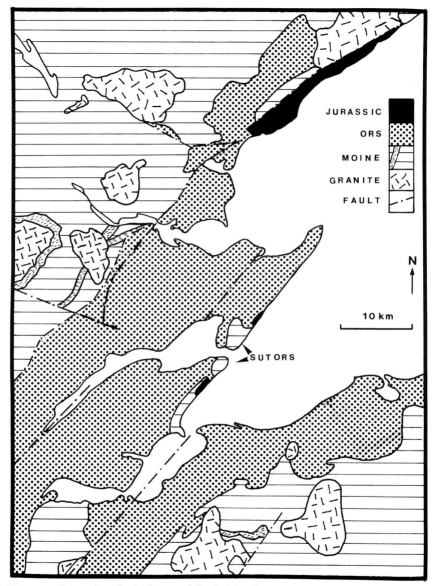

Fig. 1.2　General geological map of the firthlands.

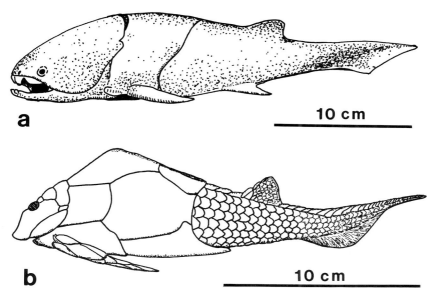

a

10 cm

b

10 cm

Fig. 1.3 Fossil fish, from the Old Red Sandstone (ORS) (a) *Coccosteus*, (b) *Pterichthys*.

sandstones of the Cromarty Firth. Reference will be made to the shape of this coastline in a later section.

Granite Intrusions

Large masses of molten granitic rock were intruded into the Moine schists at about 410 million years ago, just prior to the deposition of the Old Red Sandstone. The Fearn granite, for example, has supplied many boulders to the conglomerate at the base of the Old Red Sandstone. East of Bonar Bridge, the red colour of the Migdale granite is easily seen on crossing the bridge from the Ardgay side. The granite is made up of pink and white feldspar, clear quartz and black biotite. It is cut by many narrow (2–3 cm/1 in wide) veins of coarser granitic rock, referred to as pegmatite, which represent the last water-rich products of the cooling granite. Between Lairg and Rogart lies the Lairg or Rogart granite, the main mass of which forms rather low ground north of Strath Fleet. This rock is more properly referred to as granodiorite since it contains abundant dark minerals, biotite and hornblende, in addition to feldspar and quartz (see Brown 1983).

Old Red Sandstone

Rocks of Old Red Sandstone (or Devonian, 350–400 million years old) occupy a major NE–SW-trending synclinal fold, referred to as the Black Isle Syncline by Armstrong (1977) [Figs. 1.2; 1.4]. These sedimentary rocks

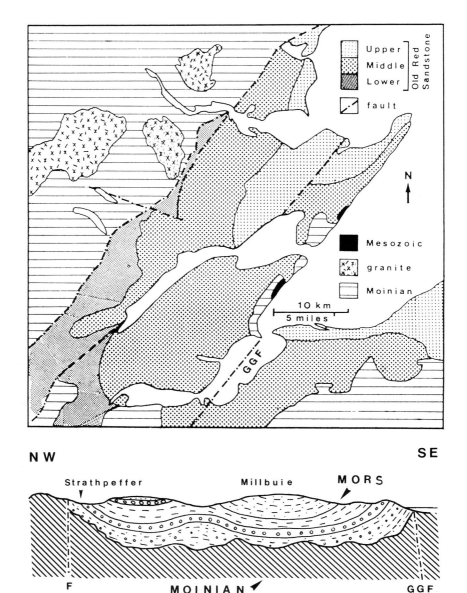

Fig. 1.4 Old Red Sandstone of the firthlands. Section shows Black Isle syncline (GGF: Great Glen Fault; MORS: Middle Old Red Sandstone).

4

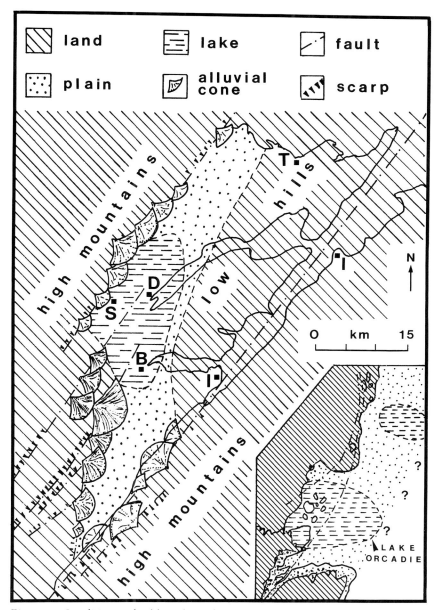

Fig. 1.5 Conditions of Old Red Sandstone (ORS) deposition. Post Devonian movement of 27 km on Great Glen Fault assumed (I: Inverness; B: Beauly; S: Strathpeffer; D: Dingwall; T: Tain). Inset shows extent of 'Lake Orcadie'.

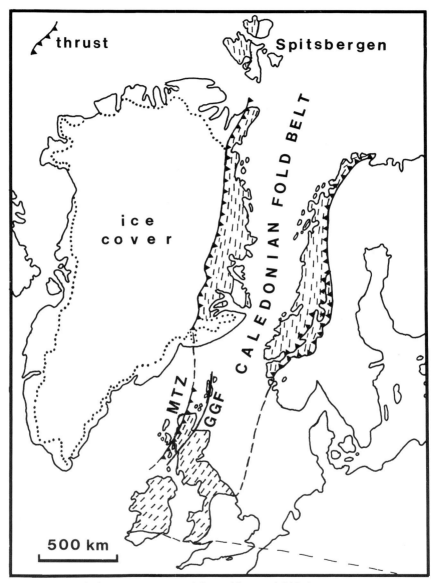

Fig. 1.6 Pre-drift reconstruction of the Caldonian fold belt.

became famous upon the discovery of fossil fish by Hugh Miller at Cromarty (NH 795673) and Ethie (NH 782642). Miller's various geological papers were collected and expanded into his book, *The Old Red Sandstone*, first published in 1841. The total thickness of the Old Red Sandstone succession in Easter Ross and the Black Isle is approximately 6,500 m (21,350 ft), made up of conglomerates, mudstones, sandstones and shales. The fish beds of Edderton, Cromarty and Balintore are Middle Old Red Sandstone calcareous shales, containing hard limey nodules with occasional fragments of primitive armour-plated fishes (mainly lustrous black scales) [Fig. 1.3].

The Old Red Sandstones are terrestrial in origin, having been laid down in the alluvial fans and on the floodplains of large meandering rivers which flowed off the young, high Caledonian mountains [Fig. 1.5]. Siltstones, shales and mudstones represent the deposits of shallow ephemeral lakes at the base of the mountain slopes. Some of these land-locked lakes became choked with sediment and decaying animal and vegetable matter. The Caledonian mountain range extended from Ireland and Wales through the Scottish Highlands, north to Shetland and north-east to Scandinavia, East Greenland and Spitzbergen [Fig. 1.6]. During the Lower Devonian, Britain lay at a latitude of 20°–30° S. Slow northward drift brought us to 10°–20° S by the end of the Devonian, some 350 million years ago (Mykura 1983). At that particular time, north-east Scotland lay in the lee of high mountains and had a hot dry climate, punctuated by torrential rainstorms which led to flash floods and the transport by intermittent rivers of the vast quantities of coarse sediment from the mountain scree slopes down onto the extensive plain at the foot of the mountain chain (Mykura & Owens 1983).

In Middle Devonian times the land sloped to the north-east and was cut by deeply incised rivers which flowed north-eastward onto the broad alluvial plains on the area in which today are found the firthlands (Mykura 1983). North of the firthlands lay the great land-locked lake or shallow inland sea known in the literature as the 'Orcadian' lake.

The Great Glen Fault

The Great Glen Fault is probably the single most important structural feature in the north of Scotland. The fault occupies a zone about a kilometre (0.6 mls.) wide along which considerable movement has taken place on several occasions during a long span of geological time, starting around 400 million years ago. Even today minor earthquakes are experienced in Inverness and other towns along the 90 km (56 mls.) of the Great Glen. During the last two centuries at least sixty earthquakes have been recorded along the fault (Wood 1978).

The Great Glen Fault is one of a set of near-parallel faults which cut the rocks of the highlands north and south of Glen More [Fig. 1.4]. The fault was initiated during the Caledonian mountain building event, long before the deposition of the Old Red Sandstone, and it remained a plane of weakness in the Earth's crust along which movement occurred in several different directions (Smith 1977; Mykura 1982, 1983). Crushing, fracturing and milling-down of rocks in the fault zone have resulted in material that has weathered more rapidly than the surrounding hard rocks, so that an early river valley was utilized by glaciers during the last ice age, and we are now left with a loch-filled long, narrow, deep valley.

While there are divergent opinions concerning movement on the Great Glen Fault, it is now accepted that the fault was initiated as a deep and fundamental structure before the deposition of Old Red Sandstone sediments. Basement rocks along the Great Glen display extensive shearing, cataclasis and recrystallization with the development of thick bands of mylonite (finely-banded fault rock, recrystallized from rock powder), indicating that the fault originated at deep levels within the crust (Smith 1977; Mykura 1983). Original attempts to determine the amount of movement on the fault were based on postulating a match between the Strontian granite at the south-west end and the Foyers granite at the north-east end of the fault. Other evidence includes matching structures, rock types and metamorphic grades in Moine schists, and when all this is taken into account we are left with the postulate that the Great Glen Fault is a sinistral (left-hand) transcurrent fault with a horizontal displacement of around 100 km (62 mls.). It should be emphasized, however, that the Great Glen follows not merely a simple transcurrent fault line, but a wide complex zone of thrusts and faults which were active at various times in the geological past.

In a recent study of the Old Red Sandstone rocks east of Loch Ness, Mykura (1982) draws attention to repeated differential vertical movements in the fault zone and along associated NE-trending faults during the deposition of the sediments, and to the existence of several compressive thrust faults and folds in the Foyers section. The conclusion is that there was a complex interplay of normal faulting, folding, thrusting and transcurrent movement in the Great Glen Fault zone in Devonian times. The Old Red Sandstone on Struie Hill, for instance, has been thrust over the underlying basement of Moine schists so that, looking up the hill from the 'Queen's View', the thrust plane can be clearly observed as a distinct near-horizontal break in slope. When the palaeogeography of Middle Old Red Sandstone rocks in the Moray Firth area is taken into account, the conclusion is reached that there was an overall dextral (right-hand) displacement along the Great Glen Fault of some 25–30 km (16–19 mls.) (Donovan et al. 1976; Smith 1977; Mykura 1982; Mykura & Owens 1983).

Evidence for movement along the Great Glen Fault zone in post-Devonian times is conflicting (Smith 1977). The concensus view, based on off-shore geophysical studies in the Moray Firth basin, is that during Mesozoic and early Tertiary times (190–55 million years ago), the Great Glen Fault behaved as one of a set of NE–SW fractures which partly controlled the location of sedimentary basins. The Jurassic sediments of the area have been affected by normal faults, with downthrow to the south-east (Bacon & Chesher 1975). Some reconstructions of the Great Glen Fault show it as continuing through the Walls Fault in central Shetland and on up to Spitzbergen, more than 1000 km (620 mls.) distant, but this correlation is uncertain and is disputed (Wood 1978; Mykura 1982).

The other major fault of the area is the Helmsdale Fault [Fig. 1.4], which brings Mesozoic rocks along the north coast of the Moray Firth down against older rocks (Old Red Sandstone, Moine schist and the Helmsdale Granite).

Mesozoic Rocks

Narrow outcrops of Mesozoic sediments occur along the coastal margins of the Moray Firth [Fig. 1.4]. An incomplete succession from Triassic (220 million years old) to Upper Jurassic (140 million years old) is found between Dunrobin and Helmsdale. Jurassic rocks are also present on the shore at Balintore and Ethie, while on the south coast of the Moray Firth a faulted succession of Permo-Triassic to Lower Jurassic sediments is exposed between Burghead and Lossiemouth.

The Jurassic rocks are mostly clays, shales, siltstones, sandstones and occasional beds of nodular limestone and ironstone. Fossils are fairly abundant, and include ammonites, lamellibranchs and plant fragments [Fig. 1.7]. At Brora, bituminous shales are overlain by a one metre (3.3 ft) thick coal seam which was worked for many years. Being a young coal, it is poor quality, with high water, gas and sulphur content. The depositional environment of these Middle to Upper Jurassic sediments is interpreted to have been a sandy shallow-water delta at Brora, and a deeper-water thin shaly sequence at Balintore (Chesher & Lawson 1983).

At Ethie and Balintore, the topmost Jurassic sediments consist of Kimmeridgian (around 137 million years old) carbonaceous shales, sandstones, grits and thin limestones. Between Brora and Helmsdale, the Kimmeridgian is represented by 60 m (20 ft) of thick sandstone units with shaly partings, overlain by 500 m (1,640 ft) of carbonaceous shales, flagstones and grits with many prominent boulder beds. Fossil evidence (the plants in the Brora coal beds for instance) indicates that the climate at the time was probably subtropical. These boulder beds contain large blocks of Old Red Sandstone, similar to rocks that occur *in situ* near Dunbeath, over 20 km (13 mls.) to the north. During late Jurassic times, large-scale normal faults developed during a period of rifting in the North Sea, with the formation of deep marine sedimentary basins. The margin of one such basin is defined by the Helmsdale Fault [Fig. 1.4]. Subsidence on the south-eastern side of this fault led to a fault scarp, down which masses of sediment flowed as debris accumulations, rock falls and mud-charged rapid turbidity currents (Pickering 1984). As the submarine slope built up, the uncompacted soft sediments were redeposited by sliding. Underwater channels were cut deeply into the slope and infilled with coarse-grained clastic sediments [Fig. 1.8]. The Helmsdale Fault continued to move as

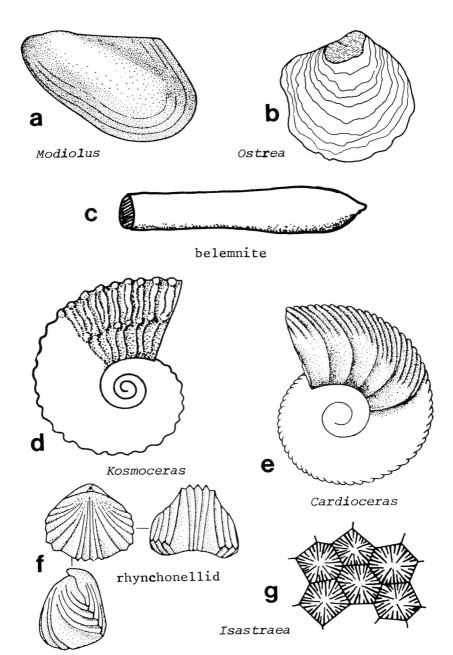

Fig. 1.7 Fossils of Jurassic age: (a, b) bivalves, (c) mollusc, (d, e) ammonites, (f) brachiopod, (g) coral.

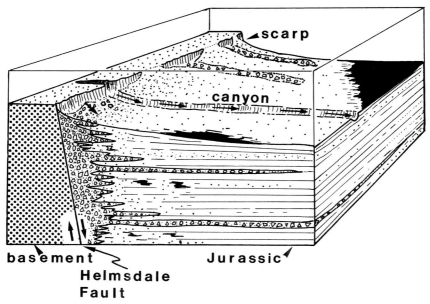

Fig. 1.8 Submarine fans along the Helmsdale Fault in Jurassic times (after Pickering, 1984).

sediment accumulated, and the regional structural pattern is of large-scale differential subsidence accompanied by the deposition of thick organic-rich muds which are locally interbedded with deposits of mass-flow and landslip origin, derived from adjacent rising fault-bounded blocks of crust (Anderton et al. 1979).

In the centre of the North Sea the Jurassic succession is some 2,300 m (7,550 ft) thick (Chesher & Lawson 1983), which is one of the thickest occurrences in the North Sea. The rock types there are alternating sandstones and shales, which overlie Permo-Triassic beds; they dip gently to the north-east. Black shales and siltstones of Lower Cretaceous age overlie Upper Jurassic Kimmeridgian beds in the North Sea. The Upper Cretaceous white chalk with flints is present in the east of the Moray Firth, where it extends over the entire width of the area. Upper Cretaceous chalk occurs on the sea bed north of Fraserburgh and east of Wick (Chesher & Lawson 1983).

The Moray Firth Basin

The Mesozoic basin of the Moray Firth was more or less coincident with the older Old Red Sandstone Orcadian basin. Mesozoic rocks are mostly marine and deltaic, whereas the Old Red Sandstone deposits are continental and lacustrine. The present-day coastline of the south Moray Firth marks the limit of the Mesozoic basin. Fault lines define the margins of the basin [Fig. 1.2], with Mesozoic strata being downfaulted against the Old Red Sandstone. Within the basin, sediments have been affected by normal faulting which was active during sedimentation, particularly in the Jurassic, and resulting in the formation of a series of fault-bounded rift valleys (grabens) and upstanding blocks (horsts). A major syncline (down-fold) is present along the line of the Great Glen Fault, which was active as a normal fault during the Mesozoic. Other major faults of the area moved during Mesozoic times along reactivated lines of weakness that were initiated in the Old Red Sandstone era, towards the end of the Caledonian orogeny (mountain-building period) or earlier (Watson 1984). Mesozoic sediments piled up thickly in the Moray Firth basin to the south of the Great Glen Fault, on its downthrow side (Chesher & Lawson 1983).

DEVELOPMENT OF THE LANDSCAPE

Tertiary Erosion

The present landscape which we see in the area of the firthlands began to be developed during Tertiary times, around 30 million years ago, when Scotland was repeatedly uplifted in a series of pulses and the land surface was deeply eroded. The drainage system of Scotland became established in the Tertiary, and great rivers flowed eastwards across the easterly-dipping tilted land surface of the highlands to the North Sea [Fig. 1.9]. During Tertiary and Quaternary times the area of the North Sea was subjected to deep and rapid subsidence (Anderton et al. 1979). Sediments of Tertiary age are absent from the land area of north-east Scotland, whereas large volumes of muddy, shaly and silty sediments were supplied to the subsiding trough of the North Sea in the form of large deltas and submarine fans. The Hebridean west coast of Scotland was an area of volcanic activity at the time, and humid tropical climatic conditions prevailed.

The long east-flowing streams cut discordantly across the major structures of the Moine schists, and for this reason the initial drainage pattern is considered to be superimposed on the geology due either to rapid uplift and the removal of a once-extensive cover of sediments (Sissons 1967), or to the emergence of a marine-planed surface from beneath the sea (George 1965). Dissection of the surface by rivers and later by the Pleistocene ice sheet resulted in the isolation of high residual hills, such as Ben Wyvis (1,047m: 3,433ft) from the main massif of the Scottish Highlands [Fig. 1.9]. West and north of Ben Wyvis the mountains are eroded into a dissected plateau, with erosion surfaces at different heights (George 1965; Sissons 1967).

Glacial Erosion

During the last two-and-a-half million years, cold waters have pushed southwards from the polar ice cap more than twenty times and large ice-sheets have built up on adjacent land masses in the North Atlantic region.

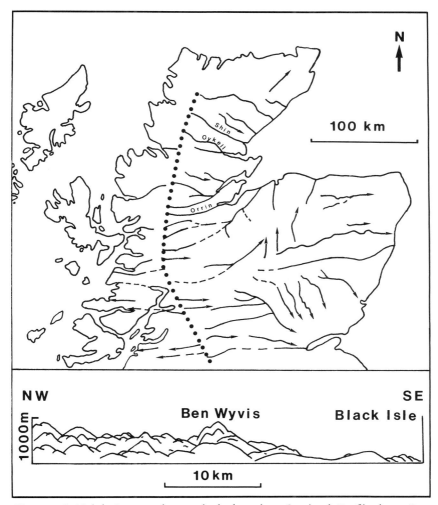

Fig. 1.9 Initial drainage and watershed of northern Scotland. Profile shows Ben Wyvis as a residual hill.

The mountainous areas of Britain became the centres of growth and as the climate deteriorated and arctic conditions set in, the mountain glaciers merged into an ice-cap and ice-sheets advanced over the lowlands. Ice-sheets well over 1,000 m (4,000 ft) thick covered most of Britain during the extensive early glaciations. The huge Scandinavian ice-sheet crossed the North Sea depression and came against the Scottish ice-sheet just off the north-east coast [Fig. 1.10]. It was not until a mere 10,000 years ago that the last ice-sheet melted from the Scottish Highlands.

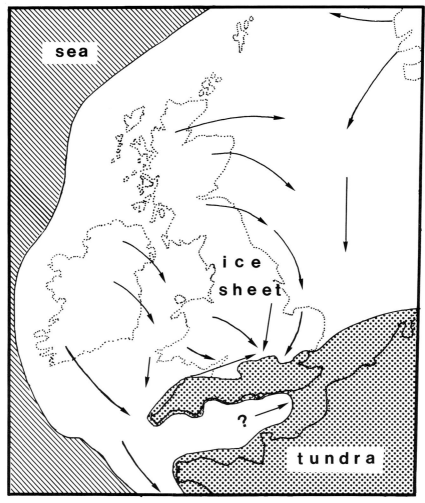

Fig. 1.10 Extent of the ice-sheet during the Pleistocene glaciation. Arrows show flow directions.

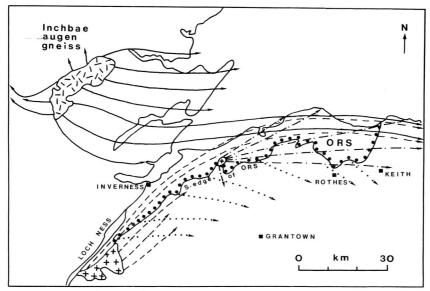

Fig. 1.11   Distribution of ice-carried erratics (ORS: Old Red Sandstone).

Many of the characteristic landscape features of the Highlands were produced by glacial erosion. As ice-sheets moved over the surface and down old river valleys, loose scree and alluvium were picked up and embedded in the base of the advancing glacier, which subsequently scraped, moulded and polished the bedrock. Glaciated valleys are now straighter than the original river valleys and tend to have steep sides and wide U-shaped profiles, in contrast to the more typical V-shaped valleys of mountain streams. The ice-sheets covered all but the highest areas of the Highlands and produced a smoother and more rounded landscape. It is not certain if Ben Wyvis was completely submerged beneath ice, though small semi-circular steep-walled corries are present on the mountain. These mark the birthplaces of glaciers which eventually outgrew their corries and flowed steadily down pre-existing river valleys. Glacial striae or scratch marks are not often preserved on the soft Old Red Sandstones, but some examples are to be found on rocks in the Black Isle, such as at Culbokie village, facing the Cromarty Firth.

Ice moved north-eastwards along the Great Glen and gouged out the rock basin of Loch Ness. Towards the Moray Firth this valley glacier was deflected eastwards on meeting a more powerful and larger ice-sheet that flowed eastwards from Ross-shire. Erratic boulders of the highly distinctive Inchbae augen gneiss were carried by the ice and are now widely distributed through Easter Ross, except on the summit of Ben Wyvis [Fig. 1.11].

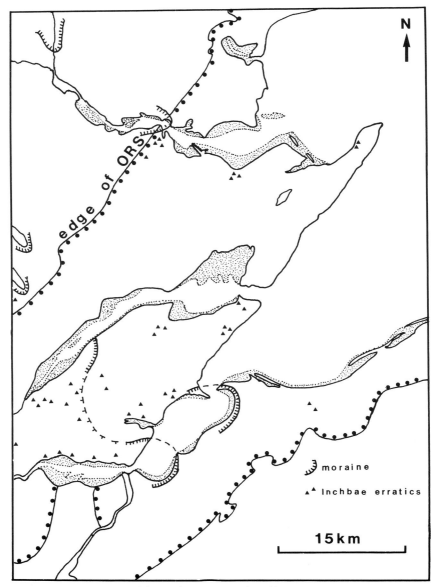

Fig. 1.12 Recent coastal forms, moraines and Inchbae augen gneiss erratics.

The Beauly, Cromarty and Dornoch firths are glacially over-deepened and drowned ancient river valleys. The presence of hard crystalline Moine schist and granite at the Sutors of Cromarty caused the ice to excavate more deeply into the softer Old Red Sandstone in the inner Cromarty Firth, which was considerably widened [Fig. 1.12]; eventually the ice broke through the Moine rocks and created a narrow entrance to the firth. An example exists at Balintraid [NH 744719], 6 km west of the Sutors, of deeply weathered sandstone similar in nature to other sites in north-east Scotland of deep glacial erosion (Smith 1977).

Fluvio-Glacial Deposition

Around the firths the low-lying land was scraped and smoothed by the ice-sheet, then largely covered by extensive sheets of glacial and fluvio-glacial drift (or moraine) deposited beneath and at the edges of the moving ice or left behind after the ice had melted and disappeared. Extensive sheets of fluvio-glacial material flank the shores of the Moray Firth.

The direction of meltwater flow on the northern side of the Moray Firth was controlled by the underlying shape of the topography. Near Dornoch and between Golspie and Brora are long sinuous mounds of fluvio-glacial sands and gravels termed eskers. Eskers record the courses of meltwater streams that flowed in tunnels beneath the ice. Systems of eskers run down Strath Brora along the northern shores of the Dornoch Firth towards Dornoch, while meltwater channels run parallel to the NE–SW strike of the Old Red Sandstone rocks in the coastal area around the firth [Fig. 1.12]. Large meltwater channels at Struie record meltwater flow from the Dornoch Firth into Strathrory, then into the Pitmaduthy esker system near Nigg Bay [NH 775765] (Smith 1977). The erosive effects of meltwater streams are well illustrated in the gorge of the River Beauly at the Falls of Kilmorack. The gorge has been cut into the basal conglomerates of the Old Red Sandstone and right down to Moine schist. The famous Black Rock gorge of Novar, near Evanton [NH 589668] is an extremely narrow, deep cleft in Old Red Sandstone conglomerate which formed in post-glacial times during a period of rapid uplift. Sediment-laden torrential meltwater cut swiftly through the rock like a saw.

An atypical landform between Ardersier and Chanonry Ness near Fortrose in the inner Moray Firth has been described by Smith (1977) as a glacial re-advance moraine, made of unsorted mixed boulders and cobbles overlain by beach deposits and formed at the front of a lobe of ice which locally advanced westwards from the retreating ice-sheet in a cold episode. The bluffs of the Ardersier-Fortrose moraine were subsequently washed by a late-glacial marine transgression and then extended by post-glacial seas to form the present-day cuspate shape of the foreland [Fig. 1.12]. Terraces at Edderton may represent the same phase in the Dornoch Firth. Smith (1977) reports that there is some morphological evidence for an ice margin in the area around Culbokie on the Black Isle.

Boulder clay was deposited directly by the ice and consists of boulders of mixed size, shape and rock type held together by a matrix of sticky grey, red or yellowish clay, the clay representing rotted and milled-down rock particles. The widespread covering of boulder clay throughout most of the Black Isle gives rise to smooth, undulating topography. The red to yellowish colour of much of the glacial and fluvio-glacial sediment indicates a local origin from the underlying Old Red Sandstone. Erratic blocks, however, are widespread throughout the north-east. These are ice-transported rounded boulders, cobbles and pebbles which have been moved some considerable distance and it is often the case that they can be matched with a unique rock outcrop, so allowing the path of ice movement to be traced. One such example is the Inchbae augen gneiss, referred to above, boulders of which have been found at Bonar Bridge [Fig. 1.11]. Erratics from Scandinavia have also been found around the coastline of north-east Scotland, indicating transport from at least 500 km (310 mls.) away by the Scandinavian ice-sheet.

Evidence for the decay of the ice-sheet is shown in the Black Isle in the form of successive moraine stripes and gravel ridges which run obliquely to the contours on the hillside overlooking the Cromarty Firth. These mounds and ridges slope gradually and increasingly towards the firth in a more or less concentric arrangement that marks successive stages in the retreat of the ice. The mounds are themselves truncated and form bluffs overlooking the 30 m (100 ft) post-glacial raised beach.

Raised Beaches

Well-marked terraces standing at heights up to about 30 m (100 ft) above sea level form a conspicuous feature along the shores of the northern firths. These terraces which skirt the shores mark the position of the sea at the end of the ice age. For when the glaciers had finally melted, the sea level rose for a time and drowned much of the coastal lowlands. At its maximum extent, the ice-sheet was over 1,000 m (4,000 ft) thick, and this enormous weight led to the land being somewhat depressed. Once the ice melted and the load was removed, the land surface began to adjust and started rising again (most rapidly where the ice was thickest) towards its pre-glacial level, so that the higher post-glacial seas began to retreat. Raised beaches with low cliffs, old caves and boulder deposits are well-preserved around the Beauly Firth and on the Tarbat Ness peninsula. Notable examples are at North Kessock and Hilton of Cadboll. Two levels at around 15 m (50 ft) and 30 m (100 ft) are seen at Munlochy in the south-east of the Black Isle. On the raised beach terraces are stratified deposits of marine sand, gravel and clay. Various levels between 15 m and 30 m have been recorded, particularly around the Beauly Firth, but usually they can be traced for only short distances and indicate a gradual uplift of the land, punctuated by occasional stand-stills when the sea was able to erode a more or less conspicuous notch into the boulder clay or the Old Red Sandstone.

The railway between Beauly and Muir of Ord crosses the wide terrace formed by the highest raised beach at the head of the Beauly Firth. The 30 m raised beach is also well-developed around the head of the Cromarty Firth, and it extends inland along the River Conon where it merges with a

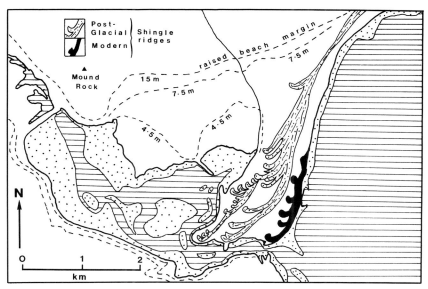

Fig. 1.13   Shingle ridges of Loch Fleet.

large ice-marginal delta (Synge 1977). On the Black Isle it forms a terrace about 500 m (1,640 ft) wide which increases in width inland. This particular terrace is made up of finely laminated light-brown clays and fine silty sand, giving rise to well-drained, good quality soils. On the north side of the firth the same beach terrace is much narrower. It extends up the valley almost as far as Strathpeffer itself, where again good arable land results. The glacial beach deposits at Strathpeffer contain sea shells (cockles, mussels and periwinkles) and whale bones. Raised beaches at 15 m (50 ft) and 7.5 m (25 ft) levels are found around the firths. Beauly stands on the wide 7.5 m terrace which is composed of marine alluvium: finely laminated grey and yellow clays with beds of sand and fine gravel. Shell banks occur within these sediments, containing remains of estuarine and shallow-water species that still exist today. Around Dingwall it is this same 7.5 m beach which gives rise to the widest extent of carse land. Raised beaches are discussed in greater detail in the paper by Synge (1977).

Loch Fleet, south of Golspie, was formed in post-glacial times when a shingle barrier was built up by wave action across the estuary of the River Fleet. The barrier is constructed of many shingle ridges, each 2–3 m (6.5–10 ft) high, which form a curved spit of land built out southwards from Golspie [Fig. 1.13]. Today the ridges are higher than and farther back from the sea, the highest parts being 10–11 m (33–36 ft) above sea-level. A number of other shingle spits are found a little to the south. Cuthill Links, Ferry Point and Ardjachie Point in the Dornoch Firth are raised post-glacial spit complexes made of well-rounded cobbles and pebbles with interlaminated lenses of coarse sand and occasional shell banks, now colonized by coastal plants and grasses. During the highest of the post-glacial sea levels there was a sea connection between the Cromarty and Dornoch Firths.

Formation of the Coast

The generally rectilinear north-east coast, in stark contrast to Scotland's highly indented west coast, depends for its origin on the underlying rocks. The NE–SW shape is parallel to the Caledonian 'grain' of the country rock, and in particular the coasts of the Black Isle and the Tarbat Ness peninsula facing the Moray Firth have been formed at the edge of the Great Glen Fault Zone [Fig. 1.4]. The eastern coastlands have been excavated from Old Red Sandstone in the main, a relatively uniform rock that extends from Orkney and Caithness southwards then eastwards along the Moray Firth. The relief around the firthlands is of a relatively uniform, low undulating plateau cut by broad valleys. Many of the shorelines are constructional, with wave action shaping the glacial deposits into long sandy beaches. Sand barriers erected by the wind since post-glacial times have caused the foreland of Morrich Mhor near Tain [NH 845855] to advance out into the firth as the higher post-glacial sea level fell; the Whiteness Sands have advanced and resulted in Tain harbour being silted-up (Whittow 1977; Ogilvie 1923); the landward margin of the Morrich Mhor is a sea-cliff cut in red boulder clay, and forms part of the 7.5 m (25 ft) raised beach.

Although some of his conclusions concerning post-glacial sea levels are questioned by Synge (1977), Ogilvie (1923) has presented a very detailed study of the coastal morphology of the Moray Firth. He considered the Dornoch Firth to be composed of three distinct segments:

(1) An 'inner firth' to the west of Struie Hill and Spinningdale. This 17 km (10.6 mls.) section consists of a steep-walled trough cut in Moine schist and overdeepened by glacial erosion. Five separate alluvial fans project into the firth, built out by stream deposition.

(2) The 'middle firth', bordered by dissected terraces, largely of glacial meltwater origin. The entire feature may have been a continuous surface of fluvio-glacial outwash.

(3) An 'outer firth', where the evolution of the coastline is mainly attributable to erosion of Old Red Sandstone rocks and the formation of marine constructions. At Cuthill Links, for example, much of the original shingle surface is overlain by recent sand dunes.

ECONOMIC GEOLOGY

The Old Red Sandstone of the area was once extensively quarried as a freestone for building construction, but this industry has now disappeared. Flagstones of Moine schist were once extracted at the Raven Rock, Strathpeffer, for local building purposes; quarries in the granites are also long abandoned. However, the extensive sand and gravel deposits are still being extracted on a massive scale for use as road metal and concrete aggregate.

The Brora coal has ceased to be worked, likewise the brick clays with which it was associated. Mineral veins are not of sufficient extent in the area to be commercially viable. Horne and Hinxman (1914) mention in their memoir that veins of silver-bearing galena, zinc blende, baryte and calcite occur in fault lines cutting the Moine schists in Strath Glass, and lead mines operated for a time during the first half of the last century.

It goes without saying that the greatest economic asset in the north-east is provided by the considerable deposits of oil and gas in the North Sea basin. Production is currently running at nearly 100 million tonnes per annum, with estimated recoverable reserves put at 2,000–4,300 million tonnes (Duff 1983). Most of the hydrocarbon deposits have been found within or around graben structures (down-faulted blocks containing thick accumulations of sedimentary rocks), though one exception is the Beatrice Field in the Moray Firth Basin where drilling platforms can be seen from the land north of Helmsdale. The source-rock for most of the oil seems to be the Kimmeridge Clay of Jurassic age, which is a black kerogen-rich mudstone. Oil occurs in traps beneath Jurassic to Tertiary shales, whereas gas is usually restricted to the Palaeocene (Lower Tertiary, 63 million years old). The source of the gas is also likely to be deeply-buried Kimmeridge Clay. Reservoir rocks are mostly sandstones of Jurassic or Tertiary age, with oil occurring in tilted fault-block traps.

Peat is another important fuel resource which is widespread as a blanket bog type of deposit in the upland areas adjacent to the firths. The Aultnabreac deposit is being exploited using mechanized methods, and there is renewed interest in the possible viability of small-scale peat-fired electricity-generating plants in various parts of the Highlands.

For over two hundred years Strathpeffer has been renowned as a spa resort on account of its natural mineral waters. Interest has declined of late, however, and the dozen or so springs which emerge from bedding planes of rocks or along fault lines at the surface are no longer of commercial use. The sulphurous spring waters, whose underground circulation is not very deep-seated (Horne and Hinxman 1914), emerge from fetid shales of Old Red Sandstone age; chalybeate springs (containing iron salts, especially carbonate) issue from glacial deposits and from muscovite-biotite gneiss in the Moine rocks (Phemister 1960).

Acknowledgement

Figure 1.1 is reproduced by kind permission of the Scottish National Portrait Gallery, Edinburgh.

References

Anderton, R., Bridges, P. H., Leeder, M. R. & Sellwood, B. W. *A Dynamic Stratigraphy of the British Isles — A Study in Crustal Evolution.* 1979.

Armstrong, M. The Old Red Sandstone of Easter Ross and the Black Isle, in Gill, G. ed. *The Moray Firth Area Geological Studies*. 1971: 25–34.

Bacon, M. & Chesher, J. A. Evidence against post-Hercynian transcurrent movement in the Great Glen Fault, in *Scott. J. Geol*. 1975. vol. II(1): 79–82.

Brown, P. E. Caledonian and earlier magmatism, in Craig, G. Y. ed. *Geology of Scotland*. 2nd ed. 1983: 167–204.

Chesher, J. A. & Lawson, D. The geology of the Moray Firth, in *Rep. Inst. Geol. Sci*. 1983. no. 83/5.

Craig, G. Y. ed. *Geology of Scotland*. 2nd ed. 1983.

Donovan, R. N., Archer, A., Turner, P. & Tarling, D. H. Devonian Palaeogeography of the Orcadian Basin and the Great Glen Fault, in *Nature*. 1976. vol. 259: 550–51.

Duff, P. McL. D. Economic geology, in Craig, G. Y. ed. *Geology of Scotland*. 2nd ed. 1983: 425–54.

George, T. N. The geological growth of Scotland, in Craig, G. Y. ed. *The Geology of Scotland*. 1st ed. 1965: 1–49.

Gill, G. ed. *The Moray Firth Area Geological Studies*. 1977.

Harris, A. L. Metamorphic rocks of the Moray Firth district, in Gill, G. ed. *The Moray Firth Area Geological Studies*. 1977: 9–24.

Horne, J. & Hinxman, L. W. The geology of the country around Beauly and Inverness, including a part of the Black Isle (explanation of sheet 83), in *Mem. Geol. Surv. Scotland*. 1914.

Mykura, W. The Old Red Sandstone east of Loch Ness, Inverness-shire, in *Rep. Inst. Geol. Sci*. 1982. no. 82/13.

Mykura, W. Old Red Sandstone, in Craig, G. Y. *Geology of Scotland*. 2nd ed. 1983: 205–52.

Mykura, W. & Owens, B. The Old Red Sandstone of the Mealfuarvonie Outlier, west of Loch Ness, Inverness-shire, in *Rep. Inst. Geol. Sci*. 1983. no. 83/7.

Ogilvie, A. G. The physiography of the Moray Firth coast, in *Trans. Roy. Soc. Edinb*. 1923. vol. 53: 377–404.

Phemister, J. *Scotland: the Northern Highlands*. (British Regional Geology). 3rd ed. 1960.

Pickering, K. T. The Upper Jurassic 'Boulder Beds' and related deposits: a fault-controlled submarine slope, NE Scotland, in *Jl Geol. Soc*. 1984. vol. 141(2): 357–74.

Sissons, J. B. *The Evolution of Scotland's Scenery*. 1967.

Smith, D. I. The Great Glen Fault, in Gill, G. ed. *The Moray Firth Area Geological Studies*. 1977: 46–59.

Synge, F. M. Land and sea level changes during the waning of the last regional ice sheet in the vicinity of Inverness, in Gill, G. ed. *The Moray Firth Area Geological Studies*. 1977: 83–102.

Watson, J. V. The ending of the Caledonian orogeny in Scotland, in *Jl Geol. Soc*. 1984. vol. 141(2): 193–214.

Whittow, J. B. *Geology and Scenery in Scotland*. 1977.

Wood, R. M. *On the Rocks — a Geology of Britain*. 1978.

NORSE AND CELTIC PLACE-NAMES AROUND THE DORNOCH FIRTH

Ian A. Fraser

The Dornoch Firth is perhaps the most important topographic feature of this part of eastern Scotland. It is divisive in terms of both topography and history since it is a natural barrier between Ross and Sutherland, and even if it is no longer significant in political terms there can be no doubt that it proved to be exactly that in past times. Nevertheless, Norse place-names successfully bridged the Dornoch Firth to establish themselves in Ross, so that parishes such as Tarbat, Fearn, Nigg, Edderton and Kincardine display some of the Norse elements that are to be found across the Firth in Sutherland, albeit in smaller numbers and in less variety.

The peninsula between the Firths of Dornoch and Cromarty is largely undulating and low-lying, with a variety of topography, and potentially fertile. It has much in common with the Moray Firth coastlands in this respect, and the presence of Pictish place-name elements in the area is a link with the littoral to the south. It can truly be said that here the place-names of both Picts and Norse intermingle in what must have been a zone of contact between the two peoples, with a later, Gaelic element being introduced as Pictish power declined in the ninth century. Certainly no other area of Scotland can present us with such an interface, so the Easter Ross peninsula is worthy of detailed investigation, if for this reason alone. Moreover, the archaeological remains left by the Picts in the area provide useful comparative material [Figs. 2.1–2.3].

Sutherland and Ross have had widely varying treatment by place-name scholars. W. J. Watson's *Place-Names of Ross and Cromarty* (1904) is a valuable reference, which is unsurpassed elsewhere in the north. Sutherland can boast of no such comprehensive survey, although John Mackay's series of articles in the *Transactions of the Gaelic Society of Inverness* (1888–94) does attempt to tackle the place-names of much of Sutherland on a parish basis. This has many suspect derivations, which is not surprising since it comes from the pen of an amateur writing nearly a century ago. Watson himself wrote a brief article entitled 'Some Sutherland names of places' in the *Celtic Review* of 1905–06, which is well up to his usual standards, although fairly limited in scope.

PICTISH NAMES

These are, as one might expect, relatively infrequent in the area [Fig. 2.4]. Apart from those containing the habitative element *pit-*, 'share', 'portion', of which there are four in Sutherland and six in Easter Ross, the only other

Fig. 2.1 Pictish Symbol Stone, Hilton of Cadboll (in Royal Museum of Scotland, Edinburgh).

Fig. 2.2   Pictish Symbol Stone, Golspie
(in Dunrobin Museum).

Fig. 2.3   Pictish Symbol Stone, Ardross No. 1 — Sittenham (in Inverness
Museum).

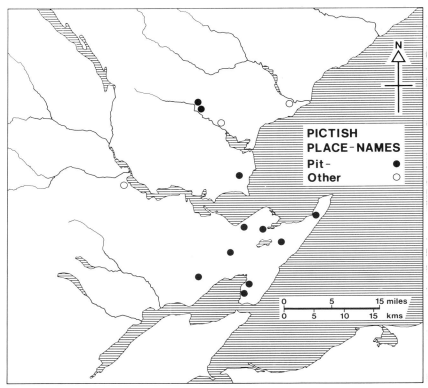

Fig. 2.4   Pictish place-name elements around the Dornoch Firth.

significant examples contain *dol*, 'meadow', *aber*, 'confluence', and *cardden*, 'thicket', 'wood'. The other important name is *Oykel*, suggested by Watson as originating in the Early Celtic *uxellas*, 'high', which became *uckel* or *uchel* by the Norse period. *Strath-ochell* 1490, *Kill-ochell* 1582 and *Strath-okell* 1582 are the earliest documentary forms which we have, apart from the *Orkneyinga Saga* reference to *Ekkjall* and *Ekkjallsbakki*, 'Oykel-bank' (Watson 1926. 209). There seems little doubt that this place referred to in the saga is the Oykel, and it reinforces the suggestion that the valley is one which is part of a frontier zone. In any case, there are Norse names in some numbers in Strath Oykell.

The names in *pit-* show similarities to examples further south, in the Pictish heartland. Many contain qualitative elements which are clearly Gaelic, or which have close Gaelic parallels. *Pitfour* in Rogart becomes Gaelic '*Baile-phùir*', from G. *pòr*, W. *pawr*, 'grazing-land', 'pasture-land'. *Pitmean* is 'mid-share'; *Pitgrudie* may be compared with the river-name *Grudie* in Ross, which Watson reads as G. *grùidich*, 'gravelly-water'. *Pitarxie* remains obscure.

26

Across the Firth, the Ross-shire *pit-* names include *Pithogarty* in Tain (*Petogarthe* 1548, *Pettogarty* 1560), 'the priest's share'; *Pitnellies* in Tain, a pluralised form which points to the fact that there were originally two — north and south — originating in G. *ianlaith*, 'birds', giving 'stead of the birds'; *Pitculzean* in Nigg, 'share of the little wood'; *Pitcalnie* in the same parish, of obscure origin; *Pitkerrie* in Fearn (*Pitkeri* 1529), perhaps from G. *ciar*, 'dark'; and *Pitmaduthy* (*Pitmadwy* 1370, *Pettecowy* 1578), 'Macduff's share', in Logic Easter.

Of the other identifiably Pictish names, *Aberscross* at the mouth of Strath Fleet may contain *aber*, 'confluence'. If so, the second element is obscure. *Doll* in Clyne is the equivalent of Gaelic *an Dail*, 'the meadow' or 'the valley', but must be pre-Gaelic. There are many parallels, including *Dull* near Aberfeldy, for example. This element becomes *dail* in Gaelic, and occurs throughout Gaelic Scotland as a settlement name, from Sutherland to Galloway. But it also appears as a simplex in such cases as *Doll* and *Dull*, and these are usually regarded as indicative of Pictish rather than Gaelic presence (see Watson 1926. 414–19). The name *Dallas* in Edderton is a variant form, *daláis*, which comes from a compound of *dul* or *dol*, and O.Ir. *foss*, 'resting-place', 'stance', and gives 'meadow-stance' or 'meadow-dwelling' as the derivation.

It is appropriate to mention *Kincardine* as being an important name which as Watson says (Watson 1904. 1) 'is of common occurrence on Pictish ground'. The elements here are G. *ceann*, 'head' and a term which is cognate with O.W. *cardden*, 'wood', and which must have been a Pictish *càrdain*. This term crops up widely, in names like Urquhart, Cardenden in Fife, Pluscarden, and several other Kincardines, so the Ross-shire example is notable, and is of course an established parish name. The earliest documentary form is *Kyncardyn* 1275.

GAELIC NAMES

Although these form by far the largest proportion of the settlement names in the area [Fig. 2.5], I do not propose to discuss them in detail. The two basic habitative elements, *baile*, 'farmstead' and *achadh*, 'field', are well represented in both counties; and their distributions nationally are mapped in Nicolaisen (1976. 137, 140). Easter Ross has a particularly high density of names in *baile*, while the parishes of Dornoch and Creich contain many *achadh-* names. *Baile* tends to be located in good agricultural land, while *achadh* is a term applied to farms in less fertile, upland country. This is a generalization, of course, but one which holds more than a grain of truth. *Bailenanalltan*, 'farm of the streams' in Creich, *Balloan*, 'pool-farm' in Dornoch, *Bailenacroite*, 'farm of the croft' in Creich, and *Balyraid*, 'street-farm' near Skelbo are Sutherland examples. In Ross, *Balcherry*, 'farm of the quarter davach' in Tain, *Balintore*, 'bleaching-farm' in Fearn, *Balnabruach*, 'farm of the banks' in Tarbat, and *Ballachraggan*, 'farm of the rock' in Logie Easter are typical. Some date from as

27

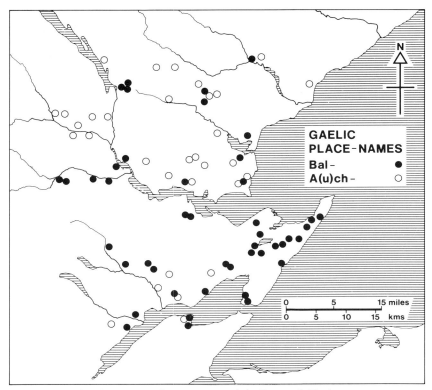

Fig. 2.5   Gaelic place-name elements around the Dornoch Firth.

late as the sixteenth century, like *Ballinroich* in Tain, which is 'Munro's farm' and recalls the acquisition of the lands of Meikle Allan by one William Munro about 1570 (Watson 1904. 43).

Of the names in *achadh*, most are conventional and descriptive, although *Achinchanter* in Dornoch is 'the precentor's field' and *Achnahanat*, 'field of the mother church', in Kincardine must be an early example. Similarly, *Achnagart*, also in Kincardine, contains *gart*, 'corn enclosure', a term now nearly obsolete in Gaelic, and occurring as a prefix in place-names in central Scotland, such as Gartnavel, Gartinsherrie, Gartmore, and many others.

A significant omission, as far as early Gaelic habitative names is concerned, is the element *cill*, 'church', which is relatively scarce in the area. *Kilmachalmag* in Kincardine is the only significant example, probably 'Colman's church'.

Topographic names feature strongly in the Gaelic material. Terms like *bad*, 'clump', 'place', abound in the southern parishes of Sutherland, with names like *Badbog*, 'wet place' in Creich and *Badninish*, 'meadow-place' in Dornoch. *Garbad*, 'rough place' in Edderton is a Ross-shire example. *Druim*, 'ridge', *cnoc*, 'hillock' (giving names in *Knock-*), *innis*, 'meadow', *ruighe*, 'hill-slope' and *lón*, 'water-meadow', are found throughout the area. *Clais*, 'hollow', 'defile', is unusually common in the parishes of Creich and Dornoch, applied usually to small farms in hilly situations like *Clashban*, 'fair hollow', *Clashcoig*, 'hollow of the fifth part', *Claiseanglas*, 'little grey hollow' in Creich, and *Clashmore*, 'big hollow' and *Clashmugach*, 'murky hollow' in Dornoch. *Camas*, 'bend', is found associated with large meanders on major rivers, or with curved coastal bays such as *Cambusmore*, 'big bend', at the south-western end of The Mound in Dornoch parish and *Cambuscurrie*, 'bay of the coracle' in Edderton. *Aird*, 'height', 'high place', 'promontory' occurs in *Ardmore*, 'big promontory' in Edderton, and *Ardjachie*, 'field promontory' in neighbouring Tain. *Eiden* in Strath Fleet is *aodann*, 'hill-face'; *Camore*, just to the west of Dornoch, is *cadha mór*, 'big path or passage'; and *Tullich* in Fearn is *tulach*, 'hillock', a very common topographic element in Easter Ross.

NORSE NAMES

With scarcely more than a dozen habitative names, it cannot be said that Norse place-names have survived here in any great strength. Yet they are of significance, and they are distributed fairly evenly throughout the area [Fig. 2.6]. As one might expect, the earliest documentary forms for most of them are late, usually no earlier than the sixteenth century, and it is noticeable that in Ross those with habitative names are on reasonably good soils. There are some fifteen extant topographic names, all relating to settlement, which contain important Norse elements, although this number could be added to if we take in 'lost' names. There is, however, sufficient Norse material of an onomastic nature to confirm the supposition that this was an area where Norse settlement was considerable, if not dominant.

North of the Dornoch Firth the most significant name of Norse origin in the study area is *Golspie*. The early forms are *Goldespy* 1330, *Golspi* 1448, *Gospye*, *Golspe* 1570. Johnston (1903. 147) suggests an ON. personal name *Gold*, or Gaelic *gall*, 'stranger', while Mackay (1894. 178) settles for *gil*, 'ravine', for the first element, with *býr*, 'farmstead' as the classifying element. *Býr* is uncommon on mainland Scotland in the north but Golspie, located on the edge of a fertile area between the mouth of the Golspie Burn and the tidal Loch Fleet, is certainly an attractive site for early settlement. The Gaelic form, *Goillsbidh*, still used by Gaelic-speakers, provides no assistance as regards derivation, and the general consensus of opinion is that this must remain obscure, since both Johnston's and Mackay's offerings do not bear close scrutiny.

The term *setr*, 'farm', 'stead', 'shieling', normally appears in Sutherland as *-side* or *-said*. Two examples occur in Creich parish, along the Oykell, above its confluence with the Shin — *Linside*, 'flax-stead' and *Bosset* or *Bowside*, 'cattle-stead'.

Ból, 'farmstead', occurs in several Sutherland names. *Embo* in Dornoch is *Ethenboll c.*1230, *Eyndboll* 1610, perhaps 'Eyvind's stead'; *Skelbo* which occurs in an early form as *Scelbol* is possibly 'shell-stead'; *Skibo* is *Scitheboll c.*1230, and may be 'Skithi's stead'; *Torboll* in Dornoch and *Torrobol* in Lairg probably share the derivation 'Thori's farm'. The only other habitative Norse term in the area is *-land*, 'land', which appears in *Merkland* in upper Lairg parish, possibly from *merki-land*, 'march or boundary-land'.

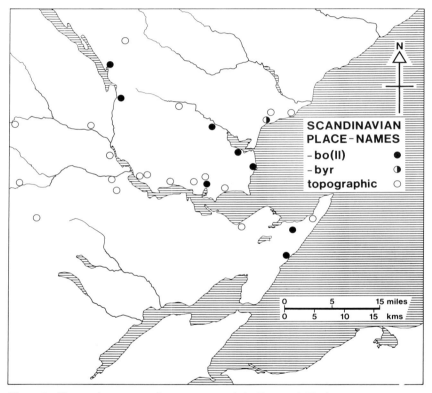

Fig. 2.6   Norse place-name elements around the Dornoch Firth.

Of the non-habitative Norse elements, the most common is *dalr*, 'valley'. *Osdale* in Lairg, *Astle* in Dornoch (which is *Askesdale* 1222, and is likely to be 'ash-valley'), *Migdale* in Creich, *Ospidale* in Dornoch (perhaps 'Ospak's valley'). *Swordale*, 'grassy valley' in Creich, and *Spinningdale* in the same parish, are the most obvious examples. The last-named is *Spanigidill* in 1464, a form which bears a close resemblance to current Gaelic pronunciation, but again the derivation is obscure. *Völlr*,

30

'field' occurs in *Rossal* in Strath Fleet which could be 'horse-field'; *Backies* in Golspie is O.N. *bakki*, 'bank', with a pluralized Scots ending; and *Uppat* a few miles to the east has been tentatively given the derivation *upp-vatn*, 'rising spring loch'.

The Norse place-names which are found in the Ross-shire section of the area (which does not include the parishes south of Strathrory) are mostly located along the Dornoch Firth shore and up the Oykell valley, although a few important examples occur in the Tarbat peninsula. Of the habitative names, *Arboll* in Tarbat is *Arkboll* 1463 and 1535. Watson (1904. 47) gives the derivation of this as 'Norse *ork-ból*, ark-stead, but possibly from *orkn*, seal, which in Skye gives *Or-bost*'. *Cadboll* in Fearn is *Cathabul* 1529, for which Watson (1904. 40) gives '*kattar-ból*, cat-stead'. Both of these derivations must be regarded with some suspicion, but subsequent attempts to provide more likely derivations have proved fruitless.

Langwell, *lang-völlr*, 'long field', and *Syal* (*Seoll* 1578, *Soyall* 1642), *sauða-völlr*, 'sheep-field', are two examples in Kincardine parish incorporating *völlr*, 'field' (for *Scatwell* in Strath Conon, see Crawford in this volume), and there are several names in *-dalr*. These include *Alladale*, 'wolf-dale', *Diebidale*, 'deep-valley' and *Gradal* in Kincardine, *Bindal* which Watson suggests as *bind-dalr*, 'sheaf-valley' in Tarbat, and *Carbisdale* in Kincardine, which appears as *Carbustell* 1548. *Kjarr-bolstaðr*, 'copse-stead', with a *-dalr* suffix is an unlikely combination, but one which fits in reasonably well with the topography.

Amat in Kincardine is *á-mót*, 'river-meet', a name found elsewhere in the Gaelic-Norse area. *Plaids* near Tain is *Plaiddes* 1560, and may well be from O.N. *flátr*, 'flat place', again with an 'englished' plural as in *Backies*.

An unusual Norse example is *Cyderhall* in Dornoch, which has the early forms *Sywardhoth* 1230, *Sytheraw* 1275 and *Siddera* 1654. This is reputed to be the burial place of Earl Sigurd who, according to the saga account, died from blood-poisoning when he was scratched by the bucktooth of Maelbrigit, Mormaer of Moray. Sigurd, having slain Maelbrigit in battle, was imprudently carrying his adversary's head home to Caithness on his saddlebow, when the fatal scratch was acquired. It is certainly the most colourful of the Norse names in the area, and one of the few which can be said to be truly commemorative.

There are few Norse names which apply to coastal features in the area. When we consider the diversity of such elements in the north and west, this is surprising. *Vík*, 'bay', occurs only in *Shandwick*, 'sand bay' in Nigg parish, just south of Balintore; and *gjá* which becomes Gaelic *geodha*, 'creek', 'inlet' appears to be absent. The presence of a Gaelic- and Scots-speaking population along the coasts of Easter Ross and Sutherland has obviously had a profound effect on coastal place-names; many in fact are Scots, displaying many of the naming characteristics of the south shore of the Moray Firth, and Buchan to the east. *Tarbat Ness* and *Whiteness* are important promontories which contain the Scandinavian *nes*, 'promontory', but it is by no means certain if these date from the Scandinavian period. They may well be late formations.

CONCLUSION

Place-name evidence must never be viewed in isolation. In this area of northern Scotland, however, there is a relative lack of archaeological research relating to the dark-age period, and consequently there is a considerable onus put on the onomastic record and the documentary evidence. If we look at the area with the highest density of names in *pit-* and *-bol*, there is a certain amount of correlation evident. The coastal strip of Sutherland from Brora to Bonar Bridge is by far the most productive not only agriculturally but in terms of habitative names from the dark-age period. The same is true of the parishes of Tain, Tarbat, Fearn and Nigg in Ross. It is in these areas that we find the most revealing place-names. The presence of Norse topographic names in the hillier areas, however, suggests that Norse settlement was not confined to the coast, but that exploitation of these less productive areas was a prominent feature of settlement.

The interface between Pictish and Norse is still ill-defined, despite the information which the place-names reveal. We are left with but tantalizing glimpses of the political and economic situation in the Dark Ages. Place-names provide only a fragmented picture and the samples of habitative elements, Pictish and Norse, are relatively small, so that the place-name record poses new questions which often remain unanswered. In the final analysis, archaeological research may be our last chance to shed light on the complex earlier history of this part of Scotland.

Acknowledgement

Figure 2.1 is reproduced by kind permission of the Royal Museum of Scotland (Queen Street); Figures 2.2 and 2.3 courtesy of the Royal Commission on the Ancient and Historical Monuments of Scotland, Edinburgh. Figures 2.4–2.6 have been redrawn by Douglas Lawson.

References

Fraser, I. A. The Norse element in Sutherland Place Names, in *Scottish Literary Journal.* 1979. Supplement no. IX.
Johnston, J. B. *The Place-Names of Scotland.* 1934.
Mackay, J. Sutherland Place Names, in *Transactions of the Gaelic Society of Inverness.* 1888–89. XV; 1889–90. XVI; 1890–91. XVII; 1891–92. XVIII; 1892–94. XIX.
Nicolaisen, W. F. H. *Scottish Place-Names.* 1976.
Watson, W. J. *The Place-Names of Ross and Cromarty.* 1904.
Watson. W. J. Some Sutherland Names of Places, in *The Celtic Review.* 1905–06. vol. 2.

THE MAKING OF A FRONTIER: THE FIRTHLANDS FROM THE NINTH TO TWELFTH CENTURIES

Barbara E. Crawford

The clash between Norse and Scots (or Picts) was a perennial feature of the northern and western parts of this country for most of the Middle Ages. Wherever the Norseman settled he came into contact, and most probably conflict, with the indigenous population. Although the apparent disappearance of the Picts in the Northern Isles is something of a mystery, it does not seem likely that they disappeared without putting up at least a show of resistance. But the impact of the Norse was so overwhelming that the Pictish population failed to retain any hold of their lands in those islands. The Hebrides provide rather more evidence of resistance at the outset, and then intermingling between the native Gaelic population and the Norse raiders and settlers. But native Gaelic culture re-asserted itself, and Scottish political control was established by the medieval kings of Scotland, ambitious to control the islands round their coasts.

The north Scottish mainland provides an area where Norse and Scots also clashed although it was never, in recorded history, under Norwegian political control. However both Caithness and Sutherland were firmly under the rule of the Norwegian earls of Orkney until their power was undermined by the advancing Scottish kings in the thirteenth century. The earls' political control was based on widespread settlement by Norse-speaking peoples as far south as the Dornoch Firth or Kyle of Sutherland, so that to all intents and purposes the territory north of that waterway was part of the Norse world from the ninth to the thirteenth century. South of that waterway was a disputed region, and the firthlands of Easter Ross were a frontier territory during the same period. Lying between Sutherland and Caithness to the north and the Scottish province of Moray to the south and west [Fig. 3.1], these low-lying peninsulas and the waterways between them were subject to the ebb and flow of Norse and Scottish control.

There was no obvious geographical reason why the Norse should have contented themselves with the Dornoch Firth as the southern limit to their expansion. It certainly became the traditional and remembered limit of Norse control, for thirteenth-century Icelandic saga writers refer to *Ekkialsbakki* as the extent of the conquests of some of the early earls; this is thought to be the banks of the Oykell River, which flows into the Dornoch Firth [Fig. 3.1]. But it is quite clear that the Norse attempted to control land to the south both politically and territorially.

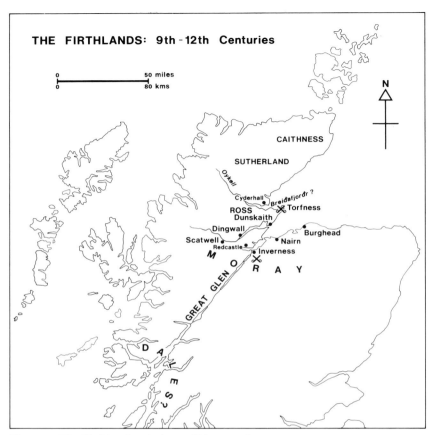

THE FIRTHLANDS: 9th-12th Centuries

CAITHNESS

SUTHERLAND

Oykell

Cyderhall
Breidafjordr ?
Torfness
ROSS
Dunskaith
Dingwall
Scatwell
Redcastle
Nairn
Burghead
Inverness
M
O
R
A
Y

GREAT GLEN

D
A
L
E
S
?

Fig. 3.1   The Firthlands: ninth–twelfth centuries.

Evidence for repeated attempts at political conquest comes from the saga of the Earls (*Orkneyinga Saga*) which tells of their campaigns in this region during three phases: the late ninth century; the late tenth and early eleventh centuries; and the late twelfth and early thirteenth centuries. Evidence for territorial settlement comes from the place-names of the Tarbat peninsula and the Black Isle, and the valleys running to the west, where there are a sprinkling of recognizably Norse place-names on the 1 in. Ordnance Survey map, and probably more on the ground. These range from the farm-names Cadboll (ON *kattar-ból*, 'farm of the cats'), Arboll (ON *ork-ból*, possibly 'seal farm'), to topographical names such as Bindal (ON *bind-dalr*, 'sheaf-dale'), Geanies (derived from ON *gjá*, 'coastal inlet'), and names of administrative significance such as Dingwall (ON *þing-völlr*, field of the assembly') and Scatwell (ON *skattr-völlr*, 'tax-field'). Some Norse names have gone out of use within historical memory, such as Scuddel (cf. Sculdale in Caithness and Orkney), replaced by Conon Bridge but recorded on the monument at Bonar Bridge [Fig. 12.21], and no doubt many others long before. In total they bear witness to the influence among the native Gaelic farmers of Norse-speaking residents whose presence we would not know about otherwise.

The attraction of good land is, of course, one reason why the Norse earls pressed south of the Dornoch Firth in the conquering phases. Easily-cultivated sandy soils such as the coastal farm-lands of the Tarbat penin-sula and the Black Isle were always a magnet for those Vikings who wished to settle rather than spend a lifetime raiding. It is very noticeable how Norse place-names are concentrated in such localities around the shores of the firthlands, including Sutherland. The apparent absence of pagan grave-goods south of the Dornoch Firth suggests that the settlement of this region took place at a time when Christianity had begun to exercise some influence on the Norse (perhaps tenth century?).

But there may have been other reasons why the earls were prepared to spend their time and resources in attempting to control these waterways. They lead to that major artery which cuts northern Scotland in two and provides access from coast to coast: the Great Glen [Fig. 3.1]. The histori-cal significance of this remarkable geological feature, which forms a 'direct and relatively easy route between the southern Hebrides and the Moray Firth' (Barrow 1981. 105) has not been sufficiently recognized. For any Scandinavian chieftain aspiring to control both the former and the latter it was the obvious means of communication between the two. As will be discussed, there were earls of Orkney and Caithness who did attempt to rule in the Hebrides also, and they were the ones who were prepared to expend resources in striving with Celtic rulers for mastery of the firthlands. This may have been in order to ensure free access to the Great Glen and the maintenance of a through route to the south-west, thus avoiding the long sail round the north-eastern tip of Caithness, the turbulent waters along the north coast of Scotland, the headland of Cape Wrath and the long sail south through the Minch.

LATE NINTH CENTURY: SIGURD THE MIGHTY AND THORSTEIN THE RED

The first phase in which Ross and the firthlands were a theatre of war was as early as the late ninth century, at a time when the whole of Scotland had been suffering from the incursions of the Vikings for some decades. In this period two powerful Norse dynasties had gained control over the two island groups, the Northern and the Western (or to the Norse, the Southern) Isles.

In Orkney the family of Rognvald of Møre had dominated the turbulent viking element and were ruling this fertile archipelago as 'jarls', either by virtue of their own military overlordship or, as later saga-writers preferred to remember, by virtue of a grant from the powerful king of Norway, Harald Fine-Hair. The first of this family to be remembered as Earl of Orkney was Rognvald's brother, Sigurd, called *hinn riki*, 'the Mighty'

EARLS OF ORKNEY: 9th–12th CENTURIES

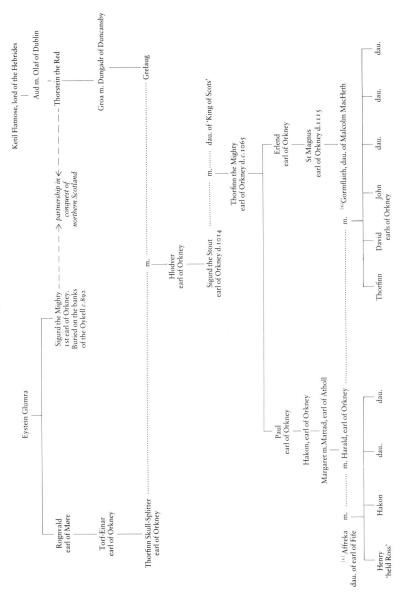

Fig. 3.2 Geneological Tree of the Earls of Orkney, ninth–twelfth centuries.

[Fig. 3.2]. In the West, by contrast, a son of one of Norway's leading chieftains, Ketil Flatnose, had gained power and was remembered later as the ruler of the Hebrides, but without title of either king or earl. He was said to have been sent by Harald Fine-Hair in the first instance, but he had abandoned any pretence of ruling as Harald's representative and established an independent empire allied with the Norse kingdom of Dublin, for he married his daughter Aud to the king of Dublin, Olaf the White. Some of the facts and much of the chronology of these early Viking entities in the west are dubious, but there was a strong Icelandic tradition about Ketil's family and particularly about the son of Aud and Olaf of Dublin, Thorstein the Red [Fig. 3.2]. This tradition remembered that Thorstein had conquered north Scotland in partnership with Earl Sigurd of Orkney. The reason why Thorstein turned his attention to the north Scottish mainland may have been connected with the difficulties which the Norsemen seem to have been experiencing in the Hebrides at this time, which led many of them to move north to Iceland in a fresh settlement phase in the third quarter of the ninth century.

The partnership between Thorstein and Sigurd seems, therefore, to have been a deliberate one designed to carve up northern Scotland between them — Sigurd moving south across the Pentland Firth from Orkney, Thorstein perhaps moving up the Great Glen from the Hebrides. Nothing is known of the terms of any agreement made between them; the recorded information about their successes is brief indeed. We are only told that they 'won all Caithness and much more of Scotland, Moray and Ross' (*Orkneyinga Saga*), and that Thorstein was actually made king over these lands (*Book of Settlements*). But this onslaught probably receives some corroboration from the contemporary record in the *Chronicle of the Kings of Scotland* that the Northmen 'wasted' Pictland during the reign of Donald Constantine's son (889–900). What was 'wasting' to the natives was 'conquest' to the Norse, for they would have raided over a much larger area than they finally exercised any permanent control over, or settled in. A symbol of their conquest was raised by Sigurd who is said to have built a castle 'in the south of Moray' thought, without any very good reason, to have been Burghead on the coast of Moray.

This aggressive partnership may not have lasted very long, however, for Thorstein was killed in battle against the Scots and Sigurd met his death in some encounter with a native earl called Maelbrigte. Legendary accretions have developed around this incident which have strong Celtic overtones, according to a recent study of the story in *Orkneyinga Saga* (Almqvist 1978–79. 97–98). These overtones are, first, the practice of cutting off the head of your adversary and hanging it on your saddle bow, as Sigurd is said to have done with Maelbrigte's head; second, the theme of the head of a slain man avenging the former bearer of the head, which is what happened when the long tooth sticking out of Maelbrigte's severed head jabbed Sigurd's leg as he was riding, from which wound he later died. This story in the saga therefore tells us rather more about the Celtic elaborations which at some point in the transmission of the story of Sigurd's death became

Fig. 3.3   The present-day farm of Cyderhall, a few hundred metres south-west of the alleged burial site of Earl Sigurd the Mighty.

attached to the actual historical details, and which, of course, are of significance for hinting at the blending of Celtic with Norse elements in the Orkney earldom.

There is little doubt, however, that Sigurd did die while establishing Norse authority in the frontier territory south of the Dornoch Firth, for the place where he was buried was well-remembered, and such early traditions are surely among the most reliable details to be found in the whole history of the colourful lives of the Orkney earls. He was laid in a mound at *Ekkialsbakki*, on the banks of the Oykell, mentioned already as forming an important frontier between Norse and Scottish territory, and strongly suggesting that this marked the southernmost limit of his and Thorstein's permanent conquests. For an earl would be buried only in safe territory, while the raising of a 'howe' which could be seen by his enemies across the Firth was an aggressive marker of Norse possession as well as of Norse paganism.

Indeed the site of Sigurd's burial became known as 'Sigurd's howe', and that name has survived in a very corrupted form to the present day. Its survival is at one and the same time a testimony to the remarkable permanency of place-names, and to the ease with which they can be corrupted and turned into something entirely different! If it were not for the survival of a thirteenth-century form of the name it would probably not be recognized today for what in reality it is. The present form of the name is Cyderhall, a farm on the north side of the Dornoch Firth, where the Oykell widens out into an estuary [Figs. 3.1; 3.3]. It was the famous

Fig. 3.4   Local tradition places Sigurd's howe on Cnoc Skardie, a hillock just to the west (left) of the farm track now bisecting the sinuous glacial ridge in the lower part of the aerial photograph (Mr Munro of Cyderhall, 29 March 1971 *comm.* to RCAHMS).

Scottish antiquary Joseph Anderson, writer of the introduction to Hjaltalin and Goudie's translation of the *Orkneyinga Saga* in 1873, who first recognized that this name (or Sidera, as it was sometimes written) was in reality the name 'Sigurd's howe'. In the first half of the thirteenth century it appears as *Syvardhoch* (*Caithness and Sutherland Records.* no. 9). Local tradition apparently locates the site to a mound known as Cnoc Skardie [NH 762 3891 5] (ON *skarð*, a 'notch' or 'defile', used of a saddle between hills), one of a line of geological deposits on the south-east bank of the Evelix River, 0.8 km (0.5 mls.) from the present farm of

Cyderhall [Fig. 3.4]. It is exceedingly difficult, however, to recognize which of the mounds could have been a burial howe, and only excavation might prove the exact location. Nonetheless the conjunction of historical, toponymic and topographical evidence in this instance provides a classic example of the interdisciplinary approach which it is necessary to take when studying this early historic period.

With Sigurd and Thorstein's deaths (c. 890 × 892) this phase of conquest came to an end. It is more unlikely that their conquests would have been maintained, for there do not appear to have been any strong successors immediately in line. In fact, it is said that great unrest ensued and that many Vikings established themselves in the north. There was also the continuation of a native line of 'earls' in Caithness who married into the families of Thorstein the Red and the earls of Orkney [Fig. 3.2].

LATE TENTH–EARLY ELEVENTH CENTURY: SIGURD THE STOUT AND THORFINN THE MIGHTY

Not until the end of the tenth century did the earls of Orkney begin another campaign to establish political control further south than their earldom lands of Caithness and Sutherland. Quite clearly the main obstacle to their progress was the native dynasty in Moray, the descendants of the branch of the Dalriadic Scots, the Cenel Loairn, who had established themselves in this area some centuries earlier. To the author of the saga they were 'kings of Scots', and their aggressive intentions towards the Norse quite clearly emerge from the saga account of battles fought between them as far north as Caithness.

Territorial Expansion

It was a second Sigurd, another powerful warrior of the calibre of the earlier Sigurd, who initiated the most successful period of the Orkney earldom when the earls extended their authority over the Hebrides and northern parts of the Scottish mainland. Sigurd 'the Stout' is said to have been a 'mighty chief, with wide dominions. By main force he held Caithness against the Scots, and every summer had a war cruise abroad. He harried in the Hebrides, in Scotland and Ireland' (*Orkneyinga Saga*).

Strong traditions about the battle of Clontarf (1014) prove that Sigurd was directly involved in the attempt of the Norse Dubliners to resist the Irish push to dislodge them, but it was an attempt in which he lost his life. According to the theory discussed above, it seems therefore likely that Earl Sigurd II would also have wished to use the direct route between his northern Scottish lands and the Hebrides and the Irish Sea, and have unhindered passage through the Great Glen. There are no references in the *Orkneyinga Saga* to this earl's activity in Ross or Moray, but the section on Earl Sigurd in that Saga is surprisingly brief, considering that he was one of the most famous of the Orkney earls and well-remembered in Icelandic tradition. However, one Icelandic saga does say that he 'owned Ross and

Moray, Sutherland and the Dales'. The latter name, although very unspecific, is later used with reference to the territory of Argyll, around the western end of the Great Glen [Fig. 3.1]. If Sigurd really did control this area then it is obvious that he would have used the Great Glen as a means of communication between the west coast and his northern possessions, and renewed Norse activity in the firthlands of Ross and Moray can be assumed.

Such activity is fully described in the saga of his famous son, Thorfinn *hinn riki* ('the Mighty') who, despite the disaster of Clontarf and the consequent reduction of Orkney power in the Hebrides, managed to rebuild his father's empire and indeed to extend it even further south. He achieved this in the firthlands by defeating a powerful member of the Moray dynasty known to the saga-writer as 'Karl Hundison' ('son of a dog'), who is also called 'king of Scots'. It seems very probable that once more this is the Norse name for a ruler of Moray, and by this stage in the history of Scotland it should be possible to recognize which 'mormaer' of Moray this might be. But different suggestions have been made. One of the successors of Malcolm of Moray (d. 1029) seems obvious, but whether Gillecomgain (1029–32) or the more famous Macbeth (ruler of Moray 1032; king of Scots 1040–57) is not clear.

Two battles between Thorfinn and Karl Hundison are described in the saga, one a sea fight off Deerness in the Orkneys, the other on land at *Torfness*, said to be 'in the south of the Moray Firth' (*Breiðafjorðr*). Here we are faced with the problem of a specific name for a location, but a name which has disappeared. Karl Hundison was in possession of a fleet, and also collected a large army together in order to attack Thorfinn and to avenge his earlier defeat off Deerness and the murder of his nephew Mumtan/Moddan by one of Thorfinn's close followers. It is likely, therefore, that he would have sailed out from Moray in order to come to battle with Thorfinn. Further, the saga says that Thorfinn and his follower Thorkell Fostri lay off the coast of Moray and that Thorkell raised a force in Ross, which suggests that they were exercising some authority in this locality. In these circumstances the battle is likely to have taken place on Tarbat Ness, accessible to fleets from both south and north. Is it possible to describe Tarbat Ness as lying in the south of the Moray Firth? Perhaps the Norse name *Breiðafjorðr* ('Broad Firth') really applied to the waters *north* of the Tarbat peninsula, and was in fact the Dornoch Firth [Fig. 3.1]?

The saga account provides a rare picture of the earl accoutred for battle at Torfness and leading his troops: he had a gilded helmet on his head and wielded his sword and a great spear. His victory was praised by his skald, Arnor, and the Scottish king fled. So assured did the young earl feel after this decisive event that he is said to have harried far and wide throughout Scotland, even as far south as Fife. His ships, however, were left in the firthlands and he marched through Scotland, suggesting that he was assured of his position indeed, not to have his fleet with him close at hand in case of a forced retreat. This victory must certainly have given Thorfinn political control of the firthlands and it would be surprising if, during his reign as earl of Orkney and Caithness (*c*.1030–*c*.1065), Norse administration and rule had not been firmly imposed on the territory between Sutherland and Moray.

In one important respect Thorfinn was different from the majority of the earls in the north: his mother was a member of a Scottish royal family and he had been brought up at his grandfather's court after the death of his father at Clontarf. It is said specifically in the saga that his grandfather gave him Caithness and Sutherland along with the title of earl; and although Thorfinn inherited a share of the Orkney earldom he seems to have been content to concentrate on his Scottish possessions for the first stage of his career. Not until his half-brothers had died did he take all the Orkneys under him and centre his power base there. Until that date (1030 × 1035), Caithness seems to have been his base of operations, and he looked south to Moray when expanding his area of rule. Even when his nephew, Rognvald Brusison, arrived on the scene and claimed his father's share of Orkney (1037 × 1038), Thorfinn seems to have resided mainly in Caithness.

It was in company with Rognvald that the next stage of Thorfinn's career unfolded and the two of them turned their attention to the west. In 1039 they 'harried during the summer round the coasts of the Hebrides and Ireland and far and wide round the west coast of Scotland' (*Orkney-inga Saga*). For the next eight years the two sailed together in company, successfully terrorizing the whole Irish Sea area and plundering in England. It seems highly likely that the Great Glen would supply the usual means of access between the west coast and the northern earldom, particularly when their control of the firthlands was maintained. Even after Thorfinn and Rognvald had fallen out and Rognvald was murdered (1046), there is no hint that Thorfinn ever lost control over any of the territories that had been brought under his sway. It was well known in tradition that 'he has been the most powerful of all the Orkney earls', and that he owned 'nine earldoms in Scotland, and all the Hebrides and a large realm in Ireland'. Whatever was meant by nine earldoms in Scotland, it cannot be doubted that Ross and Moray were counted among them.

Thorfinn's Administration

How was this part of Thorfinn's dominion ruled? According to the saga, Thorfinn gave up war cruises after his visit to Rome, settled in Birsay and turned his mind to governing his people and making laws. We can assume from this that some sort of governmental structures must have been imposed on his conquered territories for the administration of the population, and in particular the exaction of taxes. The saga hints at something of the kind when it says 'in those lands which he had brought under him by the sword, it seemed to many a hard lot to live under his rule'. Unfortunately, there is very little evidence of earldom administration in any parts of Norse Scotland apart from the hereditary territories of Orkney,

Shetland, Caithness and Sutherland, although there are occasional references in some of the sagas to the earls' tax-collectors in the Hebrides.

It is possible, however that the land divisions known as ouncelands and pennylands, which do occur throughout parts of the Western Isles and the western mainland of Scotland, may be relics of an earldom administration imposed for the collection of taxes. Such divisions are very clearly basic to the earldom administration in Orkney and Caithness; but they do not appear in Ross or anywhere south of the River Shin (see Bangor-Jones in this volume). This suggests that the earls' administrative control of the firthlands was never strong or permanent enough to leave traces of any tax-collection system in the local toponymy.

However, there are two place-names which, on the contrary, do suggest that a Norse system of administration must have been imposed in this area and to which they bear mute testimony. One is the name *Dingwall* (ON *þing-völlr*, the 'field of the Thing' or 'assembly'), a classic sign of Norse settlement anywhere in the British Isles. Remarkably, it is a place which has remained important in the administration of Ross, for it continued to be the centre of Scottish administration in the upper part of the Cromarty Firth [Fig. 3.1], although many of the 'Thingwalls' elsewhere have declined in importance. We can be sure that for a period of maybe two centuries Dingwall, conveniently located at the head of the Firth, was the meeting-place for legal assemblies of the Norse and Gaelic farmers of the rich lands of Easter Ross. But just as striking as the name Dingwall is the name *Scatwell*, a place which lies well inland and at the edge of the higher land in Strath Conon, in a location where one would never expect to meet Norse place-names at all [Fig. 3.1]. There seems no other possible explanation of this name, recorded from the fifteenth century, except a derivation from *skattr-völlr*, the field for which 'scat' or tax was paid. Watson (1904. 149), recognizing such a derivation, suggested that the 'scat' was paid for the right to use the common grazing. This is rather misleading. Although lying at the western limit of cultivable land in Strath Conon, Scatwell has extensive arable fields, and has every appearance of having been the centre of a wealthy and long-established estate. Moreover, it was divided into two holdings, Little and Meikle 'Scathole', as early as the fifteenth century. The original Scatwell, in fact, must have been a large arable holding whose name indicates that tax was paid for more than merely grazing privileges. Now payment of 'scat' was exclusively associated with the dominions of the earldom of Orkney. The earls paid 'scat' to the kings of Norway and the dues paid by the Orkney farmers were always called 'scat', while certain divisions of land were called in the rentals 'Skattlands'. It is, however, very unusual for the element to form part of a place-name, if not unprecedented. Its appearance in a name at the western limits of Easter Ross is a very strong indication that the earl's taxation system was indeed imposed in this locality; and if imposed in this corner of Ross, then undoubtedly all over the province. Why this place-name should have been given to this estate alone is one of the many mysteries of place-name studies. Could it have been because this remoter corner of Strath

Conon was not cultivated before a Norse farmer settled here in the tenth or eleventh century? The majority of existing Pictish holdings obviously retained their names, even though they may have been assessed for the payment of scat to the Orkney earls. Scatwell, however, was given a new Norse name which reflected its assessment status. This one place-name serves as a warning that the absence of ouncelands and pennylands is no proof at all that the earldom administrative system was not imposed in the Firthlands. And evidence that Ross was divided into 'quarters' may also be an indication of Norse administrative influence, as suggested by Watson (1904. xxv).

Even though governmental structures may have been established in this area, Norse control is unlikely to have long survived the death of Earl Thorfinn. The most revealing comment is made in the earl's saga that after his death 'many realms that the Earl had subdued fell away and men sought protection for themselves under the hereditary chiefs in their realms'. There is no evidence in the saga that Thorfinn's sons or grandsons attempted to maintain any control over the Hebrides or Ross and Moray, and if campaigns and battles are not mentioned we can be fairly sure that they did not take place. These earls became involved in internal struggles with rival claimants and Norwegian kings: none of them seem to have had the military qualities of the great Earl Thorfinn. Probably they did not have the resources to keep a retinue of ships and fighting men permanently employed in keeping control of territories where the population felt no loyalty to a Scandinavian dynasty. The fading of interest in the west meant that access to the Great Glen was no longer of any significance.

LATE TWELFTH–EARLY THIRTEENTH CENTURY: HARALD MADDADSSON

However, over a century later the firthlands did once more become a flashpoint between the northern earl and what was by then the Scottish establishment based in Inverness, the centre of royal administration of Moray. This marks the third and final phase in the history of the Orkney earls' attempt to assert control in the area. The earl concerned was Harald Maddadsson who, like his famous ancestor Thorfinn, was half-Scottish and who was perhaps therefore more inclined to be drawn into the northern Scottish political arena. There is also evidence from the saga of a renewed interest in Ireland in this period; at any rate by the 'ultimate' viking, Swein Asleifsson, who went on at least two expeditions accompanied by the earl's son, Hakon (1171). It may also be the case that Earl Harald was more involved in events in Ireland at this time than appears from the saga (Topping 1983. 109–12), and if so then free access through Ross to the Great Glen would once more have been desirable. The importance of an alliance with Malcolm, earl of Ross, is very evident from Earl Harald's bigamous relationship with Malcolm's daughter, Hvarflød (Gormflaith) [Fig. 3.2], and Earl Harald may have exercised some influence in Ross through this liaison, after the death of Malcolm in 1168.

If we believe Fordun, the Scottish chronicler, Harald kept himself clear of involvement in the disturbances which racked the north during the 1180s, but he finally became embroiled in rebellion against his Scottish overlord. Fordun explains Harald's behaviour as a result of goading by his wife. There is no doubt that Earl Harald was pursuing some very definite course of action when he moved south from Caithness with a military force in 1196 and 'occupied' Moray. It was a reaction to some situation, but whether it was concerned with his wife's interests in Ross or whether it was an expression of anger against some action taken by King William's representative in Moray is not entirely clear. Perhaps significantly his eldest son by this marriage possessed the name of one of the most famous of the earl's ancestors, Thorfinn; it was a name which, strangely, had never been used in the earldom family since the time of Thorfinn Sigurdsson, four generations previous.

This son was deeply involved in his father's campaigns in Moray, and the *Chronicle of Melrose* records a battle fought by him against the king's vassals near Inverness. It is quite clear that King William wished to have Thorfinn in safe custody: the English chronicler, Roger of Howden, tells the story of how Earl Harald arrived at a pre-arranged conciliation meeting at Nairn with only his two small grandsons as hostages, and was imprisoned himself in Roxburgh Castle until Thorfinn came and gave himself up to the Scottish king. Perhaps because of his blood links with the troublesome MacHeth dynasty, and maybe because of some claims through his mother, Thorfinn was a potential danger to royal authority in the north (Duncan 1975. 196). But he was finally rendered helpless by blinding and castration because, Fordun tells us, of his father's bad faith. This must relate to the turbulent events in Caithness which fill the years from 1196 to 1202 (Crawford 1976–77. 101–07).

Not only did the long arm of the king of Scots reach out to the firthlands in the late twelfth century, but right into the heartland of the earl's own domain. Two campaigns by the Scottish army penetrated right to the borders of Caithness and Sutherland, while a force even reached the earl's castle at Thurso. Meanwhile, royal castles planted at strategic points on the Beauly and Cromarty Firths (Redcastle and Dunskaith) ensured that this area would henceforth be kept under permanent royal control. Strangely enough, one of Earl Harald's sons is said in the saga to have held Ross: Henry a son of his first marriage and not therefore with any family claim to Ross through his mother. If this information can be relied upon, then it seems likely that Henry would have held Ross on a grant from the king sometime during the period before Farquhar Mactaggart was made earl of Ross in 1215.

Earl Harald and his family's involvement in the firthlands may, therefore, have been motivated by slightly different considerations from those of their ancestors who had also fought and campaigned in this frontier area. In general, however, it can be said that these low-lying eastern peninsulas, and the waterways surrounding them, were an irresistible attraction to any Orkney earl who was sufficiently powerful to be able to look southwards for expansion. Significantly, those three earls who are named by the saga writer at the very end of the saga of Earl Harald as being 'the most powerful of the Orkney earls', that is Sigurd Eysteinsson, Thorfinn Sigurdsson and Harald Maddadsson himself, are the very three earls who did focus their attention on the lands between Sutherland and Moray, showing that they regarded them as territory over which, for different reasons, they needed to exercise control.

Acknowledgement

Figure 3.4 is reproduced by kind permission of the Royal Commission on the Ancient and Historical Monuments of Scotland, Edinburgh; Figure 3.1 has been redrawn by Douglas Lawson.

References

Almqvist, B. Scandinavian and Celtic Folklore Contacts in the Earldom of Orkney, in *Saga-Book of the Viking Society*. 1978–79. xx.

Anderson, A. O. ed. *Early Sources of Scottish History*. 1922.

Barrow, G. W. S. *Kingship and Unity*. 1981.

Caithness and Sutherland Records. Johnston, A. W. & A. eds. 1909 (Viking Club).

Crawford, B. E. The Earldom of Caithness and the Kingdom of Scotland, in *Northern Scotland*. 1976–77. 2.ii.

Duncan, A. A. M. *Scotland: The Making of the Kingdom*. 1975.

Gray, J. *Sutherland and Caithness in Saga-Times*. 1922.

Orkneyinga Saga. Anderson, J. ed. 1873; Taylor, A. B. trans. 1938.

Regesta Regum Scottorum. ii. Barrow, G. W. S. ed. 1971.

Topping, P. Harald Maddadsson, Earl of Orkney and Caithness, 1139–1206, in *Scottish Historical Review*. 1983. LXII.

Watson, W. J. *Place-Names of Ross and Cromarty*. 1904.

THE MEDIEVAL CHURCH IN THE NORTH: CONTRASTING INFLUENCES IN THE DIOCESES OF ROSS AND CAITHNESS

Ronald G. Cant

The contrasting political and cultural influences and inter-relationships at work around the firthlands of Easter Ross and Sutherland have influenced a wide variety of problems here over successive historical periods. It is the purpose of this paper to examine them in relation to the medieval church.

CHRISTIAN ORIGINS *c.* 400–850

Probably no-one can be completely certain, save in a few particular instances, precisely when 'organised Christianity' first appeared in the various parts of Scotland. That the earliest indigenous centre of significant missionary activity was that of St Ninian at Whithorn around 400 is generally agreed. But beyond that is the problem of how long and how far its influence extended among the northern Britons and the Picts. In the view of A. B. Scott and Douglas Simpson it continued for at least three hundred years and, through a series of missionary saints, penetrated into the farthest north.

As against this, it may be doubted whether church dedications commemorating these saints can be accepted as proof of their personal involvement without supporting literary or archaeological evidence. Nevertheless there is good reason to believe that a strong Christian presence linked with Whithorn, by way of Strathclyde, eastern Pictland and northern Ireland, existed in the far north before St Columba established his much publicized centre at Iona in the late sixth century; and that even in his own lifetime his influence here was probably less than that of St Donnan of Eigg, and was considerably exceeded in the late seventh century by St Maelrubba of Applecross in Wester Ross.

By the time of the Viking impact, around 800, in the area of Ross, Sutherland and Caithness, we can envisage a generally Christian population grouped around a series of centres marked by cross-slabs of characteristic Pictish design as at Farr, Reay, Skinnet, Ulbster, Golspie, Creich, Edderton, Shandwick and Nigg (though some might be of a purely sepulchral character) [Figs. 4.1–4.5]. And there were monasteries of major

Fig. 4.1   Cross Slab, Nigg.

Figs. 4.2; 4.3   The Shandwick Stone.

importance at Applecross, Mid-Fearn, and Rosemarkie. A slab from the second of these commemorates its abbot Reodatius who died in 762, while the third may have acquired some kind of episcopal status over its neighbourhood as a result of the activities of St Curitan or Boniface around 700, but the relative importance of such centres clearly varied from time to time [Fig. 4.6].

POLITICAL AND ECCLESIASTICAL DEVELOPMENTS *c.* 850–1100

The change from a predominantly monastic to a predominantly episcopal form of organization in the Celtic Church took place in the period after 850. By this time Norse settlements were well established in the northern and western isles and in the coastal areas of the adjacent mainland. One consequence was the end of Iona for the time being as a major ecclesiastical and cultural centre, and the virtual destruction of the Scottish kingdom of Dalriada (in origin a fifth-century colony from northern Ireland) with which Iona had been so strongly identified since its foundation by St Columba three centuries before. Nevertheless it was a member of its royal house, Kenneth mac Alpin, surviving precariously on the eastern borders of his former realm, who took over control of the Pictish central monarchy in the 840s, so drawing together in the Gaelic-speaking kingdom of *Alba* or Scotland the parts of northern Britain outwith Nordic control.

Fig. 4.4 Cross Slab,
Edderton.

Fig. 4.5 Cross Slab from Reay
(in Royal Museum of Scotland,
Edinburgh).

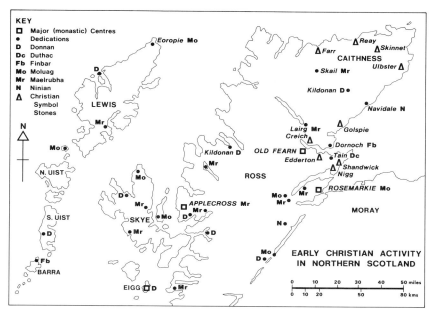

Fig. 4.6   Early Christian Activity in Northern Scotland.

This 'kingdom' was, of course, not much more than a loose aggregation of sizeable regions (whose rulers did not hesitate to call themselves kings), which were in turn aggregations of smaller communities. In the lists of the 'provinces' of Pictland — of which Alba was the essential successor — the most northerly were *Cait* or *Cathanesia* and *Fidach* or *Muref et Ros*. The first would seem to have included most of the territory north of the River Oykell and the Dornoch Firth, the second Moray and Ross. These lists, imperfect as they are in many respects, are associated with the *Pictish Chronicle* and probably give a reasonably accurate interpretation of the situation in the 'Pictish dominions' in their final form. They also make geographical sense, especially in the linking of the lands on the inmost reaches of the Moray Firth.

When territorial bishoprics can be identified in Scotland, from the later ninth century onwards, they tended to be associated with this well-established pattern. Thus in the eleventh century St Duthac (d. 1065) seems to have served as a bishop in the area of Tain and Dornoch, perhaps also of Rosemarkie, while another bishopric may have functioned in the lowlands or *laich* of Moray [Fig. 4.6]. By this time, of course (nominally since 995), the Norse settlers were also Christian, a bishopric of Orkney being in existence by 1035 and having a firm base by about 1060 at Birsay, in close association with the great Earl Thorfinn. And just as the authority of the earldom extended from Orkney to Shetland and Caithness (or nordic north-eastern *Cait*), so did that of the bishopric.

THE TWELFTH AND THIRTEENTH CENTURIES
The Diocese of Caithness

In 1098, during a period when the earldom was divided between Thorfinn's sons Paul and Erlend, the Norwegian monarchy became concerned to assert its authority over the Norse colonies 'west-over-sea'; but as an act of 'imperial stabilisation', King Magnus Barelegs agreed with King Edgar of Scotland to recognize the Pentland Firth as the boundary between their realms in this northern area and Caithness as part of the Scottish kingdom. In practice the arrangement made very little difference to the local situation, Caithness remaining under the immediate control of the dynasty of the Orkney earls, though now conceived as a separate earldom held from the King of Scots.

From 1139 Harald Maddadson, son of Earl Paul's sister Margaret and the Scottish Earl Maddad or Modach of Atholl (though then a mere boy), was accepted as joint Earl of Orkney by Earl Rognvald. This seems to have been done under pressure from King David I of Scotland who further instructed the earls to ensure the safety of a community of Benedictine monks from Dunfermline apparently being settled in Dornoch at this time. When Harald Maddadson came of age in 1150 the king took the even more remarkable step of establishing a bishopric in Caithness. As the area already had a reasonably well organized system of parochial churches and chapels in association with the bishopric of Orkney, this can only be

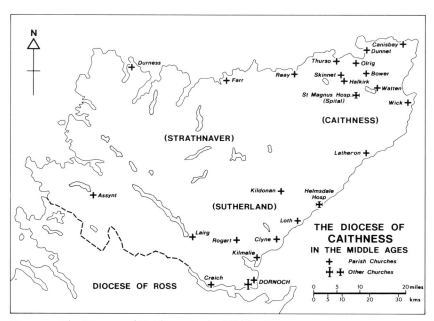

Fig. 4.7 The Diocese of Caithness in the Middle Ages.

regarded as an act of deliberate aggression, made more pronounced by the location of the new Scottish bishop at the principal church or minster of Halkirk, close to the Earl's castle at Braal [Fig. 4.7].

In fact the position of these bishops proved to be highly precarious. Not only did they lack the support of Earl Harald, but provoked his hostility and that of the Norse population in a way that led to the mutilation of Bishop John at Scrabster in 1202 and the murder of Bishop Adam at Halkirk in 1222 in the time of Earl Harald's son John. King Alexander II, having conducted a punitive expedition into Caithness (as his father King William had done in 1196 and 1202) then decided to re-locate the administrative centre of the diocese far to the south at Dornoch. Here it would be further protected by a new Earldom of Sutherland held by the great family of de Moravia or Moray, which also provided the first bishop of the reorganized diocese.

As founded by Bishop Gilbert in 1224 the cathedral of Dornoch, if of no great size and lacking its nave for two centuries more, was a cruciform structure of high architectural quality served by a community of 'secular' canons. But to sustain this central organism all twenty-two parishes in the diocese — half being in 'Caithness' in the narrower (and correct) Nordic sense, and all but three of the rest in easter Sutherland — were 'appropriated' to the bishopric, to the canonries (initially ten, later thirteen, headed by the customary 'dignities' of Dean, Precentor, Chancellor, Treasurer and Archdeacon), or for the upkeep of the cathedral fabric and services [Fig. 4.7].

As a result, the parish churches were served by *vicars* or deputies of the non-resident *rectors* drawing only a proportion of the parochial *teinds* or tithes; and although the Norwegian church order allocated one-quarter of the tithes to the bishop, the remainder was retained for parochial use and divided between the priest, the church fabric, and the poor. It may be a consequence of this that the churches of the Norse period in Caithness proper seem to have been of better quality than those in the remainder of the diocese. It would also appear that the hospital or hospice of St Magnus at Spital near Halkirk was founded by the Earls of Caithness for use by pilgrims to the great Nordic shrine of Kirkwall, and that the other hospital at Helmsdale on the approach to the Ord may have served a like purpose.

The Diocese of Ross

By contrast with the tensions involved in the creation of the bishopric of Caithness, that of Ross had a somewhat more settled history. As has been seen, there is evidence of its existence in the eleventh century and perhaps earlier. As with most Scottish sees, however, it is only from the time of King David I (*c*. 1130) that something like a regular succession of bishops appears. In the twelfth century they were usually styled 'of Rosemarkie', thereafter 'of Ross'. Although royal nominees, and generally from outside the diocese, they seem to have encountered little local hostility. Politically, however, Ross like neighbouring Moray was an extremely independent region of the Scottish kingdom, the situation being further complicated by associations of both with claimants to the throne and by the intervention of Earl Harald Maddadson from the north and Somerled from the west. By the time of King Alexander II, however, stability was established under Farquhar Mactaggart (son of a lay abbot of Applecross) who was created Earl of Ross *c.* 1215 and established a dynasty on reasonably good terms with the monarchy and the church for nearly two centuries thereafter.

At some time in the 1220s Earl Farquhar brought Premonstratensian canons (and relics of St Ninian) from Whithorn to establish a house of the order at the old monastic centre of Mid-Fearn, but about 1238 transferred it to a better site at New Fearn between Tarbat and Nigg [Fig. 4.8]. This development prompts two thoughts. The first is the apparent strength of a tradition that after more than five hundred years linked Ross with Whithorn and to the extent that the election of the Abbot of Fearn was regularly confirmed by the Prior of Whithorn. The second is the possibility that the Earl may have envisaged this abbey as a potential cathedral for the diocese of Ross, as Whithorn was for Galloway.

If so it may be more than a coincidence that about 1240 Bishop Robert decided to move his cathedral from its historic but restricted location at

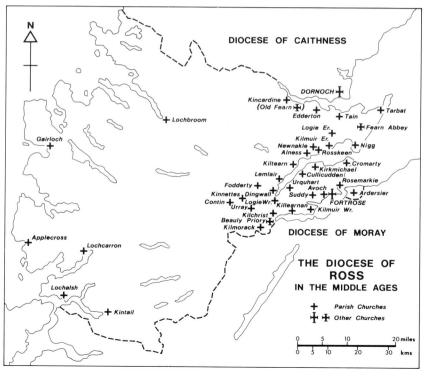

Fig. 4.8   The Diocese of Ross in the Middle Ages.

Rosemarkie, to a more spacious and level site one mile to the south-west at Fortrose. In scale and design the new structure was similar to those being built at this same time at Dunblane and Dunkeld but of a more simple form, consisting as it did of a long unaisled choir and nave separated by a massive arched screen, itself probably surmounted by a belfry. To serve the cathedral a chapter of secular canons was formed (or reorganized), consisting originally of Dean and Sub-Dean, Precentor and Succentor, Chancellor, Treasurer, Archdeacon and perhaps two ordinary canons, making nine in all at this stage of its development.

Almost contemporary with Fearn Abbey and Fortrose Cathedral was Beauly Priory, probably founded by Sir John Bisset of Lovat about 1230 for monks of the Valliscaulian order. The Valliscaulians were 'reformed Benedictines', not unlike the Cluniacs, Cistercians, and Tironians and like them dependent on their mother-house the monastery of Val de Choux in France from which, in its Latin form, they derived their name. Of this relatively small order, almost unknown elsewhere in the British Isles, Scotland had three houses, the other two being at Pluscarden in Moray and Ardchattan in Argyll. Though of more modest scale than these, the church at Beauly impresses by its relative length and the refinement of its detail.

LATER DEVELOPMENTS: 1300–1560

The thirteenth century marked the climax of the religious and architectural inspiration of the Middle Ages. But in the two ensuing centuries there was to be further development, or at least elaboration of the medieval ecclesiastical pattern. At Fearn the abbey church was rebuilt between 1338 and 1372 in a mature gothic design, still impressive despite a reduction of length and height. At Fortrose the cathedral chapter was increased to twenty-one *prebends*, a figure only slightly smaller than Dunkeld with twenty-two and Elgin with twenty-five, and not so far short of the largest Scottish examples of Aberdeen and Glasgow with thirty and thirty-two. The fabric was also enlarged by the addition of a bell-tower at the north-west corner of the nave and, in the early fifteenth century, by a south aisle and Lady Chapel of remarkably high quality compared with the simple arcaded nave added at about this time to Dornoch Cathedral [Fig. 4.9]. Surrounding the church as at Dornoch, but in a more regular form comparable to Elgin, was a precinct comprising the manses of its clergy together with the bishop's palace, the whole known as 'the Chanonry of Ross' or plain 'Chanonry'.

Regrettably, however, all this was achieved mainly at the expense of the parishes of the diocese, virtually every one of the thirty-six being appropriated to the bishopric or cathedral and served by a vicar. And almost more than Caithness, Ross suffered from a concentration of its parochial provision in the fertile lowlands of the east [Fig. 4.9], though even here the parish churches appear to have been of relatively modest size and construction. In its six vast western parishes (those of Gairloch and Lochbroom far exceeding their northern neighbours of Assynt, Durness

Fig. 4.9 Dornoch Cathedral.

and Farr in sheer extent), the main church might be supplemented by local chapels for outlying districts, but this did little to ameliorate the situation. Beyond this, the area was totally devoid of monastic foundations, for unlike Fearn and Rosemarkie in the east, such ancient centres as Applecross had no successors in the main medieval period. And although Gaelic was overwhelmingly the vernacular speech of the diocese, there is no evidence comparable to that at Dunkeld of provision for its study in the cathedral schools of Fortrose.

The Lady Chapel of the cathedral was served by chaplains supported by a special 'chantry' foundation to provide for the spiritual welfare of the Earls of Ross, and especially of the Countess Euphemia (I), last of the old Mactaggart line who died about 1395 and whose tomb was located here. Such foundations were very characteristic of the later Middle Ages, sometimes forming independent corporations associated with a 'collegiate church'. Of such the most northerly in mainland Scotland was that of St Duthac at Tain. Deriving from a much older cult in this locality, the structure of the church was certainly in existence by 1457 even if it was not until thirty years later that the foundation was formally incorporated by Bishop Thomas Hay. It was a favourite place of pilgrimage of King James IV who, like James II, endowed a special chaplainry within it. Alone of all the major medieval churches of Ross its fabric remains virtually intact, a simple but impressive design both within and without.

CONCLUSION

It will be seen, then, that the history of the medieval church in Ross and Caithness has features that tie it into the general pattern of ecclesiastical development in northern Europe at this time, the sporadic evangelizing of the early missionary saints being succeeded by the more settled 'tribal-monastic' form of 'Celtic Christianity' and then by the full organization of the 'Roman and Catholic Church'. But even in this definitive stage, developments here have a character very much their own, initially in the fact that this organization came from two sources, producing in Caithness, at least, parochial arrangements more akin to Norway than to Scotland.

There must also have been other local differences arising from the circumstance that although the liturgical language of the church, as of ecclesiastical and civil administration, was Latin, the area contained three vernaculars — Gaelic, Norn, and (in the towns) the form of northern English that would come to be known as 'Lowland Scots'. The social and political structure, too, within a broadly feudal outline, embodied ancient 'Pictish' as well as 'Gaelic' elements, represented at a higher level by the Earldom of Ross and its association for much of the fifteenth century with the Lordship of the Isles. Yet within this strongly idiosyncratic geographical and human context were to be found cathedrals and monasteries representing some of the finest qualities of medieval art; and in the parish churches, at least a semblance of the majesty of the universal liturgy so grandly, perhaps over-grandly, maintained in the two diocesan centres.

Acknowledgement

Figures 4.1, 4.2, 4.3 are reproduced by kind permission of the Royal Commission on the Ancient and Historical Buildings of Scotland; Figure 4.5, the Royal Museum of Scotland (formerly NMAS); Figure 4.8, the Scottish Tourist Board. The Society is grateful to Dr J. Close-Brookes for permission to reproduce Figure 4.4. Figures 4.6–4.8 have been redrawn by Douglas Lawson.

References

Barrow, G. W. S. *Kingship and Unity* (New History of Scotland 2). 1981.

Beaton, D. *Ecclesiastical History of Caithness*. 1909.

Bentinck, C. D. *Dornoch Cathedral and Parish*. 1926.

Cowan, I. B. The Organisation of Scottish Secular Cathedral Chapters, in *Records Scot. Church Hist. Soc*. 1960–62. XIV.

Cowan, I. B. *The Parishes of Medieval Scotland*. (Scot. Rec. Soc. 93). 1967.

Cowan, I. B. & Easson, D. E. *Medieval Religious Houses, Scotland*. 2nd ed. 1976.

Cowan, I. B. The Medieval Church in the Highlands, in Maclean of Dochgarroch, L. ed. *The Middle Ages in the Highlands*. 1981.

Crawford, B. E. The Earldom of Caithness and the Kingdom of Scotland, in *Northern Scotland*. 1974–77. II.

Curle, C. L. The Chronology of the Early Christian Monuments of Scotland, in *Proc. Soc. Antiq. Scot*. 1939–40. LXXIV.

Dunbar, J. G. The Medieval Architecture of the Scottish Highlands, in Maclean of Dochgarroch, L. ed. *The Middle Ages in the Highlands*. 1981.

Duncan, A. A. M. *Scotland: The Making of the Kingdom* (Edinburgh History of Scotland 1). 1975.

Gray, J. *Sutherland and Caithness in Saga-Time*. 1922.

Innes, C. *Origines Parochiales Scotiae* (II.2: Dioceses of Ross and Caithness) (Bannatyne Club). 1854.

Macdowall, C. G. *The Chanonry of Ross*. 1963.

MacGibbon, D. & Ross, T. *Ecclesiastical Architecture of Scotland*. 3 vols. 1896–97.

Mackay, A. (ed. Beaton, D.) *The History of the Province of Cait (Sutherland and Caithness)*. 1914.

Munro, R. W. & J. M. *Tain through the centuries*. 1966.

Omand, D. ed. *The Caithness Book*. 1972.

Omand, D. ed. *The Sutherland Book*. 1982.

Royal Comm. on Ancient and Historical Monuments of Scotland. *Inventory of . . . Caithness*. 1911.

Royal Comm. on Ancient and Historical Monuments of Scotland. *Inventory of . . . Sutherland*. 1911.

Scott, A. B. *The Pictish Nation, its people and its church*. 1918.

Simpson, W. D. Dornoch Cathedral: The High Church of Caithness, in *Proc. Soc. Antiq. Scot*. 1923–24. LVIII. Also in Bentinck, *Dornoch*.

Simpson, W. D. *The Celtic Church in Scotland*. (Aberdeen Univ. Studies III). 1935.

Smyth, A. P. *Warlords and Holy Men* (New History of Scotland 1). 1984.

Topping, P. Harald Maddadson, Earl of Orkney and Caithness, 1139–1206, in *Scot. Hist. Rev*. 1983. LXII.

Watt, D. E. R. ed. *Fasti Ecclesiae Scoticanae Medii Aevi*. 2nd draft. 1969.

THE EARLDOM OF ROSS AND THE LORDSHIP OF THE ISLES

Jean Munro

The period covered is roughly 1215 to 1476, and the subject falls into three parts: the first concentrates on building up the earldom of Ross under the first five earls, the second brings together the earldom of Ross and the lordship of the Isles, and the third gives some indication of the way in which the two fitted together in practice [Fig. 5.1].

THE EARLS OF ROSS:
EARLY THIRTEENTH – EARLY FOURTEENTH CENTURIES

The story of what the *Scots Peerage* calls the ancient earls of Ross began about 1215, when Farquhar helped Alexander II to crush rebellion in Moray and Ross and was rewarded with the earldom which, until then, seems to have been part of the province of Moray (*RMS*. II. i. App II). It was Farquhar, son of the lay patron of Applecross, who founded the abbey of Fearn in the early 1220s on a site in Kincardine parish; and it was he who, fifteen years later, moved the abbot and brethren, with their consent and 'for the more tranquilitie, peace and quyetnes', to the parish of Tarbat (*Chron.* 3–4). This was nearer the heart of the earldom and William, Farquhar's son, was recorded as dying at Earl's Allane, probably very near Fearn, in 1274 (*Cal. Fearn*). It was this first William who got a charter from Alexander III of the lordship of Skye, Norse until 1266, which was held along with the earldom but not merged with it.

There is no ready-made definition of the earldom of Ross. The earl's land covered the east of the modern county, but not the south part of the Black Isle, and we find the earls and their families dating charters and/or dying at Dingwall (Munro 4,6; Ross 163), Balconie (Ross 167), Alness (*RMS*, i. 301), Delny (*Chron.* 4, 9; Ross 169, 173), Earl's Allane (*Cal. Fearn*), and Tain (*Chron.* 4; Ross 198). The southern march was the river Beauly and the northern probably the Kyle of Sutherland, but when we consider the west, matters become much more complicated. In 1324 there was a definition of the bounds of the earldom of Moray as granted to Thomas Randolph. In the west this refers to the 'lands of Locharkaig and Glengarry and Glenelg, then by the march of Glenelg to the sea towards the west, and by the sea to the bounds of North Argyll which belongs to the Earl of Ross: and so by those marches to the marches of Ross and by the marches of Ross to the water of Forne [Beauly] and thence to the sea' (*Moray Reg.* 342). We know that Kintail and Gairloch were described as being in North Argyll in fourteenth-century charters granted by the earls

EARLS OF ROSS AND LORDS OF THE ISLES

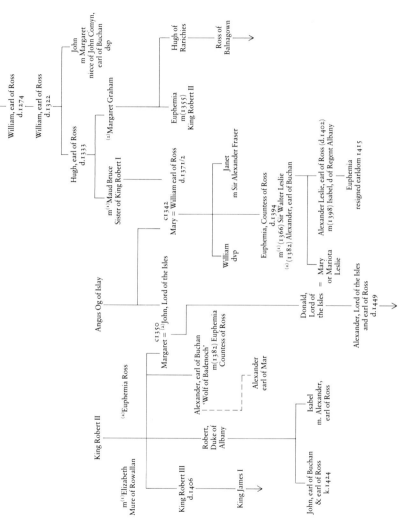

Fig. 5.1 Earls of Ross and Lords of the Isles.

of Ross to Ranald of the Isles (*RRS*. vi. 505) and Paul McTyre (*RMS*. i. 437). The Moray definition seems to tell us two things: first that North Argyll was a geographical description and has no relation to the modern county of Argyll and indeed had no common boundary with it; and second that in the fourteenth century the western coastlands were not part of the earldom of Ross, although held by the earls.

William, 3rd Earl of Ross was a supporter of Balliol and was in the tower of London after the battle of Dunbar in 1296 until about 1303/4 (Barrow 104). In 1306 he was responsible for the capture at Tain of Bruce's wife and daughter, his sister Mary the Countess of Buchan, and the Earl of Atholl (ibid. 228). During the confused events of 1308 he sent a request for help to Edward II, but when he received none he submitted to Bruce at Auldearn in October (ibid. 251–52; *APS*. i. 117). He was given easy terms, getting all his lands back with the additions of Ferincoskry (an area on the north of the Kyle of Sutherland) and the until then royal burgh of Dingwall and its castle (*RMS*. i. II. 370). Nor was this all, for William's sons Hugh and John were singled out for honours. In 1323 Hugh married the king's sister Maud (Ross 192) and thereafter added to the lands his father owned, getting Cromarty and Nairn and extending south into Strathglass (*RMS*. i. II. 54, 55, 65). John, his younger brother, also made a profitable marriage through royal influence — to Margaret Comyn, niece and co-heiress of John Earl of Buchan (Barrow 384; *RMS*. i. II. 49). The earl was an English supporter but his wife Isobel, daughter of the Earl of Fife, escaped north to crown Bruce in 1306, only to be captured a few months later with the royal ladies at Tain. Buchan died in 1308, and his lands and the marriages of his two nieces came into the king's hands. Margaret's sister married Henry de Beaumont; they became, in Professor Barrow's phrase, 'irretrievably English' and were disinherited after Bannockburn, their lands in Buchan being divided among several of Bruce's followers (Barrow 385). John and Margaret had no children and in 1316 Margaret's lands, which lay between the rivers Ythan and Don in Aberdeenshire, were entailed on John's elder brother Hugh (*RMS*. i. II. 11). This brought a great extension of wealth, power and influence to the earls of Ross. Yet another marriage seems to have been arranged, this time for Isabel, sister of Hugh and John; for a dispensation is said to have been issued by the Pope in 1317 for her marriage with Edward Bruce (*SP*. vii. 235), though they were not married when he died the following year.

Hugh was Earl of Ross for only ten years and fell at the battle of Halidon Hill in 1333 (*Chron*. 6). Just two months before he died Hugh gave charters to his younger son Hugh of lands at Rarichies, between Balintore and Nigg (Ross 165), and also of the lands in Buchan still in the hands of his uncle's widow Margaret (Ross 167).

Hugh's son William, 5th Earl, was said to be in Norway when his father died and not to have taken possession of the earldom until 1336. The family chronicle says that he returned after long banishment but gives no hint of the cause (*Chron*. 6, 9). The same chronicle also says that the abbey of Fearn built in Finlay's time was only of clay and rough stones, and that it was William who inspired the building of the kirk of hewn stones, the date of the operation being 1338–55 (*Chron.* 6, 7).

FIRST LINKS WITH THE LORDSHIP:
MID – LATER FOURTEENTH CENTURY

In spite of his close connections with the royal house, made even closer in 1355 when Robert the Steward (later Robert II) married William's half-sister Euphemia (*CPL.* iii. 574), William ends up a sad and frustrated man, seeing the split between the earldom and the traditional heartlands of Ross. He married in 1342 Mary, daughter of another Bruce supporter, Angus og of the Isles (*CPL.* iii. 85), a marriage which is a major landmark in our story. They had only one son William, who died young, probably about 1357, for in August of that year he was reported to be too ill to travel to London to take his place as one of the hostages for the payment of the King's ransom (*RRS.* vi. 175, 186; *CDS.* iii. 435). Perhaps young William was always weakly, for seven years before his death, in April 1350, the earl nominated his brother Hugh as his heir in the event of his death without legitimate heirs male of his body. This nomination had the consent of the granter's sister Marjorie, Countess of Caithness and Orkney, and was on condition of getting the King's consent. The document also states that this was done 'at the instance and request of all the great men and nobles of our whole earldom of Ross and of freeholders and others both cleric and lay' (Ross 163). Earl William was survived by his daughters Euphemia and Janet, but he supported his father's grants to Hugh of lands of Rarichies and added more lands in the heart of Ross even before his son's death (Ross 173, 181). William was already out of royal favour through his murder in 1346 of Ranald MacRuari when royal forces collected at Elcho, near Perth, before the battle of Neville's Cross, and his subsequent desertion of the King's army (Nicholson 146). Later he brought further trouble on himself by supporting his relatives the Steward and the Lord of the Isles in their defiance of David II during the 1360s, and with them earned the dislike of David's queen, Margaret Logie.

This is probably the background to the marriage of William's elder daughter Euphemia to Sir Walter Leslie, which took place in or about 1366 (*RMS.* i. 258; *CPL.* iv. 59). Walter was a younger son of the Fife family of Leslie of Leslie. He and his brother Norman were soldiers of fortune in Prussia, France and Italy, and had been on crusade with King Peter of Cyprus to Alexandria in 1365. His marriage to Euphemia may have been arranged, and was certainly supported, by King David II, probably in the hope of detaching the heir to the earldom of Ross from the strong Highland party forming round the Steward and the Lord of the Isles. After their marriage Walter was much about the court, and in high favour with the king and queen. The marriage was followed by the resignation by William of all his earldom lands into the hands of David II for a re-grant, dated 23 October 1370, giving succession to heirs male of the body, followed by Euphemia and Walter and their heirs (*RMS.* i. 354).

Very soon after this, in February 1370/1, David died, and on 24 June 1371 William addressed a complaint to his half brother-in-law, now Robert II (Ross 193; *Chron.* 33–38; *AB Ill.* ii. 387–91, English trans. in Innes 70–72). He says that David had given to Walter and Euphemia 'all my land and also those of my brother Hugh within Buchan, without our leave and without legal process'. It appears that Hugh had been 'in foreign parts as a banished man'; William says that he tried to object, and travelled to see David at Aberdeen. There when he 'was invited to dine with my lord the king, I asked, after dinner, an answer about my affairs; but the king, after consulting, sent me a great schedule of questions to be answered, wherein were put forward many authorities of the civil law; which, when I had read, I said I did not come to dispute at law with my lord the king, and then, without seeking leave, I journeyed to Ross'. He met the king again in Inverness and was forced to agree to make grants to Sir Walter Leslie, and so the earldom was restored. But William ended strongly '. . . never was my daughter spoused with the said Sir Walter with my will, but quite against my will. Nor did I make to them any grant or gift of lands or agreement of any kind of succession at any time up to the day of the death of my lord King David your predecessor, except by compulsion of my lord the king and through fear of his anger'.

Robert II did not act on this complaint, and after William's death on 9 February 1371/2 (*Cal. Fearn*) the earldom was confirmed to Walter and Euphemia. The Buchan lands had reverted from John and his widow Margaret Comyn to Earl Hugh in terms of the 1316 charter (*RMS.* i. 11. 11), and in 1333 Hugh settled them on his younger son Hugh (Ross 167). Before his death, Hugh the younger had apparently returned them to his elder brother Earl William so that he might 'make a better defence in them' while Hugh was abroad, but as we have seen they descended to Walter and Euphemia, and they were given by them on 4 June 1375 to Euphemia's sister Janet on her marriage to Sir Alexander Fraser, ancestor of the Saltoun family, as recompense for Janet's share of the earldom of Ross (*AB Ill.* iv. 87–88). Meanwhile Hugh seems to have died shortly before his brother and was succeeded in his Ross-shire lands by his son William (*RMS.* i. 619; Ross 176). From William descended the Rosses of Balnagown, chiefs of the clan, landowners in Ross but not in Buchan, heirs male of the old earldom but no longer earls of Ross. William held his lands from Walter and Euphemia, as his son Walter was to do from his cousin Alexander (Ross 178, 179).

The Leslies had a son Alexander, and a daughter Mary. Walter Leslie died at Perth in February 1381/2 (*Chron.* 9) and within five months Euphemia was married to Alexander Stewart, the Wolf of Badenoch, who took the title of Earl of Buchan (*RMS.* i. 736, 742). Alexander Leslie seems to have succeeded to the earldom of Ross on his mother's death *c.*1394, but he died at Dingwall in May 1402 (*Cal. Fearn*). By his wife Isabel, daughter of Robert, Duke of Albany, Regent of Scotland, Alexander had a daughter, yet another Euphemia, who was taken over by her grandfather Albany who by 1405 was calling himself lord of the ward of Ross (*Cawdor Bk.* 5).

It is now that the Lords of the Isles come directly into the picture because Mary Leslie, aunt of the heiress of Ross, was married to Donald Lord of the Isles. The battle fought at Harlaw in 1411 by Donald is regarded as his challenge to the Regent for the earldom of Ross. There are two extremes of interpretation of Donald's motives in undertaking the invasion of the east of Scotland: one is that he was aiming to take over the earldom of Ross, and the other is that he was aiming to take over the crown of Scotland. Donald's claim to Ross was in right of his wife Mary Leslie. This was fairly straightforward, as in the normal way she would have been heir presumptive to her niece Euphemia who was still very young, certainly under thirteen, in 1411. The succession had already gone through the female line when Mary's mother had followed her father in 1371/2. On the death of Alexander in 1402 Donald might have expected the official wardship of the infant heiress. But as we have seen, by 1405 Albany had taken over his grandchild. The power of the Albanys was getting very strong in the Highlands. Recently Mar had been acquired by one of them in very dubious circumstances, and Donald may well have had good reason to suspect that Ross would be similarly swallowed up. There may have been more to it than that, for after the mysterious death of David Duke of Rothesay in 1402, and the death of Robert III in 1406 at the time of the capture by England of his son James, the Regent Albany looked like swallowing up not just Ross but all Scotland. Donald was probably one of the few magnates and certainly the only one in the Highlands capable of withstanding Albany. In 1407 his nephew Hector Maclean of Duart got a safe conduct to visit James in England and in the following year English envoys visited Donald (Nicholson 234). Was he perhaps setting up assistance for James against Albany with English support?

Whatever Donald's exact motive or objective may have been is hard to determine because the result of the battle of Harlaw was indecisive. Donald had seized Inverness and marched east. In July 1411 he was caught by an Albany army under Mar and fought at Harlaw near Inverurie. Both sides claimed to have won, but Donald withdrew to the Isles and later in the season Albany had an army in Dingwall and a garrison in the castle there. In 1412 he raised more men, but Donald submitted, handed over hostages and took an oath to keep the peace (Nicholson 235).

Three years later Albany persuaded Euphemia, still under seventeen, to resign the earldom to his son John, already Earl of Buchan, whom failing to his other sons in turn and finally to Albany himself (*Reg. Ho. Charter.* 243). Even so, in 1421 Donald referred to himself in petitions to the Pope as Lord of the Isles and of the earldom of Ross (*CSSR.* i. 268–69, 271–72), and in a document written in Scots in 1420 his wife appears as Lady of the Isles and of Ross (Brodie).

The date of Donald's death is uncertain, probably 1423. His son Alexander called himself Lord of the Isles and Master of the earldom of Ross in 1426 (*CSSR.* ii. 133–34) and also in 1427 (*RMS.* ii. 2287). By this time Buchan was dead, killed at Verneuil in 1424, and the Albany family all dead or disgraced by the newly released King James; but Alexander's mother was still alive. After some ups and downs of fortune, including prison in Tantallon, Alexander was recognized as Earl of Ross before January 1436/7 (Gordon Cumming 5; Macfarlane 12*a*).

From about 1436 then, the earldom of Ross was held jointly with the lordship of the Isles, first by Alexander until 1449, and then by his son John until the forfeiture of the earldom to the crown in 1475. The story of the period appears in *The Middle Ages in the Highlands* (Maclean 23–37), and only the place of the earldom is relevant here. Under these two lords the north Argyll lands seem to have been included with the earldom of Ross, and Skye with the lordship: John granted Lochalsh, Lochcarron and Lochbroom to his natural brother Celestine in 1463 (*RMS*. ii. 806), and in the same year Celestine also received from his brother 28 merklands in Sleat, now described as in the lordship of the Isles (ibid.). Also later, in 1498, Alexander MacLeod of Dunvegan (Alasdair Crotach) was confirmed in lands in Skye within the lordship of the Isles (*RMS*. ii. 2420), although presumably his ancestors once held them from the Ross lords of Skye. Although Alexander and John both spent some time on the eastern seaboard, there is no surviving record of either of them being in the northern part of the west coast, even though what was once north Argyll was now definitely within their earldom.

The island lords had until the 1430s spent their time in Islay, Mull, Morvern and Lochaber, to judge by the place/dates of their charters. From similar evidence we can judge something of the movements of Alexander and John. Many of the surviving documents reflect their dual role, and deal with lands and affairs of the Isles and the earldom of Ross. Alexander seems to have been somewhat Ross-oriented, but this may have been because for some years in the late 1430s and early 1440s he was Justiciar north of Forth (as Earl William had been a century earlier), holding his courts in Inverness. He died at Dingwall in 1449 and was buried at Fortrose (*Misc. Scot.* iv. 130) as Earl of Ross, rather than with his predecessors as Lords of the Isles in Iona. But he and his son John, who was never Justiciar, seem to have regarded their roles as interchangeable. The charters issued in either territory did not concern lands in that territory only: for example two concerning Urquhart lands in the Black Isle were dated at Islay in 1472 (Laing 1. 453) and 1475 (Cromarty Box. 1), and a Thane of Cawdor was confirmed in his father's lands in a document dated in Kintyre in 1468 (*Cawdor Bk*. 51–52). Similarly many charters of lands in the west were drawn up at Dingwall.

The appearance of island chiefs as charter witnesses at Dingwall and Inverness is also recorded in this period. The Lords of the Isles had a council to advise them, and while accounts of its functions and composition are traditional, ten of the documents that survive state that they are granted specifically with the consent of the council. Three out of the six in which witnesses are named are dated at Dingwall, and a fourth at Inverness. Maclean of Duart figures in all four of them, Macleans of

Lochbuie, Coll and Ardgour each make one or two appearances, and even lesser chiefs like Mackinnon and MacQuarrie of Ulva and MacDuffie of Colonsay are included (Monro 140–42). Some of the earl's mainland vassals such as Munro of Foulis and Ross of Balnagown also witnessed his charters in Ross, but there is no indication that they dominated the men from the Isles. We have found only one record of the meeting of a council. This took place on 28 May 1450 within the earl's chamber in the castle of Dingwall, to consider some business concerned with grants by the old earls of Ross of lands in Ferincoskry (Inverchassley and Ospisdale). The witnesses named, and presumably attending, were John Stewart lord of Lorn, Lachlan Maclean lord of Duart, William thane of Cawdor, John Maclean of Coll and an unidentified Rolland son of Alexander (surely from the west) (Ross 191). Not the traditional island council, you may say, but hardly a council of the earl of Ross either.

ANNEXATION OF EARLDOM AND LORDSHIP: LATE FIFTEENTH CENTURY

The end came for the earldom of Ross nearly twenty years before the end of the lordship of the Isles. John's treaty with Edward IV came to light and he was summoned before Parliament in the autumn of 1475 — summoned not in the Isles, but at Dingwall Castle and at the crosses of Dingwall and Inverness (*APS*. ii. 108–10). He failed to appear and action was taken by Huntly before 28 March 1476. In July, John submitted to the king and was stripped of his earldom of Ross, of Kintyre and Knapdale, and of the office of sheriff of Inverness and Nairn (ibid. 113). The earldom of Ross was annexed to the crown and later given to the king's second son, while the lordship of the Isles (transformed into a lordship of Parliament) was given back to John (*Reg. Ho. Charter.* 457). Clearly the king had not the power or resources to capture the lordship (it was different twenty years later); the earldom was rich and handy and was the obvious choice for forfeiture. John's estranged wife Elizabeth Livingston was provided for from rents of lands in Ross and in Buchan confirmed to her by the king (*RMS*. ii. 1227, 1272, 1318 etc).

The arrangement of 1476 was not permanent, however, and by the end of August 1493 John had been deprived of the lordship also (*RMS*. ii. 2172). The pretext for this was a series of rebellions, including unrest in Ross, engineered by younger members of John's family. But by then the earldom had been turned into a royal dukedom, and its affairs were no longer the direct concern of any of the families who had held it during the previous centuries.

References

Manuscript:

Brodie	Papers at Brodie Castle.
Cromarty	Ross of Cromarty papers, SRO GD159.

Gordon Cumming	Papers in National Library of Scotland.
Macfarlane	Papers of Walter Macfarlane, NLS MS 35.4.
Munro	Munro of Foulis papers, SRO GD93.
Reg. Ho. Charter	Collection in Scottish Record Office, RH6.
Ross	Balnagown papers (per J & F Anderson), SRO GD297.

Printed:

AB Ill.	*Illustrations of the Topography & Antiquities of the Shires of Aberdeen and Banff*. (Spalding Club). 1847–69.
APS	*Acts of the Parliament of Scotland*. 1814–75.
Barrow	Barrow, G. W. S., *Robert Bruce* 2nd ed. 1976.
Cal. Fearn	Calendar of Fearn, in *Historical Manuscripts Commission of Report II*. 1871.
Cawdor Bk.	*The Book of the Thanes of Cawdor*. (Spalding Club). 1859.
Chron.	*Ane Breve Chronicle of the Earlis of Ross*. 1850.
CDS	*Calendar of Documents relating to Scotland*. ed. J. Bain, 1881–88.
CPL	*Calendar of Entries in the Papal Registers relating to Great Britain and Ireland: Papal Letters*. 1893–.
CSSR	*Calendar of Scottish Supplications to Rome*. (Scottish History Society). 1934–.
Innes	*Ane Account of the Familie of Innes*. (Spalding Club). 1864.
Laing	Laing, H., *Descriptive Catalogue of Impressions from Ancient Scottish Seals*. (Bannatyne Club). 1850.
Maclean	*The Middle Ages in the Highlands*, ed. L. Maclean. (Inverness Field Club). 1981.
Misc. Scot.	Fragment of 'A briefe Chronicle of the Earles of Ros', in *Miscellanea Scotica*. 1820.
Monro	*Monro's Western Isles of Scotland*. ed. R. W. Munro, 1961.
Moray Reg.	*Registrum Episcopatus Moraviensis*. (Bannatyne Club). 1837.
Nicholson	Nicholson, R., *Scotland: The Later Middle Ages*. 1974.
RMS	*Registrum Magni Sigilli Regum Scotorum*, 1882–1914.
RRS	*Regesta Regum Scottorum, vol. vi David II*. ed. B. Webster, 1982.
SP	*The Scots Peerage*. ed. Sir J. Balfour Paul, 1904–14.

Fig. 6.1 Cromarty and the Cromarty Firth towards Invergordon.

THE MORAY FIRTH PROVINCE:
TRADE AND FAMILY LINKS
IN THE EIGHTEENTH CENTURY

Ian R. M. Mowat

It remains all too common for even relatively distinguished historians to treat all the territories north and west of an unspecified 'Highland line' as integral parts of a broadly unified, cultural and economic unit. More sophisticated interpreters of the past have drawn their Highland line to exclude more obviously non-Highland areas such as Aberdeenshire and the Laigh of Moray, while few who have looked seriously at the evidence would be prepared to defend the belief that Caithness is Highland, rather than a southern outlier of Scandinavian Scotland.

The delusion that the eastern portion of the present district of Ross and Cromarty has, at all times, been an indivisible segment of the north-west Highlands is more difficult to lay at rest. Undoubtedly, the links between Easter Ross (the two peninsulas circumscribed by the Dornoch, Cromarty, Beauly and Moray Firths) and the land mass to the north and west are strong. Yet it can be argued that the links binding the area in question to the low country on the southern shore of the Moray Firth are at least as strong, and that in historic terms as well as in the view of 1960s' planners, Easter Ross can be held to be part of the province of Greater Moray.

The particular purpose of this paper will be to examine the case for this wider Moray Firth province in the eighteenth century, as seen primarily from Easter Ross.

THE LAND-OWNING CLASSES BY
THE EIGHTEENTH CENTURY

Much of the earlier history of the area bears out the strength of the Moray Firth connection, with the close links between the Mormaers and then the first earls of Ross and Moray. It could be argued, perhaps, that these links can be seen within the wider context of the northern Highlands as a whole but, from the thirteenth century at least, some of the connections which bound together the various parts of the Moray Firth littoral also served to distinguish this littoral from surrounding Highland territories.

While the modernizing tendencies of the Canmore dynasty first hit Easter Ross in the twelfth century, with the reorganization of the diocese of Ross and the establishment, by the king, of royal castles at Redcastle and Dunscaith, the following century marks the real point of departure (Watson 1976. xix, xxvi). The foundation of episcopal seats and royal castles in the western Highlands did not significantly alter the essentially Celtic nature of the local society there in the middle ages. The first Bishop of Ross, Macbeth, would appear from the evidence of his name to have been of Celtic origin, perhaps even connected to the local nobility; and despite David I's best intentions, there must have been a danger that the church in Ross would go native. However, without exception, Macbeth's successors bore non-Celtic names, and the church above all other institutions can be seen as the Trojan Horse by which southern influence penetrated to this part of the world. This role was maintained throughout the centuries, irrespective of irrelevant upheavals such as the Reformation and Presbyterian/Episcopalian controversies. Nor was it only at the top of the ecclesiastical structure that southern influence was felt. By 1227 all but one of the chapter of Ross, composed mainly of parish priests from the Black Isle and eastern parts of Ross, bore English names (ibid. xx).

The imposition of an initial royal presence in the twelfth century was followed by the arrival of other more significant secular influences in the next century. The Freskin family, already well established in Moray and with a scion holding the earldom of Sutherland to the north, had obtained the lands and castle of Avoch by the middle of the thirteenth century and continued to hold it as one of their principal residences during the next hundred years. At the same time the first sheriff of Cromarty known to history makes his appearance, an Anglo-Norman by the name of Mowat (ibid. xix, xxiii).

If the king, the church and incoming landowners represent three main elements of southern influence, the fourth (and in many respects one of the most significant in the long term) was the burgh. Again, the early to mid-thirteenth century was a turning point. Although the burghers of Tain have been known to claim that the status of their community dates back as far as the middle of the eleventh century, the oldest burghal charter for which evidence remains relating to Easter Ross pertains to Dingwall. Alexander II erected the town a royal burgh in 1227. By 1264, Cromarty [Fig. 6.1] also was established as a royal burgh while it is possible that Rosemarkie, which certainly was a bishop's burgh by 1286, received its first charter as early as the first quarter of the century. Although Tain's precise status remained debateable for some centuries, it seems unquestionable that it had privileges equivalent to those of a burgh by the end of the thirteenth century (Pryde 1965. 18–19, 24, 28).

None of these four influences by themselves need significantly have altered the historical development of the area. Royal castles along the west coast were only significant centres of royal influence on those rare occasions when the king chose to visit them; many of the traditional Highland clans descended, or claimed descent from Anglo-Norman barons; and the foundation of isolated royal burghs such as Tarbert in Knapdale did little in the long term to further the economic development of Argyllshire.

In Easter Ross, as in Moray, the combination of all four factors, together with a sympathetic geographic environment, produced a cultural shift which was to survive. Even so, the survival was touch and go. In the fourteenth century the greater part of the area came under the domination of the Earls of Ross. Robert the Bruce added the royal burghs of Dingwall and Cromarty and the sheriffdom of Cromarty to the already substantial holdings of the earls north of the Cromarty Firth, and it was only with the forfeiture of the title towards the end of the fifteenth century that there was a reversion to the crown. Domination by the earldom was serious enough when the title was held by the male descendants of Farquhar Macintsaggart of Applecross, the first earl, but became an even greater threat to the survival of non-Gaelic culture when the title passed at the beginning of the fifteenth century to the Lords of the Isles. Although it might be unwise to emphasize the Celtic bias of the Macdonalds, the period during which they held the earldom cannot have been noted for any significant extension of southern influence (Reid 1894. 1–10).

It is perhaps significant that English speech and Lowland ways survived most obviously at the eastern tip of the Black Isle, where the Church maintained its position and where the Freskin family was succeeded in Avoch by a number of families with connections across the Moray Firth, such as the Douglases of Balvenie. Certainly by the middle of the fifteenth century English place-names were widespread in the Black Isle, whereas in the rest of Easter Ross their appearance was very intermittent (Watson 1976. 113–46; Cromartie 1979. 110).

After the Reformation the church stronghold in Rosemarkie fell under the influence of the Mackenzies who, from the fifteenth century, had spread rapidly from their original base in Kintail. By 1560, however, the anglicization of the area was too far advanced to be reversed and in any event it may be doubted how far the acquisitive Mackenzies, who continued to add to their holdings in Easter Ross well into the eighteenth century, made serious attempts to retain their links with their Celtic past. Like the Campbells of Argyll and Glenorchy, the leading Mackenzie magnates were, at most, both Highland chieftains and Lowland lairds. By the start of the eighteenth century, although the Mackenzie links with the west remained strong, their presence in Easter Ross was already two centuries old and they could be considered local landowners in the same way as the other dominant landowning families, the Munros, the Rosses and the Urquharts, all of whom had been established since the early middle ages. Some of the Mackenzie proprietors also held property in the Highland areas of Ross and a few even had their main estates there; but the majority of Mackenzie landlords were firmly and exclusively based in Easter Ross (Mackenzie 1885–86. 293–324). Indeed, lairds with no territorial connection outside the area formed the great majority of landowners in Easter Ross throughout the eighteenth century. Most were representatives of families whose connections were of long standing, although the particular branch of the family owning any given estate varied considerably over the centuries.

Representing as it did, therefore, an oasis of fertility in the generally barren desert of the north-west Highlands, Easter Ross for long had been a magnet attracting incomers from surrounding Highland districts. In the distant past the O'Beolain Earls of Ross and their relatives the Mackenzies of Kintail had taken this route, while towards the end of the seventeenth century they were followed by the Mathesons of Bennetsfield, the Gordons of Invergordon and (somewhat involuntarily) the Macleods of Assynt. Although they made their mark during their period of tenure, none of these families, with the partial exception of the Macleods, proved to have staying power (Mackenzie & Macbain 1900. 30; Macleod 1970. 15, 18; Bulloch 1906. 2, 13–14).

Throughout the centuries there were also landlords who were total incomers to the north of Scotland. Apart from the period immediately after the Reformation, however, when there was a temporary influx of a number of southern families such as the Murrays, Stewarts and Keiths, their number was small before the end of the eighteenth century, and nouveau riche purchasers of estates in Easter Ross almost invariably had an existing family connection with the area. The Davidson who purchased Tulloch in 1762, for example, was a cousin of Kenneth Bayne, from whom the estate had been sequestrated the previous year (Warrand 1965. 68; Ross 1768. 1; Macrae 1974. 58; Mackintosh 1865. 135).

The final element in the composition of the landowning community in eighteenth-century Easter Ross was that of the Moray lairds. Over the centuries the Moray Firth acted as a bridge whereby landowners established links in both directions. The Earls of Ross obtained territory in Moray in the fourteenth and fifteenth centuries, the Mackenzies in the sixteenth, the Urquharts from at least the seventeenth and the Munros in the eighteenth. From Moray came a whole sequence of landlords, including many well-established names such as the Cawdors holding Ferintosh in the Black Isle, the Dunbars holding Bennetsfield also in the Black Isle, and the Inneses owning extensive properties in Easter Ross proper (Reid 1894. 1–10; *OSA*. v. 205; Ross 1777. 7; Wallace Brown 1899–1906. 24; Mackenzie & MacBain 1900. 30; Tayler 1946. 132, 187).

Although the number of lairds owning property on both sides of the firth was never more than a small proportion of the total (seldom more than half a dozen at any time in the eighteenth century), several Moray lairds held extensive properties in Easter Ross and they formed the most significant body of landowners after those purely indigenous to the area. In the middle of the century, for example, Urquhart of Meldrum, Forbes of Culloden, Leslie of Findrassie and Rose of Kilravock all figured in the top twenty largest owners of land in the seventeen parishes which make up the area designated as Easter Ross for the purposes of this paper (E 901/28/1).

But even amongst the smaller gentry it was not unknown for property to be held on both sides of the firth. In 1751 Hugh Rose of Geddes, a middling Moray landowner, held a small estate in the county of Cromarty; and during the latter part of the century at least, the Robertsons, seventeenth-century incomers from Inverness who by this time held the small property of Kindeace in the parishes of Kilmuir and Rosskeen, also held the equally small estate of Urchany in Nairn (NLS ms 108.78; GD 146/8).

Family ties, of course, regularly were strengthened by marriage, such as that of Sir Hugh Munro of Foulis to the daughter of Hugh Rose of Kilravock in 1758; and as the century wore on and such older established Moray families as the Roses of Kilravock themselves sold their Ross-shire estates, the links across the water were maintained by the arrival of new names. James Grant, for example, a native of Moray who lived for some time in Cromarty before going south to make his fortune, purchased the estate of Redcastle from the bankrupt Mackenzies at the end of the century to add to his other estates elsewhere (Mackenzie 1898. 145; Barron 1903. I. 42).

'LOWLAND HIGHLANDERS' AND 'LOWLAND BODIES'

While the gentry in Easter Ross constituted a society set apart from their peers to the west (a writer in 1780 lamented the fact that a split amongst the Easter Ross voters had given political control of the county to the gentlemen of the west) (GD 146/14), the pattern was more varied lower down the social scale. It is probably true to say that in the Easter Ross peninsula a thin veneer of Lowland culture sustained by the gentry, the clergy and a few substantial farmers and merchants was superimposed upon a peasant society which remained basically Gaelic in its orientation. The term 'Lowland Highlanders', used some years ago as the title for a history of Tain, is a not inappropriate description of the society in the surrounding parishes as well, and it is possible to point to eighteenth-century Easter Ross as an agrarian, rather than a pastoral, Celtic community (Robertson 1972).

The Gaelic element in this society constantly was being strengthened by immigration from the west, particularly towards the end of the century as those evicted from the Highland straths found new homes in the towns and villages and on the recently-divided commonties of Easter Ross. Even in mid-century, however, this trend is apparent. Of forty-one disbanded soldiers settled at Newtarbet by the Commissioners of Annexed Estates in 1765, only nineteen came from Easter Ross itself. Four were incomers from Caithness (whether Highland or Lowland Caithness is not clear), and no less than fifteen came from Wester Ross and Sutherland. Of the remainder, one came from Banff and, more surprisingly, one from Renfrew. The last of the set came from as far away as Devon though this can be explained on the assumption that the individual in question was probably a retainer of the forfeited Earl of Cromartie who had been exiled to Devon after being reprieved from the sentence of death passed on him in 1746 (E787/28/5).

The pattern was very different in the eastern Black Isle. In the three parishes of Cromarty, Rosemarkie and Avoch the general population spoke the Moray dialect of English and were regarded with contempt by their near neighbours across the Cromarty Firth, 'being looked upon in a Despicable Light — no more than Lowland Bodies' (E787/24). In their turn the 'Lowland Bodies' were equally contemptuous of those about

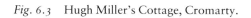

Fig. 6.2   Fisher families, Big Vennel, Cromarty. Old postcard.

Fig. 6.3   Hugh Miller's Cottage, Cromarty.

Fig. 6.4   Sculptured stone panel at no. 7 Braehead, Cromarty, dated 1727.

them. The townspeople of Cromarty [Figs. 6.2–6.4] referred scathingly to the country people of Nigg as 'Gaelickers' and the schoolboys of Cromarty in Hugh Miller's day picked fights with the Nigg ferrymen whom they derided for their broken English (Miller 1869. 43; Mackenzie 1928. III. 75).

Even in the Black Isle, however, the flood of landless Gaelic-speaking immigrants could affect the cultural balance. The numbers drawn to Cromarty by the prospect of work in the various industrial enterprises established there, more particularly after 1772, were enough to lead to the construction of a Gaelic chapel to serve their needs. In Avoch and Rosemarkie too, incoming Gaelic-speaking servants and labourers constituted a significant minority (*OSA*. XII. 257; *NSA*. XIV. 27, 30; CH 2/66/7).

MORAY FIRTH LINKS

Outside the Black Isle, as in it, the main bastion of English language, as of Lowland culture in general, was the town. For much of the eighteenth century Fortrose was regarded (though without any official justification) as the capital of Ross, while Tain was pre-eminent on account of its larger population and central position in the richest part of the county. Dingwall, anciently the chief seat of the Earls of Ross and subsequently the officially-recognized county capital, ranked a poor third in the eighteenth century. In fact, in terms of population, wealth and prestige it was inferior also to Cromarty. Cromarty had ceased to be a royal burgh towards the end of the seventeenth century and its succeeding status as a burgh of barony lapsed after the Jacobite rebellion of 1745. Only in the nineteenth century did it regain burghal privileges but this should not disguise the fact that during the second half of the eighteenth century Cromarty was the most active centre of population in the whole area.

None of these towns was of major importance in national terms at the beginning of the century. Thirty-eight of the sixty-five royal burghs paid more *cess* than Tain, the largest contributor from Easter Ross, and even by the end of the century Tain's population still did not exceed 1,500 people (*CRBS*. 1870–1918. V. 122, 236, 421–22; VI. 631; *Abstract* 1802. 542).

By comparison with the major burghs to the south of the Moray Firth (Inverness, Elgin and Banff), Tain, Fortrose and Dingwall put up a poor show. None could match the commercial enterprise and social life of the former, and the dowagers of bonnet lairds who constituted the genteel society of late eighteenth-century Cromarty were very small beer compared to the wealthy landlords and nobles whose town houses were such a distinguishing feature of the three large towns to the south during this period (Miller 1863. 307; 1869. 402).

Economic and Trading Links

Although by the eighteenth century the burghs had long since ceased to have a monopoly on trade, in Easter Ross at least they did constitute, along with Cromarty, the main trading centres; and much of this trade was local, within the Moray Firth area. Throughout the century Inverness and Elgin dominated as suppliers of imported goods, and particularly at the start of the period Dingwall, Tain and Fortrose had almost no trade which went beyond these two burghs. In return Inverness above all provided a ready market for the local agricultural produce (CRBS. 1870–1918. VI. 640, 659, 662).

After 1748 a new market appeared within the area with the start of work on the construction of Fort George [Fig. 6.5]. It would be difficult to exaggerate the short term impact of Fort George on the economy of the inner Moray Firth. The fort represented by far the largest public work ever undertaken in the north of Scotland and its impact was felt in a number of ways. Local materials, especially stone, were used in its construction, with up to one hundred boats carrying materials from quarries at Munlochy, Cromarty and Covesea. The demands of the large garrison for fresh provisions forced up prices throughout the Black Isle, as well as more locally, and gave the fishermen of Avoch a captive market; and the soldiers themselves, though largely unproductive in economic terms, were used on occasion to improve the economic infrastructure by building roads in the region. Culturally, too, the fort made its mark. The ready availability of the Adam family as masons-in-charge at the fort over two decades meant that more landlords than would otherwise have been likely, had access to the sophisticated architectural styles of the south of Scotland (SLSP. 35:33. 2–3; OSA. xv. 613, 616; NLS. ms 108. 406).

If Inverness and Elgin were the main trading centres, other Moray ports took their share of the market. Findhorn was important in the first half of the century, while in the 1770s the enterprising merchants of Portsoy [Figs. 6.6; 6.7] sold items such as lime for fertiliser in Easter Ross and bought in return the marketable surpluses of grain from local landowners (Wight 1774–84. IV(i). 258, 268; Sinclair 1795. 63; GD 129/24/81; CH 2/350/1; GD 146/13). For grain was the staple export of Easter Ross. On both sides of the Cromarty Firth and on the Dornoch and Beauly Firths the various estates had girnals where oats, bere and latterly wheat were brought for dispatch to markets outside the region. Much of this business was handled by merchants from Portsoy or from much further afield, but

Fig. 6.5   Fort George across to Chanonry Point and Fortrose.

from the middle of the century Cromarty took an ever more active part in trade across the firth. In 1759 flax was being shipped from Cromarty to Inverness, while in the last quarter of the century Inverness provided the main market for the produce of the Cromarty brewery, built after 1772 by George Ross, the new proprietor of the Cromarty estate and probably the most far-sighted and unselfish landlord to hold property in the area during the century (*BLC*. 10 July 1749; Wight 1774–84. IV(i). 254–56). However, the man who probably deserved more credit than anyone else for the growing importance of Cromarty as a trading port was William Forsyth who, shortly after 1739, bought a freighting boat for coastal trade (Miller 1863. 290; Dunlop 1978. 50–51, 61). During the following decades his example was widely followed.

Although much of the commercial intercourse between the two sides of the firth was concerned with the exchange of commodities, there was also an exchange of services. Inverness continued to be a centre for lawyers and physicians, while at a lower level tradesmen from both Moray and Easter Ross competed with each other for business both in the north-west Highlands and in their own backyards. Even at this social level, therefore, there were opportunities for social intercourse across the water (Meldrum 1935. 6; Miller 1869. 191–92; Chambers 1827. II. 307). Thus William

77

Fig. 6.6 Feu Plan of Portsoy, Banffshire. Robert Johnston 1802 (Cullen House Drawings).

Fig. 6.7 Shorehead, Portsoy.

Forsyth's father, James, a mason and builder who had settled in Cromarty before 1722 when a herring boom brought temporary prosperity to the town, was a native of Moray. William himself, though born in Cromarty, returned to Moray for his wife, Elizabeth Russell of Earlsmill, the daughter of the Chamberlain to the Earl of Moray. Similarly, another Moray mason, James Anderson, formerly of Forres was settled in Milton of Newtarbat on the north side of the Cromarty Firth by 1785 (Miller 1863. 285–306; E 766/45).

Professional, Cultural, Political and Ecclesiastical Links

Inevitably, when family and trading connections were strong, cultural bonds were also of importance, quite apart from the use of a common dialect. Even in the early seventeenth century, masons from the north-east clearly found their way across the water to build castles at Cromarty and Castle Leod which were of a degree of sophistication unmatched elsewhere in the Highlands at the time (Cruden 1960. 170; Mackenzie 1947. 60–68). At the end of the same century the architectural link may have been maintained in a far more significant way. It has long been known that Colin Campbell, the main exponent of neo-Palladianism, the architectural style favoured by the early eighteenth-century British Whig establishment, was a member of the Cawdor family. It is now suggested that James Smith, who is held to be his stylistic mentor, may have belonged to a family of Moray masons settled in Easter Ross at the time when Viscount Tarbat was engaged in erecting his splendid new mansion of Newtarbat (Colvin 1974. 8).

More generally throughout the eighteenth century Moray and Easter Ross were distinguished from their Highland neighbours by the comparative excellence of their educational establishments. Even before the creation of a rash of academies at Inverness, Fortrose, Tain, Elgin and Fordyce at the end of the eighteenth and beginning of the nineteenth centuries, the burghs of the region had made considerable efforts to maintain better-than-average grammar schools. The existence of established schools in almost every parish, a feature not matched in the north-west Highlands as a whole, was supplemented by a whole range of private establishments; dame's schools, charitable schools, subscription schools and the like. While most of these schools served only their own immediate community, the top schools attracted students from a much wider area.

A memorial from the Burgh of Fortrose to the Commissioners of Annexed Estates in 1772, for example, pointed out that 'Now, and generally, there are from seventy to eighty boys attending the Grammar School of the Burgh; among whom are several gentlemen's sons, not only from the Country around, but from other counties at a considerable distance' (E 787/16/1). In the following decade the school of Mr Strath in Nairn had a high enough reputation to attract the sons of at least one Ross-shire gentleman, Robertson of Kindeace; although by 1793, John Robertson, the youngest of Kindeace's sons and still at school, had transferred to the recently established academy at Fortrose (GD 146/8; GD 146/8[a]).

Politically the counties of Ross, Cromarty, Inverness, Nairn, Moray and Banff each had their own individual Members of Parliament, but there were links which bound the two shores of the firth together. Cromarty and Nairn, it should be remembered, alternated MPs, with each county in turn being disenfranchised for the length of a Parliament (Ferguson 1968. 134). Though the linking of the two counties was on account of their small size, the geographical link was close as well since the estate of Ferintosh in the Black Isle, lying almost adjacent to the main portion of the fragmented county of Cromarty, was administratively part of Nairn (*OSA*. v. 205). And at the level of the burghs there was a further connection, with Fortrose being included in the Inverness group of burghs electing a member of Parliament (Pryde 1962. 54).

Another feature possibly common to both Moray and the Black Isle may be the pattern of ecclesiastical allegiance. After the abolition of Episcopacy in 1688, most of the north of Scotland remained antagonistic to the new Presbyterian regime. However, beginning with a series of revivals in early eighteenth-century Nigg, an enthusiasm for evangelical Calvinism quickly swept through the north-west Highlands with the Easter Ross peninsula very much at the heart of the movement (Forbes 1886. 157, 217–19, 276; CH 1/2/95; Hall 1807. II. 491–93). By way of contrast, large numbers of both landlords and tenants in the Black Isle and in the neighbourhood of Dingwall remained attached to the Episcopal Church, as did many in Moray and the north-east of Scotland in general (Forbes 1886. 16, 66, 68, 103, 122–24, 126–28, 131–32, 273; Pryde 1962. 102; Cant 1976. 153). Whether this common religious affiliation is merely coincidental or part of the more general cultural correspondence it is hard to say.

Transport and Communications

The principal element pulling the north and south shores of the Moray Firth together was the firth itself. Nowadays, it is all too easy to see water as a barrier to communication but in the eighteenth century, as earlier, water transport was much easier than transport on land. It is said that no wheeled transport was seen anywhere north of Inverness before the end of the first quarter of the eighteenth century, and even as late as 1740 an attempt by Fraser of Lovat to travel by coach from Inverness to Edinburgh ended in ignominious failure when, after numerous breakdowns, the coach finally disintegrated (Gardiner 1961. 44–45).

Roads and, more particularly, bridges remained less than satisfactory throughout the century, although within Easter Ross itself there were improvements on a fairly dramatic scale. Most of the major rivers and many of the minor streams were bridged and the main roads at least were capable of taking wheeled transport by the middle of the century. Exaggerated reports of the dreadful state of roads in Easter Ross were found by Bishop Forbes in 1762 to have been quite misleading, and even an eccentric like Sir John Gordon of Invergordon is unlikely to have taken the air in his carriage in 1773 if it involved risk to life and limb, or even a strong chance that he would not be able to complete his journey (Forbes 1886. 150; GD 146/13[a]). Nonetheless, occasional stretches of passable road did not make a good road system. Even in the latter part of the century movement by road was very restricted and not until 1771 did the Ross-shire Commissioners of Supply attempt a major initiative to improve the roads in the Black Isle. Only in 1777 was a road made for wheeled traffic from Geanies, the seat of the most road-conscious laird in the county, to the public road; and in 1778 it appears that it was still commonplace for goods to be transported on men's backs (SC 24/21/7; GD 146/13[b, c]).

By way of contrast, it was easier to get around by water in the eighteenth and early nineteenth centuries than it has been since. Within the bounds of the Presbytery of Chanonry (the area of the Black Isle), there were no less than six ferries operating in 1766. Some of them, at least, operated on Sundays, much to the disgust of the Presbytery. Four of these ferries operated in the Cromarty Firth — Cromarty to Nigg, Balblair to Invergordon, Resolis to Alness and Alcaig to Dingwall; the remaining two covered the Beauly Firth — Chanonry to Ardersier and Kessock to Inverness (CH 2/66/7[a]). By the end of the century, at least two additional services were running, from Castlecraig to Foulis and at Scuddale (*OSA*. v. 214). Quantity of course did not guarantee quality, and opinions varied as to the services on offer. Some of the ferries, such as that from Alcaig to Dingwall, were never more than passenger ferries; and because of the absence of harbours and slipways, use of even the more significant ferries could cause some inconvenience. As late as 1825 travellers on the Cromarty ferry had to be carried ashore on the north side on a woman's back (Sutherland 1825. 88). Travellers from the south regularly commented unfavourably on the size and seaworthiness of the ferryboats, comments which were occasionally all too drastically confirmed by major accidents. Bishop Forbes in 1762 found that the Chanonry ferry was not large enough to take horses, carriage and passengers all in one trip, while Sir John Sinclair in 1795 held all the ferries to be in a wretched state. He attributed the blame, interestingly enough, to the fact that they were in private ownership. Well into the nineteenth century little had changed, with the Chanonry ferry being described as a 'crazy boat' (Forbes 1886. 151; Sinclair 1795. 46–47; Sutherland 1825. 77).

These criticisms must be taken in perspective. While Ross-shire roads were compared unfavourably with those elsewhere, Ross-shire ferries might be as good as those operating in other parts of the country. Kessock ferry, for instance, which came in for its own share of criticism, was nonetheless found by Southey (1929. 167) in the early nineteenth century to be the best in Scotland. His enthusiasm, it has to be said, in the words of W. S. Gilbert, was only a form of 'modified rapture' for he went on to acknowledge that 'the best ferry is a bad thing'. Poor though they may have been, the multiplicity of ferries did provide ready means of crossing the firths and their numbers compare favourably with the number of crossing points which are in use today.

It was not until the early nineteenth century and the arrival of steam that a regular service was established crossing the Moray Firth proper, but well before 1800 it proved relatively easy to travel by sea, even when no established route existed. In 1780 Sir John Gordon's plans to cross from Invergordon to Balblair, en route to Cromarty, being thwarted by unfavourable winds and tides, he hired instead a boat which took him directly from Invergordon to Cromarty. The previous year it was suggested to Robertson of Kindeace that he might take a fishing boat across from Cadboll to Nairn as an alternative to returning home by chaise, while in 1787 Captain David Ross of Tain determined to transport himself to London in the company of Admiral Hood and Lord Reay 'by the first smack that sails from Cromarty', because of the great expense of travelling to London overland (GD 235/7; GD 146/13[d]; Macgill 1909. I. 215).

NATIONAL AND INTERNATIONAL PERSPECTIVES

Even the remotest Highland areas maintained some contact with the outside world, whether through the trade in black cattle, through the kelping industry, or by seasonal or semi-permanent migration to southern farms. Such contact was intermittent, however, and for most of the population was extremely limited. Even for the large number of soldiers serving in Highland regiments, contact with non-Highlanders was restricted by language.

Nevertheless, the ready availability of sea transport gave an outward-looking orientation to society around the Moray Firth, and in both Easter Ross and in Moray the picture was very different. If external trade from Easter Ross was dominated before 1700 by Inverness and Elgin, as the eighteenth century progressed the local inhabitants took an increasingly independent role in marketing their own produce and in importing the outside goods they required. Grain was always the main export commodity of the area, although until the middle of the century, when Britain as a whole moved from surplus to deficit production, southern markets cannot have been easy to find. From at least the 1750s, however, grain was supplied to a wide variety of United Kingdom markets. In 1757 Ebeneezer Munro of Glasgow purchased local bere and meal; in 1759 it was the turn of an Edinburgh merchant; while by 1778 cargoes were being dispatched to Perth and North Uist. Towards the end of the century increasing quantities were sent to the industrialized cities of England, particularly Newcastle, Sunderland and above all London (GD 146/11; 146/11[a]; GD 146/13[b]; *Farmer's Mag.* 1811. XII. 128).

It would be a mistake to think of trade as restricted only to contact with the rest of Britain. Cargoes of grain were sent to Hamburg as late as the last quarter of the century, and the European littoral of the North Sea was probably the major market, directly or indirectly, for much of the exports from Easter Ross in the preceding century. Moreover, for much of the second half of the eighteenth century the Baltic trade was an important element in the Easter Ross economy. This Baltic trade, of course, was primarily associated with the linen industry (Macgill 1909. I. 187; *BLC.* 10 July 1749). Archibald Menzies, the General Inspector to the Board of Annexed Estates in 1768 reported that there was 'hardly a person in Fortrose and Rosemarkie who is not a weaver (E 787/24. 11). He elaborated with the statement that in the east of the Black Isle flax had been raised for centuries past, and that the spring market at Fortrose had supplied all the north with coarse linen from time immemorial.

In fact, by 1768, the importance of Fortrose had already declined because of the spread of the industry elsewhere in Easter Ross. The expanded industry was dominated by southern firms such as the British Linen Company and Sandemans of Perth, and unlike the earlier Black Isle weavers it did not depend upon home-grown flax. Instead, Baltic flax was imported from St Petersburg and Riga. At first it was taken into Edinburgh and sent north by coastal vessels, but gradually the north became more directly involved. In the late 1750s Cromarty developed as the entrepôt port for much of the north of Scotland, with cargoes of flax disembarked for trans-shipment to places at least as far apart as Wick and Inverness; and by 1770 the British Linen Company was refusing to order yarn from Riga for William Forsyth, believing that he could do it as advantageously himself (*BLC.* 10 March 1770).

In his pen portrait of William Forsyth, Hugh Miller suggested that Forsyth imported his flax from Holland, but there is no contemporary evidence for this and all eighteenth-century pointers indicate that the Baltic was the main source of supply. Miller may have been more accurate in his recollection that Forsyth imported iron from Sweden and tar and wood from Norway, products which would certainly have been required by the nail and spade manufacturers and the coopers of Cromarty (Miller 1863. 293; *BLC.* 10 March 1770). There is no direct evidence of what was sent to the Baltic and Scandinavian ports in return, but the local products most likely to have been successful in these markets were once again grain and salted herring.

As the century progressed, the range of products being exported expanded. London was supplied with pigs killed and cured in, and shipped from, Cromarty, while the Ferintosh whisky industry supplied large quantities of liquor to the capital even after the revocation in 1786 of the excise privilege it had enjoyed since 1688. And of course the linen yarn and sacking produced from all the imported flax and hemp went mainly for sale outside the region, much of it latterly to London (Wight 1778–84. IV(i).254–56; *Sc. Dist. Duties* 1798. 5; Hall 1807. II. 490; Mackenzie 1810. 335).

Despite the trading connections, personal links between Easter Ross and the Baltic and Scandinavian countries appear to have been fairly limited. In the seventeenth century the army of Gustavus Adophus of Sweden, Lion of the North during the 30 Years War, had been but an enlarged Clan Munro on the march; and it may have been a residual recollection of this which persuaded Lord Macleod, the heir of the forfeited Earl of Cromartie, to follow a military career in Sweden after 1746 (Fraser 1876. II. 243–44).

Moreover, early in the eighteenth century the estate of Ankerville in Nigg was purchased by 'Polander' Ross who had made his fortune as one of the innumerable Scottish merchants trading in Poland at the end of the seventeenth century (Meldrum 1935. 95). Such links were isolated, however, and did not indicate a close-knit, continuing contact.

Obviously the closest social links established outside the region were with the rest of Britain, and Easter Ross exiles were established as merchants in Glasgow, professionals in Edinburgh and businessmen in London from the start of the century and before. After 1707 and the Union of the Parliaments, the English connection could at last be broadened indisputably to become the empire connection. To take but one example, by the end of the 1780s Charles Robertson of Kindeace had one son in London, a second in India, a third in the West Indies managing a Jamaican estate, and a fourth in business in New York (GD 146/15; 146/15[a, b]). By the end of the century at least one Carribean island was covered with estate names stemming from Easter Ross, and such connections were used for the benefit of the area itself. Financial support for the new Fortrose Academy, for example, came from as far afield as Bombay, Calcutta and the island of Granada, while returning exiles used fortunes made in far-flung places to improve their old or newly purchased estates (Barron 1903. I. 42). Sir Hector Munro of Novar, at one extreme, is said to have spent over £100,000 on the Novar estate on his return from India, while at a more modest level were numerous small proprietors such as James Fowler, whose Jamaican-generated wealth allowed him to purchase the estate of Raddery near Fortrose and set himself up as a comfortable country gentleman (Southey 1929. 120; *SRO* CH 2/66/7[b]).

Even lower down the social scale the amount of foreign experience was surprisingly varied. Much of it was derived from service in the armed forces (the navy press-gangs were active in Easter Ross, as well as the recruiting sergeants for the Highland regiments), but if Hugh Miller's Cromarty was not wholly exceptional, there were numbers of civilians with sometimes extensive experience of foreign travel (Miller 1869. 2, 35, 55, 58, 246).

CONCLUSION

A short account of limited aspects of the history of Easter Ross in the eighteenth century can do little more than point to some of the more obvious characteristics linking the area with Moray. More detailed parallels could be instanced: shipbuilding at Fortrose in Ross and at Kingston in Moray, afforestation at Balnagown in Ross and at Darnaway in Moray, the construction of harbours at Cromarty and Lossiemouth, common access to the fisheries in the Moray Firth and so on. Many of these developments could be matched throughout Lowland Scotland, but only a limited number in the Highlands and then seldom in any concentration. In Easter Ross the development took on a local flavour which was similar to, and often inspired by, practice in Moray, so that although much agricultural improvement in Easter Ross, for example, was spearheaded by farmers from the Lothians, improved stocks were brought across the firth from Moray.

There can be no doubt that the eastern Black Isle was to all intents and purposes an extension of Moray across the water. If the position of the rest of Easter Ross was less clear cut, its links with its southern neighbour were still very strong. Given Easter Ross's close trading links with the Baltic in the eighteenth century, it is perhaps fitting to suggest that the Baltic provided a close parallel, although on a very much larger scale. Easter Ross could be likened to a Scottish Lithuania, attached to a Poland composed of Moray and the eastern Black Isle.

Acknowledgement

Figures 6.2–6.5 and 6.7 are reproduced by kind permission of the Royal Commission on the Ancient and Historical Monuments of Scotland; Figure 6.6, the Scottish Record Office; Figure 6.1, the Scottish Tourist Board.

References

Manuscript:

Scottish Record Office (SRO)

CH 1/2/95	*Unto the very Reverend the Synod of Ross. The complaint of William Urquhart of Meldrum, Esq., patron of the Parish of Cromarty, et al. Dingwall 14th April, 1752.*
CH 2/66/7	Presbytery of Chanonry *Minutes* 29th March, 1813, 26th April, 1836; [a] 5th May, 1766; [b] 21st June, 1803.
CH 2/350/1	Tarbat Kirk Session *Minutes* 8th. July, 1754.
E 766/45	*Report ... of the Milns ... of Milntown 1785.*
E 787/16/1	*Memorial for the Burgh of Fortrose.*
E 787/24	Archibald Menzies, *Report to the ... Hon[ble] the Board of Annexed Estates* [1768].
E 787/28/5	*List of disbanded soldiers settled on the Annexed Estate of Cromarty as Tradesmen and Day Labourers under the denomination of King's Cottagers — Newtarbet 1784.*
E 901/28/1	*Ross valuation book 1756.*
GD 129/24/81	*Letter, Sir John Ross to William MacCulloch, Plymouth, 24th. January. 1798.*
GD 146/8	*Charles Robertson of Kindeace Esq. ... to John Straith, Nairn 1788.*
GD 146/8[a]	*Mr. John Robertson Student in the Academie of Fortrose to James Grigor Shoemaker 1793.*
GD 146/11	*Letter, Ebeneezer Munro to Charles Robertson of Kindeace, Glasgow, 1757.*
GD 146/11[a]	*Letter, David Munro to Charles Robertson of Kindeace, 1759.*
GD 146/13	*Letter to Charles Robertson of Kindeace, 2nd August, 1797.*
GD 146/13[a]	*Letter, Sir John Gordon of Invergordon to Charles Robertson of Kindeace, Invergordon, 8th February, 1773.*
GD 146/13[b]	*Letter, Roderick Macleod to Charles Robertson of Kindeace, Edinburgh, 31st January, 1778.*
GD 146/13[c]	*Letter, Donald Macleod of Geanies to Charles Robertson of Kindeace, Geanies, 9th April, 1777.*
GD 146/13[d]	*Letter, Roderick Macleod to Charles Robertson of Kindeace, Edinburgh, 1779.*

GD 146/14	Letter, Roderick Macleod to Charles Robertson of Kindeace, Edinburgh 2nd August, 1780.
GD 146/15	Letter, Charles Robertson to Charles Robertson of Kindeace, London, 1790.
GD 146/15[a]	Letter, Hugh Robertson to Charles Robertson of Kindeace, Jamaica, 1790˝8.
GD 146/15[b]	Letter, Charles Robertson to Charles Robertson of Kindeace, New York, 1790.
GD 235/7	Letter, Sir John Gordon of Invergordon to the Lord Advocate, Invergordon, 18th October, 1780.
SC 24/21/7	Memorial of George Munro of Poyntzfield to the Hon. the J.Ps. & Commissioners of Supply for the Shire of Cromarty, 14th May, 1771.

National Library of Scotland (NLS)
ms 108   Sir John Gordon, *Pocket Book.*

Signet Library
SLSP   John Adam, *Unto the Right Honourable the Lords of Council and Session, the Petition of John Adam, His Majesty's Master Mason for Scotland* [1758]. Signet Library Session Papers 35:33.

Bank of Scotland Archive
BLC   British Linen Company *Scots Letter Books 1748–49,* 10th July 1749.
BLC[a]   British Linen Company *Scots Letter Books 1769–70,* 10th March 1770.

Printed:

Abstract of the Answers and returns made pursuant to . . . an Act for taking an account of the Population of Great Britain . . . 1802.

Agricultural Intelligence Scotland, Rosshire Quarterly Report, in *Farmers Magazine.* 1811. vol. 12.

Barron, J. *The Northern Highlands in the Nineteenth Century.* 3 vols. 1903.

Bulloch, J. M. *The Families of Gordon of Invergordon, Newhall, also Ardoch, Ross-shire, and Carroll, Sutherland.* 1906.

Cant, R. Early Modern Times, in Omand, D. ed. *The Moray Book.* 1976.

Chambers, R. *Picture of Scotland.* 2 vols. 1827.

Colvin, H. M. A Scottish Origin for English Palladianism, in *Architectural History.* 1974. vol. 17.

CRBS. Convention of the Royal Burghs of Scotland *Records.* 7 vols. 1870–1918.

Cromartie, Earl of. *A Highland History.* 1979.

Cruden, S. *The Scottish Castle.* 1960.

Dunlop, J. *The British Fisheries Society 1786–1893.* 1978.

Ferguson, W. *Scotland from 1689 to the Present Day.* 1968.

Forbes, R. *Journal of the Episcopal visitations of the Right Rev. Robert Forbes, M.A. of the dioceses of Ross and Caithness.* 1886.

Fraser, Sir W. *The Earls of Cromartie: their kindred, country and correspondence.* 2 vols. 1876.

Gardiner, L. *Stage Coach to John o' Groats.* 1961.

Hall, J. *Travels in Scotland.* 2 vols. 1807.

Macgill, W. *Old Ross-shire and Scotland as seen in the Tain and Balnagown Documents.* 2 vols. 1909.

Mackenzie, A. *History of the Munros of Fowlis.* 1898.

Mackenzie, A. & Macbain, A. *History of the Mathesons.* 2nd ed. 1900.

Mackenzie, D. A. Cromarty Dialects and Folk Lore, in *Trans. Rymour Club.* 1928. vol. 3.

Mackenzie, Sir G. S. *General View of the Agriculture of . . . Ross and Cromarty.* 1810.

Mackenzie, Sir K. S. Changes in the Ownership of Land in Ross-shire, 1756–1853, in *Trans. Gael. Soc. Inv.* 1885–86. vol. 12.

Mackenzie, W. MacK. Old Cromarty Castle, in *PSAS*. 1947. vol. 82.

Mackintosh, C. F. *Antiquarian Notes: a Series of Papers regarding Families and Places in the Highlands*. 1865.

Macleod, M. L. *Three Centuries of Falsehood Exposed*. 1970.

Macrae, N. *The Romance of a Royal Burgh*. 1974.

Meldrum, H. *Kilmuir Easter: the History of a Highland Parish*. 1935.

Miller, H. *Tales and Sketches*. 1863.

Miller, H. *My Schools and Schoolmasters*. 1869.

NSA. The New Statistical Account. 15 vols. 1843.

OSA. Sinclair, Sir J. ed. *The Statistical Account of Scotland*. 21 vols. 1791–99.

Pryde, G. S. *Scotland from 1603 to the Present Day*. 1962.

Pryde, G. S. *The Burghs of Scotland: a Critical List*. 1965.

Reid, F. N. *The Earls of Ross and their Descendants*. 1894.

Robertson, A. G. R. *The Lowland Highlanders*. 1972.

Ross, A. of Calrossie et al. *Petition January 29th 1777*.

Ross, J. *Information ... against the heirs and creditors of the deceased David MacCulloch of Mulderg, defenders, 30th July 1768*.

Sc. Dist. Duties. Report respecting the Scotch distillery duties. Ordered to be printed 11th June 1798 (Readex Microcard).

Sinclair, Sir J. *General View of the Agriculture of the Northern Counties and Islands of Scotland*. 1795.

Southey, R. *Journal of a Tour in Scotland in 1819*. 1929.

Sutherland, A. *A Summer Ramble in the North Highlands*. 1825.

Taylor, H. *History of the Family of Urquhart*. 1946.

Wallace Brown, W. L. Alness in the Eighteenth Century, in *Trans. Inverness Scientific Society and Field Club*. 1899–1906. vol. 6.

Warrand, D. *Some MacKenzie Pedigrees*. 1965.

Watson, W. J. *Place Names of Ross and Cromarty*. (1904) 1976.

Wight, A. *Present State of Husbandry in Scotland*. 4 vols. 1778–84.

Fig. 7.1 George Mackenzie, Lord Tarbat and later first Earl of Cromartie.
Painting attributed to M. Dahl, *c.*1708.

THE CROMARTIE ESTATE, 1660–1784:
ASPECTS OF TRADE
AND ORGANIZATION

Monica Clough

THE FORTUNES OF GEORGE MACKENZIE

We start with a summary of the career of George first earl of Cromartie (1631–1714), and single out the aspects of the grain trade and the building of the mansionhouse of New Tarbat.

George Mackenzie, Lord Tarbat and later first earl of Cromartie [Fig. 7.1] will be referred to throughout as 'Tarbat', for convenience. He was born in 1631, son of Sir John Mackenzie and grandson of the redoubtable Tutor of Kintail, Sir Rory, the man most feared in the north after the Devil. The Mackenzies, as Rosalind Mitchison has well said, were Imperialists; they were consistently loyal to the Crown, and fell at Flodden for it. This loyalty also brought gains, the trust of the Crown which gave them the reversion of the lands of the Earls of Ross, and later of the Bishops of Ross. Mackenzies fanned out from Kintail over a wide arc in the Black Isle and Easter Ross, and as the surviving Hearth Tax returns for Ross clearly show, were the leading landowners and tacksmen; only one of the name of Mackenzie has a single hearth in 1691.

George Mackenzie was next to the Chief, Seaforth, by virtue of joint descent from the eponymous Kenneth, and as the Seaforths of the late seventeenth and early eighteenth centuries were either Catholic or Minor, or both, a lot of the administration of the family, and the trust of the Crown, devolved on Sir George Mackenzie of Tarbat and his cousin, also Sir George Mackenzie, of Rosehaugh. Both were lawyers, and registered as Advocates after the Restoration of 1660. However, before that, Tarbat had been out with the Engagers at Worcester and with Glencairn in his Rising, much of which was based on Easter Ross. Tarbat was a man of great personal charm and ability, a man who needed a big stage, and in his long life he served five Stuart monarchs — of course he needed to be as agile as an eel to have done this. His political career need not detain us, only to note that Tarbat was for most of his career in Edinburgh or Whitehall, and not in Ross, except for a brief eclipse in his fortunes soon after the Restoration. From 1676 until 1709 he was almost continuously in office, as Lord Clerk Register and later as Secretary of State for Scotland under Queen Anne, and that came expensive. He retired to Ross in 1712 and died a few days after hearing of the accession of George I in England; he is buried under a crooked obelisk in the car park at Dingwall, opposite the Kirk with St Clement's aisle.

The salient point to remember in Tarbat's career is that he championed the episcopalians and the interest, just beginning to be called Tory, which later became identified with the Jacobites. Ross was strongly episcopalian at this point. The Whig rivals to the Tory episcopalian Mackenzies were the Rosses of Balnagown and the Munros of Foulis, who were staunch presbyterians but very much dominated in this period by the episcopalian majority. Easter Ross suffered quite severely during the troubled years immediately after the ousting of James VII and the arrival of King William; as it was a known disaffected area, troops were quartered all over the cornlands, and exacted all they could from the inhabitants.

Sheriff Ross of Balnagown used his term of office to harass the Mackenzie interest, and Tarbat's papers are full of petitions from leading men of the name of Mackenzie complaining about the exactions of Balnagown. It was of course the time of Glencoe, where quartering troops had led to worse troubles. Tarbat had been in command of the pacification of the Highlands until the Argyll faction had him replaced, and he did what he could for his tenants and interest in Ross. He was, however, in a delicate position because he was afflicted with a tiresome son, the Master, who had been a tearaway Restoration buck in Edinburgh until an affray in a Leith inn had nearly had him up on a murder charge, and it took all his father's adroitness to get him off and rusticated to Tarbat House. Regrettably once there he took to drink and to open adherence to the Catholic church, and had come out with his cousin Lovat in support of King James. General Mackay had put both Lovat and the Master of Tarbat under arrest. The Master did not take much part in politics again, but he did get through a lot of his father's money, as did his brothers and sisters, and his direction of affairs in the north was erratic and unsatisfactory.

ORGANIZATION OF THE GRAIN TRADE

That is the background: now the grain trade. This was a long established one. A document of 1621 among the Cromartie papers is a bond between the baillies of Tain and an agent in Bergen for shipment of bere barley, and when he inherited the estates in 1654 Tarbat must have found a framework to extend. There are only a few odd documents in this connection until the late 1670s, thereafter there is a pretty complete run until 1707 or so, and evidence of a rapid decline in grain export after 1716, when the great Whig distillery of Ferintosh was extended and took in most of the surplus of the area.

So, here is how Tarbat organized his trade. In the winter months the tenants *raused* the grain — a nice word which I have not identified but which I take to mean either to winnow or to dry in a kiln, probably the latter. The Chamberlains of the three baronies of Easter Aird, Tarbat and Strathpeffer took in the rents at Candlemas (2 February), and soon thereafter they sent a note of quantities and quality to Edinburgh where Tarbat was living. One Chamberlain was affronted to be asked to send a sample and wrote 'Our grain is well enough known and as good as any in

Lothian'. Now we would obviously expect details of the quantities involved, but there is a problem. The rental in 1703, a well documented crop, was 934 bolls of bere barley, but we do not know how much grain actually went to the great Boll of Tarbat which was the local measure. This was a copper vessel, evidently of some antiquity, kept in the old kirk of Tarbat until this year of 1703 when it was sent on a grain ship to Edinburgh for repairs, and did not return for some years. However, another measure was kept at Meddat of Milton where the Chamberlain lived, and was of the same capacity. The standard Linlithgow Boll was equivalent to 308 imperial pounds weight of barley. A Moray Boll is vaguely referred to as 'bigger'. I suspect this Tarbat Boll, I suspect it deeply, because in the great famine of 1783 the benevolent government diverted a ship full of supplies which was to have gone to America (only the war had ended there), to Dingwall for the use of the inhabitants of the Annexed Estate of Cromartie — pease, potatoes and oats, sold at give-away prices to the distressed tenants. The tenants, however, created an outcry, not at the price but at the measure, when asked to buy it by the peck. 'The people in this neighbourhood would take no other measure but their own ordinary Peck, which upon trial weighed 42 lbs. or 672 lbs. per boll', wrote the troubled Factor to the Annexed Estate. Six hundred and seventy-two pounds against a standard of just over 300 . . . ? Tarbat would seem to have done very well out of his grain rents! The commissioners sent up a standard set of weights and measures from Edinburgh on the next ship. At what point the switch took place (or even *if* it took place) is not clear; did 800 bolls of Tarbat measure leave Portmahomack and arrive as 1600 bolls of Leith measure? Because there were several shipments each year, often to different buyers, and because they took at least a year to pay in a good season, it is never possible to present a complete balance sheet. So it is just a query in the margin, but an intriguing one.

In March, on receipt of the news of intake, Tarbat negotiated a bond with a buyer, one of the great Edinburgh brewers such as Cleghorne, who undertook to take a stated amount at a stated price, with failure clauses and interest charged for non-payment. It was a long business-like document, binding on the few occasions when it was taken to the courts, and a pretty standard wording in all the surviving examples. Usually, though not always, Tarbat was responsible for the shipment, and this involved signing a Charter Party with a skipper of a reliable vessel based in Leith, Alloa or Anstruther. Some of the same Masters turn up year after year. They undertake to present themselves in a named boat off the collecting points on the estates (Dingwall, Nigg Bay, Cromarty or Portmahomack), and to take on board a specified amount of grain in ten weather-work days. Insurance was arranged, and a small amount of Captain's perquisites were specified, such as 'the boll of oatmeal and ane barril of aile as *Caplegan*'.

Naturally the arrival of a ship on contract for only ten weather-work days entailed a great deal of shore organization on the part of the estate chamberlains. They had to have the grain bagged, and they had to have boatmen to transfer the bags from the Girnal to the barque lying out in the

roads, so that I cannot help feeling that when the Chamberlain could add
'To Drink money for the completion of the lading', he must have been
thankful. The bags came from Dundee (where else would you get bags in
Scotland); they were called *sarks* and cost a penny a dozen.

No sums in the scanty accounts we have for this period ever seem to
relate to a credit to the estates for the value of the crops, roughly between
800 and 1,000 bolls sold annually at prices between £4 and £8 Scots per
boll. It is only too likely that all was spent in Edinburgh where the expenses
of Lord Tarbat were always in excess of his income, and where he was
building a mansion house at Royston. This of course represented a capital
drain from the area.

BUILDINGS FOR THE GRAIN TRADE

I have mentioned the Girnal House, the grain store, which is a feature of
the Moray Firth (see Beaton and Stell, in this volume). Tarbat was
prepared to make heavy capital investment in the grain trade, and the most
complete set of accounts deals with the building of the girnal and pier
of Portmahomack, on old foundations, in the 1690s. The builder was
Alexander Stronach of the neighbouring tack of the Milldam of Tarbat.
His girnal is still there, and his stonework was used for the foundations of
the present pier, as can be seen from Rennie's map and designs in Register
House, *c.*1821. Another girnal was built at the port of Cromarty, but
neither New Tarbat nor Strathpeffer had one; at the former the Barony
Court building was used, at Strath the ground floor of Castle Leod. I
should have said that one of the services exacted from the tenants was the
'leading of the bere', conveying it to and from those points to the ports of
embarkation. Nowhere in the papers can I see any hint of how this was
done: pack ponies, sleds, or the backs of the womenfolk? — only guesses.

But of all the capital investments on the grain account, the most
impressive was undoubtedly the long campaign to acquire the best port in
the area, the burgh and lands of Cromarty. This had long been the
property of the Urquharts, and the burgh was a fifteenth century royal
creation. Tarbat went into partnership soon after the Restoration with his
cousin Mackenzie of Rosehaugh and with Brodie of Asleck, across the
Firth, to capture the properties. The Urquhart fortunes were in decline,
and the burgh was 'much decayit' and in arrears over its dues to the Royal
Convention. The intricate steps by which these three property-developers
enveloped two successive Urquhart lairds in a web of obligations and
bonds, and finally foreclosed, are too long to detail here. It took nearly
twenty years. The partnership was an uneasy one as Brodie was a stern
presbyterian and his diary is full of biblical quotation, especially when he
considers the peril to his soul of doing business with Tarbat and Rosehaugh. However, he was inclined to write 'After I sought direction of God,
I yielded to treat...', and it was a successful partnership. By 1683 Tarbat
was confirmed as owner of most of the Urquhart estates; Rosehaugh had
died and his heirs had got Navity, a fine farm, and when his widow began

to make more demands she was briskly married to a brother of Tarbat's whose own wife, providentially, had just died. Brodie sold out his interest in the Burgh, and Tarbat was confirmed by the Crown as owner of the lands and port. For years thereafter the Royal Burghs unavailingly tried to get the back dues from Tarbat.

Tarbat was a trusted servant of James VII. In 1685 he was made a Viscount in the accession honours and got all his land holdings elevated into a Sheriffdom, subsuming the old Shire of Cromarty. The shire as a political entity, though not all as a family holding, lasted until 1894 — Ross and Cromarty. Naturally this meant that the royal ports of Dingwall and Tain were outclassed by the shire ports of Portmahomack and Cromarty, and few dues came their way. They too became 'much decayit'. Not only did the Cromarty deal bring in a fine port and good corn lands, but also the fishing of Conan, a great profit maker. On Queen Anne's accession Tarbat was made an earl and took title from Cromarty, his great strategic acquisition.

Now to the building expenses: we have none for Cromarty port, though the ruins of Tarbat's Girnal remain beside the harbour, merely stumps of stones. But there are many details for Portmahomack and for the building of the mansion house at New Tarbat, the predecessor of the one so sadly derelict at the present time. For Portmahomack the fullest account is a *Brief Survey of the workmanship of the pier of Castlehaven* in the Cromartie Papers, summarizing the building and charges for it for the benefit of Tarbat who was in Edinburgh. The work had been contracted to Alexander Stronach, of the Milldam Quarter of Tarbat, a local mason of some distinction who had started work in 1690, finished in 1698, and was awaiting full payment in 1700 when this survey was made. Tarbat had extended his requirements and been dilatory, according to Stronach, in payment. The cash charges had been fully met, £700 Scots by the first contract and several smaller sums, but not the grain payments due. Tarbat proposed that his chamberlain, Merchant of Wilkhaven, should take up the overdue grain rents of the previous year to pay himself and Stronach for their work. This was far from satisfactory, as in a sense Tarbat was gambling on futures in a commodity market: if the grain harvest was good his tenants could pay back rents, if it was too good the prices would fall unduly, if it was another bad year the reckoning could be put forward to another year . . . Stronach had built the pier 'by the first contract of 3 score yairds length and 3 ells brod and four ells high'; by the second contract he extended it with a sheltering wall six feet higher than the pier and its full length, and made shoulder-works at the shoreward end. It is probable that these included the building of the Girnal house, the use of which is referred to in subsequent letters from the chamberlains of the estate.

CROMARTIE CASTLES AND MANSIONS

When Tarbat inherited from his father, in 1654, their main residence in Easter Ross was the castle of Ballone, on the Tarbat estate [Fig. 8.10]. But

Fig. 7.2 The mansion house and policies of New Tarbat facing Nigg Bay, showing arable, woodland, pasture, rough land with whins, and water mills (top left). From a plan for the Commissioners for the Annexed Estates, 1754.

Fig. 7.3 Royston House, Edinburgh, also known as Caroline Park House.

the centre of gravity of the estate had moved to Milton, facing the Cromarty Firth, where there was a decayed castle which had belonged to Sir Robert Monroe, and which he renamed New Tarbat. Tarbat's rebuilding began about 1666, and the house was a very fine one. All that remains is a sketch in the papers from which a Victorian lithograph has been made, together with the admirable ground plan and plan of the policies made for the Commissioners for the Annexed Estates in 1754 [Figs. 8.11; 7.2].

Tarbat was connected through the marriage of a daughter with Sir William Bruce, and he had also lived in an apartment of Holyrood House while Lord Register, shortly after Bruce had completed his rebuilding there. It is clear that New Tarbat was in the Bruce manner, with four drum-towers at the corners, a marble hall and an oval staircase, and a 'piano nobile' on the first floor. Three generations of Stronachs built there. The grounds were laid out in the formal style of the late seventeenth century, the old raised beachline was built into a handsome terrace with sweeping steps and statuary and a fountain ordered in London. Royston House, the earl's other house just outside Edinburgh [Fig. 7.3], was at the same time rebuilt equally grandly; it was part of Tarbat's lifelong emulation of his political opponent, Lauderdale, that he wanted an Edinburgh house as modern as Ham House, and a country seat that also emulated Lauderdale's. The similarity between Royston and Ham can still be seen. The same plasterer, George Dangerfield, worked for all of these houses including Holyrood and New Tarbat in 1678; and Dick, the master mason, was recommended as having 'worked for the Earls of Errol and Marishal and at Panmuir'.

The best idea of the work involved in New Tarbat comes from a single set of Factor's accounts for the year 1686, the only complete set to survive. From this we can see that building was in full swing: Transport of '760 pieces of square stone, and the masons for hewing 300 of the number', plus the 'transport of 1600 loads of wall stones from the quarry of Apidauld, and a further 660 loads of wall stones from Cromarty' indicate its scope. The work was in the hands of James Dick, who in that year was paid £95 Scots and 4 bolls meal. Other named workmen were George Mackenzie, Carpenter, who was tenant of the estate, the foreman M'Cluskie who 'worked the horses that led the stones', and Donald Miller, wright, who repaired the cart-wheels and also was paid for 'the rigging of Kilmuir Kirk' of which Tarbat was principal heritor. George Mackenzie the carpenter was also paid for two 'voyages' in connection with the deal needed, some of which were brought to Tain from Sweden. Sash windows were ordered; painters, a glazier and a slater were also paid. From other evidence in these accounts it is not only clear that wheeled carts were in use, but there is a tantalizing suggestion that these carts ran on a wagon-way of wooden rails from the quarry down a gradual slope to the mansionhouse two miles away. It is impossible to prove this.

The third mansionhouse of the Cromartie family was Castle Leod in the Barony of Strathpeffer [Figs. 8.8; 8.9]. The only one to survive in family hands today, it was improved about 1606 by Sir Rory Mackenzie from an original Z-plan fortalice, and Lady Tarbat supervised further improvements in 1692, complaining of the slowness of Highland labour and the difficulty of obtaining lime, as John (the heir) needed so much at Tarbat.

In 1712 Tarbat, the old earl, in his eightieth year, retired from Edinburgh and two years later died. His son, the second earl, had already contributed to family financial difficulties so much that he was only left a life interest in Tarbat, and all the property was left direct to his minor son who later became the third earl. George, the third earl, thus inherited many problems from his feckless father but married, very happily, a neighbouring heiress, Isabella Gordon of Invergordon, by whom he had a large family.

It is possible to follow the fate of both Tarbat House and Castle Leod from the thorough inventories taken from time to time. Inventories of the contents of Royston House, however, survive only from the first earl's day, proving it to have been furnished with Chinese lacquer cabinets, sets of walnut chairs covered in green spanish leather, a number of writing cabinets of walnut wood and several great beds with bedhangings and 'tour-de-loos' or ostrich-feathered corners. On his return to Tarbat most of this furniture came with him, and was recorded in two ship's manifests as well as in subsequent inventories. Even his great coach with horse-furnishing for six horses was sent north to roadless Ross, where much of his gear was not even unpacked by the time the inventory of 1717 was taken. It looks as if the Countess of the day was not a fastidious housewife; apart from the boxes of the first earl's unopened possessions she had 'Ane vat of foul honey for the bees in winter' kept in her linen cupboard. The third Countess, Isabella Gordon, was of sterner stuff, and she and her husband restored and repainted both houses, and charming they sound. But the third earl was a Jacobite and took up arms for Prince Charles Edward; so the final 'Inventar' is taken for the Government about six weeks after Culloden, and the series ends in the Roup of the contents of both houses (E 746/74/28.1). Most of the furniture, some of it recognizably the lacquer of walnut of Queen Anne's day, was bought by neighbours and returned after a generation, when the third earl's son got back the estates but not the title in 1784. In the long time of the Annexation the house of Tarbat was neglected and decayed, though Castle Leod stood firm as a billet for soldiers garrisoning the passes to the west.

The Factor, Capt. Forbes of New, tried to let Tarbat and to keep it in repair, but he was starved of funds and had no takers. According to Thomas Pennant's account (1772. 1. 167), the tenantry gave him a lot of trouble too:

> I beg leave also to acquaint the Hon. Board that some wicked fellowes have cutt off a part of the Lead of one of the statues at New Tarbat in the night time and have disfigured one of them very much. It is a statue of Cain and Abel which stood before the entry of the House and it is a pity that such insolence should pass unpunished . . . some time ago there was an Arm cutt from another of the Statues.

Forbes also sold a quantity of mature timber planted by the first earl, some of it so exotic that the carpenter from Cromarty could make no guess as to its price. But, perhaps the only reference to Dangerfield's Restoration baroque plasterwork is that in Pennant's description of:

> the ruins of New Tarbat once the magnificent seat of an unhappy nobleman who plunged into a most ungrateful rebellion destructive to himself and family. The tenants, who seem to inhabit it *gratis* are forced to shelter themselves from the weather in the very lowest appartments while swallows make their nests in the bold stucco of some of the upper.

When Lord John McLeod inherited in 1784 he gave orders to pull the old house down, and to rebuild according to the plans of James McLeran. It is this fine building, the only Grade A listed building in Ross, which now lies derelict again.

References

All references are to the Cromartie Papers, with acknowledgement to the Earl of Cromartie, with the following exceptions:

Manuscript:
E 746/74/28.1 (Scottish Record Office).

Printed:
Pennant, T. *A Tour of Scotland*. 4th ed. 1772.

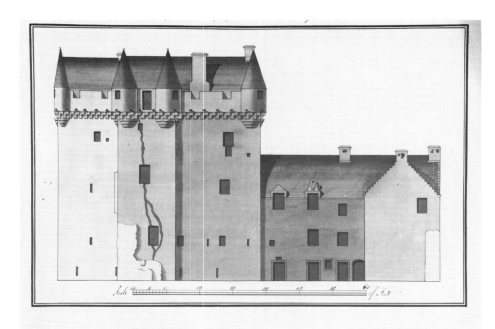

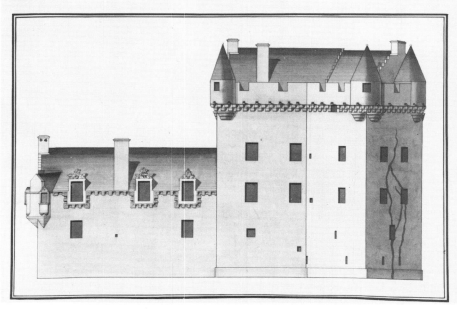

Fig. 8.1   Cromarty Castle; elevations, 1746.

ARCHITECTURE AND SOCIETY IN EASTER ROSS BEFORE 1707

Geoffrey Stell

LANDSCAPE AND BUILDINGS

The eastern seaboard of Ross and Cromarty[1] contains, and has always contained in historical times, some rich and fertile tracts of agricultural land. Within this broad geological belt of Middle Old Red Sandstone many localities have been well endowed with good sources of freestone for building purposes (Phemister 1960. 75–79, and Fig. 21; *OSA*. I. 288; IV. 288; VI. 426, 435, 613n). In times gone by, there were also plentiful supplies of timber from the woods in neighbouring Strathcarron, and especially from the western hilly district of Kincardine parish known as the Forest of Freevater (Anderson 1967. I. 324–7, and refs cited from MacGill 1909).

Not surprisingly, the natural endowments of this desirable area have given rise to a pattern of landownership, settlement and building of a variety and density that is quite exceptional for the Scottish Highlands. It bears comparison with the well-favoured lands on the southern shores of the Moray Firth with which there was a regular traffic by sea prior to the advent of the railway and the motor car. Its agricultural capacity is perhaps best exemplified by an area such as Killearnan parish in the Black Isle which boasts two major castles, Kilcoy and Redcastle. According to Sir John Sinclair (Sinclair 1795. 6n) this parish had a considerable proportion of good quality soils and the harvest there was usually earlier by a fortnight than in any other surrounding district of the northern Highlands. He also noted that the soil in Nigg and Easter Fearn in the Tarbat peninsula was 'rich and friable' and would 'carry any crops produced in the Lothians' (ibid. 94).

However, Easter Ross cannot be characterized so simply: it has a considerable variety of physical landscapes, and, with the Highlands proper all around, its lands have an uneven productive capacity and farming use. Furthermore, most of the better-favoured lands have been subjected to such intensive agricultural, and occasionally industrial, re-organization during the past two centuries that it is now difficult to appreciate the early eighteenth-century setting of many of its early surviving buildings.

PROBLEMS OF INTERPRETATION

The pattern and style of Easter Ross architecture, like that of many other parts of Highland and Lowland Scotland, underwent a transformation alongside the changes in the agricultural landscape and in general life-style in the century following the Jacobite Rebellion of 1745 (Mowat 1981. passim). There is no doubt that the surviving historic architecture here is disproportionately of later eighteenth- and nineteenth-century date: mansion houses, villas, farmhouses and cottages, matched by ecclesiastical and other institutional or commercial building on a similar scale and pattern, all to some extent following national canons of style and taste but embodying various idiosyncracies of design and materials (Omand 1984. 207–18).

Here, as elsewhere, this period of 'greatest rebuilding' was grafted onto an earlier pattern of building that is now more difficult to discern behind its Georgian and Victorian 'screen'. In assessing earlier building activity and patronage in this ancient county palatine we enter the familiar world of medieval (and sub-medieval) castles, houses and churches. But there are still many assumptions about the nature and purpose of the secular buildings of this earlier age that remain insufficiently scrutinized: hence the unanswered questions concerning their siting, the circumstances of their creation, and the manner in which the buildings were actually conceived and constructed. Can many of their sites be interpreted as mainly military or defensive in nature when, simply as well-favoured spots like Castle Leod, a significant proportion have continued in use from medieval into modern times? And, given that a castle-builder needed to be sure of his ground, both legally and physically, before embarking on an expensive building campaign of longish duration, can stone castles and towers really reflect highly disturbed unstable conditions at the time when they were actually put up?

The traditional account of the building of Milton Castle is the proverbial exception that proves the rule. Sir Robert Gordon (Gordon 1813. 146) records that John, 5th Earl of Sutherland who died in 1567, was a great supporter of the Munros, especially of Milton (to which was attached the head stewardship of the old earldom of Ross: *OPS.* II. 2. 464), against the nearby Rosses of Balnagown. According to him:

> when the Monroes began first to build the house of Milntown, Earle John went himselff in persone, to defend them against Balnagown his braging, who indevoared to stop and hinder them from building that castell. Then returning home into Southerland, he left a company of men at Milntoun for their defence against the Rosses, vntill most pairt of the castle was finished; which kyndnes the Monroes of Milntoun doe acknowledge vnto this day.

Other recorded instances of lawlessness and disorder affecting buildings were not unknown (e.g. MacGill 1909. nos. 94, 677, 859).[2] Stands of arms that appeared in household inventories (MacGill 1909. nos. 341, 960) also show a considerable potential for aggressive behaviour, but the more martial aspects of pre-eighteenth-century building design and detailing can be all too easily overstated.

BUILDING CONSTRUCTION: MATERIALS, COSTS AND CALAMITIES

Timber as well as stone was much prized for building purposes, for as the Earl of Cromartie remarked in a letter to his son in 1688 'good timber is the strength of a building' (Fraser 1876. I. no. 41, p. 56), particularly under the stressful climatic conditions of northern Scotland. Here, as elsewhere, assessments of timber and house size were often made in accordance with commonly understood modes and measurements of roof construction. Hence we find an instruction of 1637 to the foresters at Kincardine to 'cut and carry ... twelve couples with their furnishings of cabir rails, balks and huis' (MacGill 1909. no. 1073), and a record of 1584–85 referring to two partly built-up spaces in the former burial-ground at Chanonry of Fortrose assessed at eight and thirteen 'cupill biggings', both five ells wide (*OPS*. II. 2. 572–73).

It is not hard to imagine that the transport of building materials overland and by sea was difficult, time-consuming and costly. Figures giving some indications of building costs are relatively few (e.g. Fraser 1876, I. 307; MacGill 1909. nos. 329, 458, 483–85, 488–92, 677) and cannot now be easily matched against a measurable amount of building. It was not until the end of the eighteenth century that the costs of building construction were fully and clearly set out (MacKenzie 1813. 75–78), and can be more easily related to what we see today.

Most of the information on building costs relating to corporately funded public buildings and churches has been the result of the ever-present problems of maintenance and repair. Natural phenomena have accounted for many of the difficulties. The partial collapse of Tain Tolbooth tower in 1703 affords an example of storm damage (Munro 1966. 73–74), whilst rather more unusually, according to tradition (Miller 1835. 69–71) the medieval burgh of Cromarty suffered and eventually succumbed to the effects of marine erosion. According to the Kalendar of Fearn, Milton Castle was burnt when a crow's nest accidentally caught fire there in 1642, but some fires, like the later one at Invergordon Castle, occurred in unexplained circumstances (Mackenzie 1813. 70), whilst others such as those at the churches at Tain and Kilchrist are alleged to have been the result of arson (Macgill 1909. no. 42; *OPS*. II. 2. 524; Miller 1854. 167–68, 172). But the history of building calamities in Easter Ross could almost be written solely with reference to the abbey church at New Fearn which has experienced over the centuries an unfortunate catalogue of accidents. The most disastrous incident took place in 1742 when the heavy slated roof fell on the congregation during divine service.[3] Concern about the serious condition of the roof had, however, been expressed since at least 1695 (NLS. Advocates' MS 29.4.2(xi), f.287v).

FAMILIES AND ARCHITECTURE

These background themes can usefully be borne in mind when considering such apparently basic questions as 'who built, modified or repaired what, and when?'. Furthermore, in order to get a clearer measure of the needs, the resources and the shortcomings of the architectural patrons and the building industry that served them in Easter Ross, there is a case for escaping from conventional methods of architectural analysis. For whilst the sources and comparison of plan-forms, details and styles assist in the assessment of date, fashion and wealth, the methods of the architectural historian are only a means to any of several ends. If the aim is to relate the buildings to their social background, then it follows that they should be grouped according to the framework of the society that produced them. In Easter Ross medieval lordship was based on the unit of the family in all its widely ramified and complex forms, so the buildings have been arranged here accordingly, placing the families and their buildings in a rough hierarchical order that contemporaries might have understood. What follows is an attempt to view the architectural effects of patronage on the part of the kings of Scotland, descending through the social scale to the baronage and lesser lairds.

Royal Works

Royal works in Easter Ross are few, but the indirect effects of royal involvement and interest in the area are rather more widespread. The first exercise of royal overlordship that has left definable archaeological trace was William the Lion's campaign of 1179 into the Moray firth area to overawe actual or potential opposition centred around the claims of Donald MacWilliam, descendant of the mormaers of Moray and connected indirectly with the royal house through William fitz Duncan. One chronicle account, which possibly conflates events, relates to a further campaign of 1181, but all accounts otherwise agreed that a major effect of the expedition(s) was the creation or strengthening (*firmavit*) of two castles, Dunscaith and Edirdowyr (Anderson 1922. II. 301–02 & n; Barrow 1971. II, 292; see also 454 (no. 500)).

Dunscaith occupies a coastal site on the North Sutor, commanding the narrows and the former ferry-crossing at the mouth of the Cromarty Firth. It takes the form of a promontory earthwork surrounded on the landward side by a broad ditch with traces of internal and counterscarp banks. The site was considered sufficiently useful to assist in the protection of the twentieth-century naval base at Invergordon, but is now disfigured by a tangled half-demolished mass of ferro-concrete dating from this later phase (Mackenzie 1947–48. 60–61).

Edirdowyr has been identified as Redcastle [Fig. 8.16] on the northern shore of the Beauly Firth. The site occupies a good commanding position above the shoreline on the edge of a ravine but, unlike Dunscaith, it has retained a residential purpose until recent times; there appears to be little, however, of the early earthworks beneath or around the later buildings. Along with neighbouring Ormond Castle at Avoch, Redcastle had been one of the principal centres of the lordship of Ardmeneach, which, on the forfeiture of the Douglases in 1455, reverted to the Crown. Thereafter it

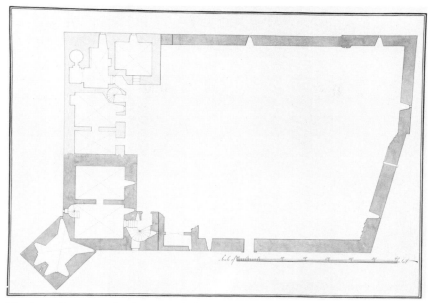

Fig. 8.2 Cromarty Castle; ground plans, 1746.

was held by royal constables until its acquisition by a branch of the ubiquitous MacKenzies in the early seventeenth century. The core of the present ruinous building is an elongated L-plan tower of sixteenth- and seventeenth-century date, extensively altered in the eighteenth and nineteenth centuries (MacGibbon & Ross 1887–92. III. 623–25; NMRS record sheet RCR/5/1).

Other royal and quasi-royal castles came to be associated with the sheriffdoms of Cromarty and Dingwall that first appeared on record in the thirteenth century, Cromarty [Figs. 8.1; 8.2] was the administrative centre of a small sheriffdom (MacKenzie 1922), and in 1470 the Urquharts, hereditary sheriffs since the mid-fourteenth century, were granted royal permission to build a tower or fortalice on the motte of Cromarty and to equip it with suitable defences (Macfarlane *Genealogical Coll.* II. 375; MacKenzie 1947–48). Judging from the evidence of later architectural drawings and descriptions, the stone castle that was erected in the later fifteenth century appears to have been a very substantial L-plan tower, bigger and more sophisticated than any surviving late medieval structure in this area. An extensive range of domestic buildings was added in 1632 by the father of the great Sir Thomas Urquhart, but the proposals to rehabilitate the castle as a barracks after the 1745 Rebellion came to nothing, and, except for a few fragments, the last traces of the castle were effaced upon the construction of Cromarty House in 1772 (Miller 1835. 129–35).

Fig. 8.3   Dingwall; view by J. Clark, published 1824.

Fig. 8.4   Tain; view by J. Clark, published 1828.

Dingwall Castle, one of the principal centres of the vice-regal earldom of Ross, came into full royal possession in 1476 on the forfeiture of the earldom by the MacDonalds, Lords of the Isles, and was considerably strengthened by James IV in the early sixteenth century (Macrae 1923. 49–61 citing *Exch. Rolls.* passim; see also McInnes 1940. nos. 5, 6, 8, 12, 15, 18, 21). It occupied a low-lying and ditched, probably moated site close to the canal of the River Peffery in the position where the present Dingwall Castle, a pleasant castellated villa of 1821, now stands [Fig. 8.3]; it was 'situated close to the shore, ... and a little river with a deep slimy channel, into which the sea flowed, winded about two of its sides' (*OSA.* III.15). Bishop Lesley (1578. 27) noted what he called a wealth (*copia*) of salmon close to the castle. The only visible portions of medieval masonry are attached to a later garden pavilion to the south-west of the house, close to which there is also a subterranean vaulted chamber. Part of a ditch still survives, the remains of a circuit around an enclosure of about 0.2 ha (0.5 acre).

The use and upkeep of Dingwall was, like Redcastle, assigned to a royal keeper or constable, and the office of constable of Dingwall Castle came to be linked with the ownership of nearby Tulloch, one of the many towers that sprang up in the middle and later sixteenth century on former earldom lands. The Bains of Tulloch, like so many in this second tier of lordship, owed their more secure position and building abilities to a confirmation of their possessions by James V, in this case towards the end of his reign in 1542 (*OPS.* II. 2. 492–93; Macrae 1923. 103–14).

Royal interest in the ferry-crossing between Dunscaith and Cromarty was connected with another important focus of royal attention, the shrine of St Duthac at Tain, the saint's birthplace and the site of his relics [Fig. 8.4]. The ferry was occasionally used by James IV on his regular royal pilgrimage to Tain, and Crown revenues out of the vill and ferry of Dunscaith had already been assigned to a chaplainry in Tain by his grandfather, James II, in 1456 (*Exch. Rolls.* VI. 216, 463, 465). The actual lines of the overland section of the pilgrimage routes into Tain cannot be established clearly: one probably crossed the head of the bay opposite Nigg, travelling thence via Balnagown and 'King's Causeway'; another may have followed a more easterly route from Nigg, entering the burgh from the direction of Loch Eye and St Katherine's Cross.

The cult of St Duthac acquired considerable renown and veneration among the kings and nobles of fourteenth- and fifteenth-century Scotland (Durkan 1962; Mackinlay 1914. 223–28). The saint's shirt, which allegedly protected its wearer, was one of the more prized relics, although Hugh, 4th Earl of Ross, was killed wearing it at the Battle of Halidon Hill in 1333 (Major *History.* 273 and n). The rebuilding of St Duthac's chapel has been attributed to Hugh's successor, William, 5th Earl of Ross (d. 1372), and while reconstruction may have commenced in the third quarter of the fourteenth century, much of the existing architecture of the collegiate church seems to reflect the more intense royal interest in St Duthac in the middle and later decades of the fifteenth century. During this

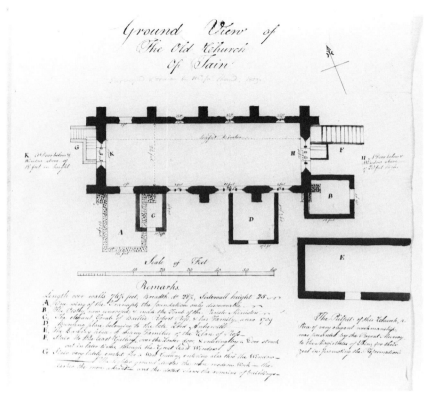

Fig. 8.5 Tain Collegiate Church; plan by J. Shand, 1819 (NLS, *Advocates MS* 30.5.23, 142a).

period the church received endowments and built up a proto-collegiate organization of chaplains, finally acquiring full collegiate status at the instigation of James III in 1487 (MacGibbon & Ross 1896–7. II. 539–42; Durkan 1962; Cowan & Easson 1976, 227–28). It acquired an additional chaplainry from James IV, and during his reign became one of the foremost pilgrimage-centres in Scotland, ranking alongside Whithorn in the frequency of royal visits (Paul 1904). A number of burial-aisles were added after the Reformation, and, although removed as a result of a thoroughgoing restoration completed in 1877, they appear in some detail on early nineteenth-century drawings prepared for General Hutton by James Shand, a Tain schoolmaster [Fig. 8.5] (NLS. Advocates' MS 30.5.23, 142a–b; for General Hutton see *DNB*. x. 353 and Ross 1964). Shand records his opinion that the nearby structure in the churchyard, now commonly interpreted as the old parish church, had never been roofed.

The great lordship of Ardmeneach passed into royal hands on the forfeiture of the Douglases in the mid fifteenth century, and through the name of its main centre at Ormond Castle near Avoch gave the title to an earldom and royal marquessate (*Scots Peerage.* VI. 585–86; VII. 245–46). The earlier owners of this castle were members of the exceptionally rich and powerful de Moray family; it is known that in 1338 Sir Andrew de Moray died at Avoch and was buried at the cathedral about a mile to the east of the castle (*OPS.* II. 2. 543–44, 547; *Chron. Wyntoun* (Laing) II. 437, 440). While the fragmentary remains at Ormond do not immediately convey an impression of the family's power and wealth — reflected so dramatically in the thirteenth-century architecture of Bothwell Castle in the Clyde Valley — it has nonetheless been a large establishment. The foundations comprise a double system of curtain walls around the summit, set within what might have been earlier ditches, and an inner quadrangle with towers and internal buildings (Beaton 1884–85). There is no clear evidence for its continued occupation after its annexation by the Crown, and by the later fifteenth century the 'moothill' of Ormond seems to have retained only residual titular importance.

Earls of Ross

How much of the exiguous remains at Dingwall Castle might be ascribed to the earls of Ross themselves is hard to say, although from the thirteenth century onwards it had served as one of their principal centres. Their residences in the eastern half of the province included Balconie and Delny, 'our manor house' of Delny as it appeared in at least one fifteenth-century MacDonald charter (MacDonald and MacDonald 1896–1904. I. 603–04; see also *OPS.* II. 460–62, and description of the chapel in *OSA.* VI. 194–95n). Virtually all medieval traces have disappeared and the site at Delny is now occupied by a large farmstead and a late nineteenth-century villa. It is possible that Delny, like the head manor at Dingwall and like the earthwork known as 'David's Fort' in Balavil Wood, south of Conon Bridge, was a wet moated site. 'David's Fort' has a raised central platform of trapezoidal plan, measuring 25 to 30 m in each direction, and is surrounded by an impressive wet moat with a water-inlet and -outlet system (Beaton 1883. 416–20; NMRS. RCD/3/1). It appears to be the most northerly recorded example of a medieval moated homestead, a type of earth-and-timber structure which in southern Scotland and England generally dates from the thirteenth century onwards.

Surviving evidence of the secular works of the medieval earls of Ross is thus somewhat scarce and enigmatic, but the results of their patronage of church building is fortunately more tangible. However, both New Fearn Abbey [Fig. 8.6] and Fortrose Cathedral [Fig. 8.7] are now considerably less than what they were in the Middle Ages, and Fearn has been much altered. This abbey, which was a house of Premonstratensian or white canons, survived for about fifteen years in apparently inhospitable surroundings at Mid Fearn in Kincardine parish before it was refounded at

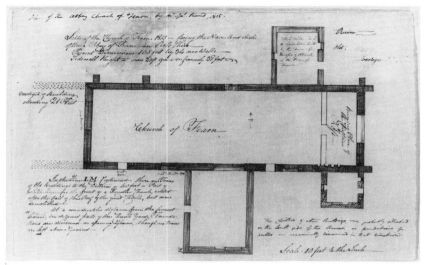

Fig. 8.6 Fearn Abbey Church; plan by J. Shand, 1819 (NLS, *Advocates MS* 30.5.23, 1306).

'New Fearn' in the more settled and richer domains of the earldom in about 1238 (Cowan & Easson 1976. 101–02 and refs cited; for English houses of this order see Colvin 1951, and for some of their architectural characteristics Bond 1913. 1. 164–65). Even after this early removal, it remained the most northerly major religious house of the reformed monastic orders in the British Isles. The abbey owed its existence and much of its character to its major lay patrons, the earls of Ross, and in particular to its founder, Farquhar Mactaggart, 3rd Earl of Ross, whose choice fell upon Premonstratensian canons from Whithorn. Fearn remained closely linked to its distant mother-house, especially in the election of abbots, and this link was probably responsible for the introduction into this locality of families of south-western origin such as the Vasses of Lochslin (Munro 1971),[4] and possibly the MacCullochs of Plaids (Munro 1971a).

The successive native earls remained solicitous for the abbey's upkeep. The Chronicle of the Earls records that in 1336 William, 5th Earl, seeing that the abbey church was built 'bot of clay [mortar] and rouch staine alutterlie rewinous appeireindlie', became 'trubbilit of mynd with anguish that the sepulture of his parentis and quhair he tendit to be buryit' should be in this condition, even to the extent that 'the dropis descending frome Heavin distilled in the challice and upon the altar quhair the sacrament was ministrat' (MacGill 1924. 320). He convened a meeting of the clergy and 'all the great men in Ross' and, whilst they presumably gave what help they could, seven canons agreed 'to beg and thig through the countrie'. The rebuilding in 'hewin stanis' was carried out between 1338 and 1372, and the Kalendar of Fearn records the obit of Earl William 'qui fabricavit et

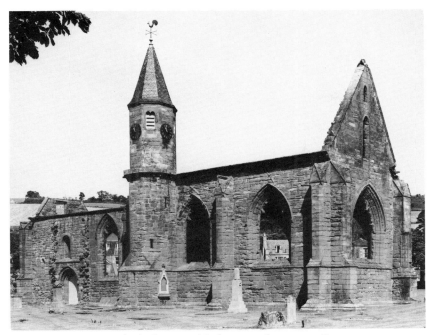

Fig. 8.7   Fortrose Cathedral; nave-aisle from south-east, 1968.

reparavit ecclesiam Nove Farine' and died at Delny on 9 February 1371 (*Hist. MSS Comm.* 1871. 179).

The institutional life of the abbey evidently became divorced from the later MacDonald earls, and building work came to depend more on the efforts of the abbots themselves. Abbot Finlay MacFaid, who died in 1485, was commemorated by a canopied tomb-recess and effigy. His successor, Abbot John, is said to have built St Michael's Aisle, in which the tomb is located, to have founded the dormitory and built the cloisters, as well as adding various church fittings. Secular benefactions after the Reformation led to the reorganization of the eastern end of the church and to the building of monumental chapels, the roof of the Ross Aisle on the north side being of a noteworthy stone-arched construction (NLS Advocates' MS 29.4.2 (xi), ff.225–300 passim, especially 242–50, 252–64, 287–90; MacGill 1909. nos. 97–101, 1029 etc).

What we are looking at today, however, is but a remnant of the former layout, particularly at the western end of the nave which is known to have been some 12.19 m (40 ft) longer; the wallhead is about 4.57 m (15 ft) lower than it was and the claustral buildings have now almost entirely disappeared from view, although in the early nineteenth century they were still traceable for a further 18.29 m (60 ft) southward along the line of St Michael's Aisle and the erstwhile Denoon chapel [Fig. 8.6] (NLS, Advocates' MS 30.5.23, 130a-b and 131; MacGibbon & Ross 1896–97.

II. 542–47). All things considered, the scale and modest quality of the abbey of New Fearn is not an unworthy tribute to the native earls of Ross and to the late medieval abbots.

Another index of fourteenth- and fifteenth-century building activity in this area is provided by the cathedral church of Ross at Chanonry, now Fortrose, whose quality and elegance bespeak handsome funding from its chief patrons, the later earls of Ross. The most obvious feature of the surviving remains is the south nave-aisle which appears to have been part of an amended fourteenth-century design, possibly to provide a setting for the church's main benefactors and dignitaries. This aisle was probably founded by the Countess Euphemia (d. 1394), or her son Alexander, Earl of Ross (d. 1402), but the vaulting which bears the arms of Bishop Bulloch was not completed until at least two decades later (MacGibbon & Ross 1896–97. II. 394–402; Cowan & Easson 1976. 207; Dunbar 1981. 50, 55; see also NLS, Advocates' MS 30.5.23, 133–39 for architectural drawings, mainly of 1815 (including plans by John MacQueen), and Scott 1873).

Bishops of Ross

At least one and possibly two of the three identifiable tombs at Fortrose commemorate later medieval bishops who, with their deans and chapters, were of course major landed proprietors and building patrons in their own right. The south nave-aisle and the chapter-house-cum-sacristy on the north side are all that is left upstanding of their cathedral church, but the outline of the nave and chancel shows that it was indeed a sizeable structure by Scottish Highland standards. An unfortunate programme of destructive quarrying commenced in 1572 with a royal grant to Lord Ruthven of lead from the church 'throw being ... no parroch kirk bot ane monasterie (sic) to sustene ydill belleis' (Reg. Sec. Sig. VI. (1567–74) no. 1653); pillaging continued with the construction of the Cromwellian citadel in Inverness (NLS Advocates' MS 29.4.2 (xi), f.225).

The bishop's house in Fortrose was apparently another Cromwellian victim. It was described by one of its occupants, Bishop John Lesley, as being in beauty and magnificence (splendore et magnificentia) 'inferior to few others with us' (Lesley 1578. 27; see also OPS. II. 2. 591–92). Many of the cathedral manses appear to have suffered a similar fate, but some may still survive in modified form, hidden in later housing. What was possibly the manse of the Dean of Rosemarkie, for instance, is approached from Rose Street through an arched pend wrought with a seventeenth-century moulding.

Sites associated with the bishops of Ross outside Fortrose include Craig Castle and Nigg House. Craig Castle stands on the Cullicudden shore of the Cromarty Firth in an area where the bishops and the Urquharts of Cromarty shared the roles of principal landholders. The castle comprises the surviving wing of a well-detailed late sixteenth-century tower which stands in the corner of a stone-walled enclosure; parts of the enclosure may be of earlier date, but the traditional association with the bishops of Ross may well relate to the use of the site as an occasional episcopal residence in the post-Reformation period (MacGibbon & Ross. III. 465–67; OPS. II. 2. 555–56).

The site of Nigg House, on the other hand, does have documented connections with the pre-Reformation bishops and their demesne lands. In the words of the parish minister in the late eighteenth century (OSA. XIII. 17):

> Nigg is one of the mensal churches that belonged to the bishoprick of Ross. Behind the church is still to be seen the foundation of a large house above 90 feet in length, which goes under the name of the Bishop's House, though not the place of his constant residence; and the hill ... is, in old charters of the lands of the parish, called the Bishop's Forest. One of the vaults of the house remained entire in the year 1727.

Property transactions of the 1580s refer specifically to 'the manor-place, mansion, orchard, garden, moothill, stanks [fish-ponds] and granary' belonging to the bishop at Nigg (OPS. II. 2. 457). The land around the church and house (which bears a 1702 datestone in re-use) has an interesting topography comprising man-made platforms, ditches, hollow-ways and a terraced way, locally called the 'Bishop's Walk', leading down to the foreshore; cropmarks revealed by aerial photography in a nearby field may also relate to the medieval use of the site.

The MacKenzie families

The greatest architectural contribution in Easter Ross in the post-Reformation era was that made by the two main branches of the MacKenzie family and their widely ramified cadets (Macfarlane Genealogical Coll. I. 54–102; MacKenzie 1899; Dunlop 1953). Largely through royal service and advantageous marriages in the sixteenth century, the MacKenzies gathered to themselves many of the forfeited possessions of their former superiors, the earls of Ross. By 1600 there were twenty-five landed families of the name, most of them based in Ross-shire, and after 1600 five cadets founded a further sixteen. By 1623 the chief of the senior branch in Easter Ross had acquired the title of Earl of Seaforth, the power and influence of this line reaching its zenith shortly before his death in 1633 (Scots Peerage. VII. 495–515). The other main branch reached its peak later in the century in the person of Sir George MacKenzie, later Viscount Tarbat and 1st Earl of Cromartie (d. 1714), whose architectural patronage was quite outstanding (Clough 1977, and this volume).

Eilean Donan Castle was the centre of the family's parent lordship of Kintail on the west coast, acquired by the MacKenzies in 1509 but possibly incorporating remains dating back to the fifteenth century (OPS. II. 2. 394; MacGibbon & Ross 1887–92. III. 82–85; see also NLS. MS 1648, Z3/26, and Dunbar 1981. 57). Unfortunately MacKenzie Jacobite sympathies led to the partial destruction of the castle by government naval forces in 1719, but it was lovingly rebuilt by the MacRaes, descendants of former constables of the castle, between 1912 and 1932.

From Kintail the family scenario shifted to the rich and fertile lands around the lower reaches of the Peffery and Conon Rivers, possibly occupying temporarily the island-refuge on Loch Kinellan (Fraser 1916–17; *OPS*. II. 2. 504, 507). The principal residence of the senior branch of the family became Brahan Castle now demolished (*OPS*. II. 2. 521–2; MacGill 1909. no. 340; NMRS photographs and record sheet RCR/3/1; RCAHMS 1979a. no. 251). In its final form Brahan was a substantial pile, but by no means the most prepossessing of mansion houses. Sir George MacKenzie (MacKenzie 1813.68) considered that there was no justification for

> a man ... divesting himself of comfort, and injuring the beauty of the country, by propping up and patching an aukward [*sic*] and ugly mass of building, such as Castle Brahan ... Numerous progenitors of different families which bear the name MacKenzie ... would not be displeased to see an elegant modern mansion inhabited by their chief, although, perhaps, their pride might be a little flattered by the exertions which have been made to keep up the ancient castle.

Whatever its defects, the seventeenth-century nucleus evidently contained some reasonably high quality stone carving, judging by surviving fragments like the ornate strapwork-decorated fireplace lintel now lying outside the former stables-block.

The first eastern seat of the second son of Colin MacKenzie of Kintail, Sir Rorie MacKenzie, founder of the Tarbat branch of the family, was Castle Leod [Figs. 8.8; 8.9] (Fraser 1876, I. xlii; II. 436–37; MacGibbon & Ross 1887–92. III. 625–28), built on the lands of Culteleod acquired from his father in 1585. Marriage to a MacLeod heiress in 1605, considerable activity in settling west coast disputes on behalf of King James VI, and his role as Tutor to the Chief of Kintail in the second decade of the seventeenth century were the major aspects of his early career, paving the way to a programme of additions to Castle Leod in 1616 (Fraser 1876. I. xxv–liii). The appearance of this handsome five-storeyed tower is reminiscent of contemporary styles in Aberdeenshire; originally of a stepped L-plan form, it incorporates a commodious scale-and-platt stair in the seventeenth-century addition, and the entrance-doorway is surmounted by a well-detailed but worn three-bay MacKenzie armorial.

The onward and eastward progress of this remarkable branch of the family continued in the seventeenth century, establishing themselves first at Ballone then at Milton, a former Munro possession (see this paper), replaced in turn by the present Tarbat House in 1787. Ballone Castle [Fig. 8.10] (MacGibbon & Ross 1887–92, II, 248–51; NMRS record sheet), an elaborately detailed Z-plan tower, stands on the edge of a coastal terrace above the north-eastern shore of the Tarbat peninsula. Described as the 'fortalice of Easter Tarbat', the sixteenth-century tower

Fig. 8.8 Castle Leod; view from south-west, 1958.

Fig. 8.9 Castle Leod; entrance-doorway and armorial panel, 1958.

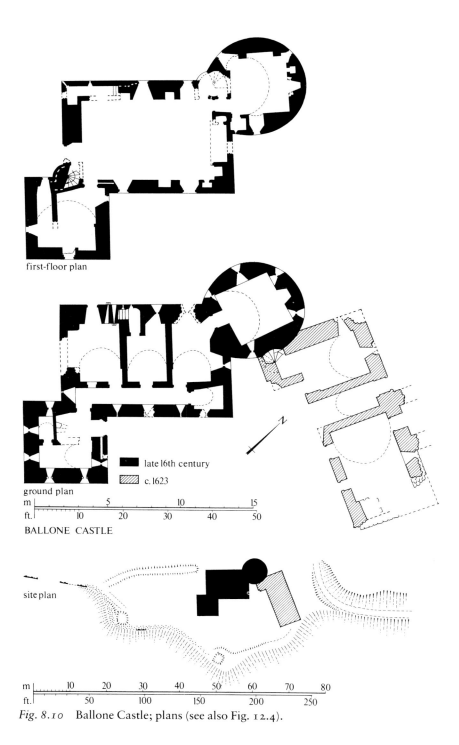

first-floor plan

late l6th century

c. 1623

ground plan

m | 5 | 10 | 15

ft. | 10 | 20 | 30 | 40 | 50

BALLONE CASTLE

site plan

m | 10 | 20 | 30 | 40 | 50 | 60 | 70 | 80

ft. | 50 | 100 | 150 | 200 | 250

Fig. 8.10   Ballone Castle; plans (see also Fig. 12.4).

first comes on record in the early seventeenth century during the last phase of its possession by the Dunbars of Tarbat. This family had held these lands in *feu ferme* of the earls of Ross in the fifteenth century, and a series of royal confirmations of the lands and fishings was issued in their favour during the reign of James V (*OPS*. II. 2. 443–45). After a brief period in the hands of the Munros of Meikle Tarrel the lands and castle were absorbed in 1623 into the growing empire of Sir Rorie MacKenzie of Coigach, and this part of his purchase thenceforth provided the territorial title for his family (Fraser 1876. II. 427–29).

The tower, which has been well protected by gun-ports of various kinds, comprises ground-floor cellarage and kitchen ranged *en suite* with a service-stair and a relatively spacious newel stair to the first floor in the square south-eastern tower. A sizeable north-eastern range, which now survives merely as a vaulted service basement, was added by the MacKenzies. But they did not reside here for long. Ballone was soon superseded by New Tarbat House at Milton, a property that was purchased in 1656, and tradition avers that Ballone has not been occupied since the later seventeenth century.

Although the building and maintenance of the first Tarbat House has a reasonably well documented history from the 1650s onwards (Fraser 1876. II. 431–35) its actual appearance is known only through a nineteenth-century lithograph of a lost original [Fig. 8.11]. Some impression of a similar but scaled-down version of this house may, however, be gained by viewing Royston House (better known by its later name of Caroline Park) in the northern suburbs of Edinburgh [Fig. 7.3]. This house was built in 1685–87 and extended in 1696. Viscount Tarbat reckoned that, including the additions, the building had cost him upwards of £6,000 sterling, although in attempting to sell it in the early eighteenth century he was evidently prepared to settle for half that price (Fraser 1876. I. 307; II. 451–57; RCAHMS 1929. no. 41).

Viscount Tarbat's building activities extended to the commercial development of the village of Portmahomack, involving the construction of a pier and the erection of a sizeable meal girnal there between 1697 and 1701 (Beaton and Clough, this volume). The girnal's layout and details have been modified by its later use as a drying-shed, but it still retains an original oak roof of coupled collar-rafter construction, secured at the wall-head by stub- and ashlar-pieces (NMRS record sheet RCR/17/1). It is one of the earliest surviving intact roofs in Easter Ross.

Uncorroborated tradition points to the castle of Lochslin as the birthplace of Viscount Tarbat in 1630, and it has been described, rather more plausibly, as the 'cradle' of the MacKenzies of Allangrange (Fraser 1876. I. lxvii–lxviii; Miller 1835. 192) [Fig. 8.12 and annotations]. The castle used to stand close to Loch Eye on the boundary of Tarbat and Tain parishes, taking its title from the older name of the loch. The last upstanding portion fell in the night of 31 January/1 February 1953, but old photographs [Figs. 8.13; 8.14] clearly show that it had a high-level corbelled angle-turret like Ballone and cable-moulded decoration comparable with that at

Fig. 8.11   Tarbat House; from Fraser 1876 (*1*, opp. p. clxxii).

Castle Craig. A sketch-drawing of the building illustrates a building of stepped L-plan form; the kitchen was on the ground floor, and although the position of the stair is not shown nor easily inferred (cf. description in *OSA.* IV. 296–97), the layout appears to be similar to Castle Leod and other MacKenzie residences. However, it is very doubtful whether the MacKenzies actually built this castle. Lochslin came into their possession in 1624, and the first mention of the castle is in a charter of their Vass predecessors in 1590, a date that would correspond much better with the known architectural evidence. The Vasses had been in possession of Lochslin from the fifteenth century down to 1603 when for a second and final time they were declared rebels (MacGill 1909. nos. 204, 410; *OPS.* II. 2. 450–51; Munro 1971).[4]

Their successors at Lochslin were the Munros of Meikle Tarrel and then, briefly, the Cuthberts of Drakies. James Cuthbert of Lochslin, former provost of Inverness, and his wife, Jean Leslie, both of whom died in 1623, are commemorated by mural monuments in the north aisle of Tarbat parish church at Portmahomack [Fig. 8.15]. Sir John MacKenzie of Tarbat, father of the 1st earl of Cromartie, acquired the rights to that aisle in 1634 (Fraser 1876. I. lix).

In addition to Redcastle (above) [Fig. 8.16], the principal local residences of the other branches of the MacKenzies included towers at Fairburn, Kinkell Clarsach and Kilcoy. The lofty mid-sixteenth-century

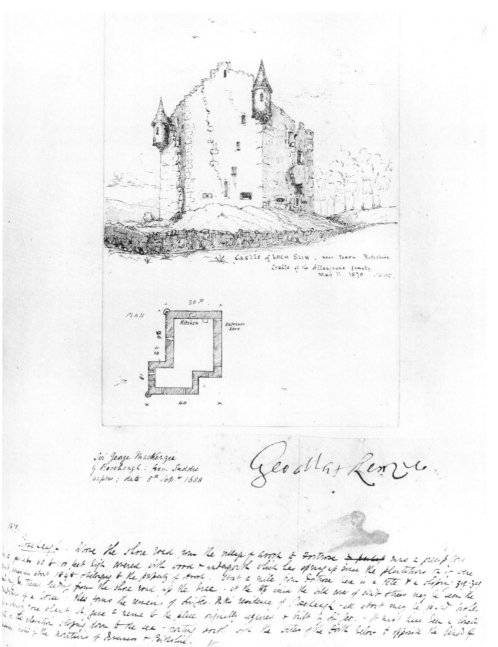

Fig. 8.12   Lochslin Castle; drawing by Sir J. D. MacKenzie, 1870.

Fig. 8.13   Lochslin Castle, *c.*1870.   *Fig. 8.14*   Lochslin Castle,
*c.*1950.

tower at Fairburn is most commonly remembered as the subject of two prophecies by the Brahan Seer. Noteworthy features of a more tangible kind consist of an early seventeenth-century stair-tower placed in front of the original first-floor entry, the remains of a single-storeyed and cruck-framed kitchen annexe, and in the east wall a wooden-lintelled window with stone hood-mould above (MacGibbon & Ross 1887–92. III. 462–65; *OPS*. II. 2. 519–21).

The 'manor place' of Kinkell Clarsach [Fig. 8.17] was built by the MacKenzies of Gairloch in 1594 following their acquisition of the property. It was added to in the late seventeenth or early eighteenth centuries, and has been restored in recent times (MacGibbon & Ross 1887–92. IV. 129–30; NMRS record sheet RCR/4/1; Laing 1974; *OPS*, II. 2. 549–50).

The four-storeyed Z-plan tower of Kilcoy was erected by yet another cadet of the MacKenzies of Kintail in the early seventeenth century (MacGibbon & Ross 1887–92. II. 252–56), and incorporates a fine MacKenzie fireplace lintel dated 1679 (MacDonald 1901–02. 702–04;

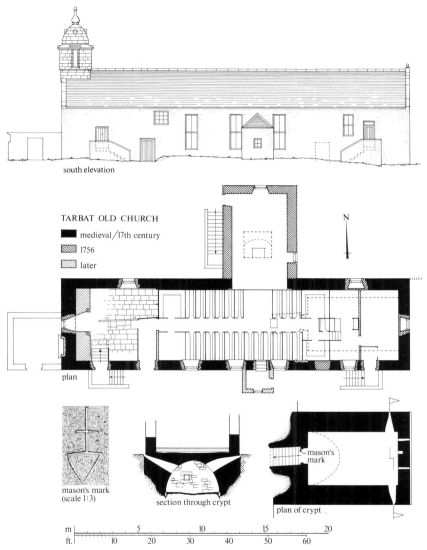

south elevation

TARBAT OLD CHURCH

■ medieval/17th century

▨ 1756

▧ later

N

plan

mason's mark
(scale 1:3)

section through crypt

mason's mark

plan of crypt

m | 5 10 15 20
ft. | 10 20 30 40 50 60

Fig. 8.15   Tarbat Old Church, Portmahomack; survey-drawings.

Fig. 8.16   Redcastle; view from east, 1966.

Fig. 8.17   Kinkell Castle; view from south, 1966.

Fig. 8.18 Balnagown Castle; view from south-west, 1958.

MacGill 1909. no. 859, for details of a forced entry into Kilcoy in 1687). Old photographs (NMRS) show how far the building had reached a ruinous condition prior to its first restoration and extension in 1890.

The Rosses of Balnagown

Prominent among the landed families in the district around Tain were the Rosses of Balnagown, who as descendants of the 4th earl of Ross established a cadet branch here in the fourteenth century and eventually assumed the chiefship of their clan (Reid 1894. 8–11). A late medieval L-plan tower, reconstructed in the seventeenth century, may conceivably be incorporated in the western portion of Balnagown Castle [Fig. 8.18] (Macgill 1909. nos. 483–85, 492 (1763)); the tower house is illustrated in the background of a seventeenth-century child portrait (National Galleries of Scotland 8814), but the existing mansion appears to be very largely of nineteenth-century character. The detailed architectural history of Balnagown has yet to be fully investigated, however, especially for the period before 1711 when the old line of the Rosses died out.

Little Tarrel [Fig. 8.19] (NMRS record sheet RCR/28/1; *OPS*. II. 2. 448–50; Reid 1894. 37–39) in Tarbat parish is a small, recently-restored L-plan house, originally built in the mid sixteenth century by a Ross of

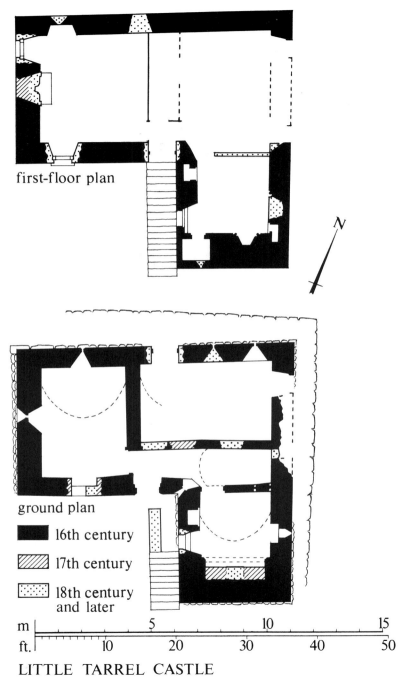

first-floor plan

N

ground plan

■ 16th century

▨ 17th century

▦ 18th century
and later

m |____5____10____15

ft. |__10__20__30__40__50

LITTLE TARREL CASTLE

Fig. 8.19   Little Tarrel Castle; plans.

Balnagown cadet. Its builder was Alexander Ross, legitimated son of Walter Ross, 8th of Balnagown, and his wife Elizabeth. An inscription beneath a first-floor window records their initials and date '155–', and a late nineteenth-century source (Reid 1894. 37) assumes that the missing digit is a 9. The house is known to have remained in the possession of succeeding generations of Rosses of Little Tarrel down to 1715. The building was subsequently sub-divided and modified on more than one occasion; an external forestair was introduced and part of the ground floor was set aside for farming purposes, an alteration that involved the removal of a vault and of an internal stair in an area that later collapsed. But much of the original detailing still survives, most notably in the vaulted kitchen and the first-floor chamber above it in the east wing.

The Rosses of Balnagown were also responsible for a portion of the work undertaken at the Denoon family castle at Cadboll. The vaulted interior in the main block of this one-time L-plan tower is of an unusually confused construction and arrangement. It may indeed relate to the episode in 1572–74 when Alexander Ross of Balnagown was ordered to make good 'the doune casting of the battelit towr of Catboll' by building up the vaults again at an estimated cost of 500 merks (MacGill 1909. no. 677; see also OPS. II. 2. 441–43).

The Munro families

The Munros have experienced a succession of residences at Foulis since at least the later thirteenth or early fourteenth centuries, but the small mount in the garden is unlikely to represent their earliest (motte-castle) home in

Fig. 8.20   Old Parish Church, Alness; view from south-west, 1966.

this neighbourhood (McInnes 1940. no. 5; and cf. Bain 1899.15). It is usually assumed that the present elegant neo-Classical mansion was built *de novo* on a cleared site to replace a burnt-out stone castle. The house and its adjacent ranges bear datestones of 1754, 1777 and 1792, but there are some features that clearly antedate this eighteenth-century building: the plan and details of the northern wing to the rear of the kitchen are probably ascribable to the later seventeenth century; sixteenth- or seventeenth-century architectural fragments are grouped in re-use in the central basement area; and a barrel-vaulted chamber in one of the court-yard buildings appears to be of similar age. Inherited modes of thinking may also account for the eccentric positioning of the stair-tower in relation to the main frontal block, but it remains difficult to gain any visual appreciation of the likely layout and appearance of the mansion's immediate predecessor (NMRS record sheet RCR/21/1).

The Munros of Foulis were principal heritors of the old parish church of Kiltearn, and the central loft and retiring rooms in the wing of this T-plan building reflect their patronage in the later eighteenth century. But

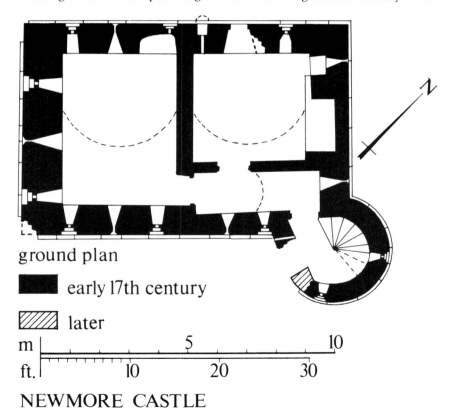

ground plan

█ early 17th century

▨ later

m |————————————5————————————10

ft. |————————10————————20————————30

NEWMORE CASTLE

Fig. 8.21   Newmore Castle; ground plan.

Kiltearn is built around a much older structure. At the east end there are clasping angle-buttresses and the remains of a hood-moulded window, survivals from the church's late medieval predecessor (Hay 1957. 89; NMRS record sheet RCR/6/1).

Another former parish church in Munro territory, that of Alness [Fig. 8.20], likewise reflects the influence of the Munros of Novar. It has a 1672 Novar Aisle together with a later extension to the north and a burial-enclosure of 1671 to the east. Datestones commemorate the fact that the main body of the church in its existing form dates from 1625 and was renovated in 1775. However, its basic rectangular plan and orientation suggest a medieval origin, and on the inner face of the north-east wall there is a blocked-up arched opening, in all likelihood a medieval tomb-recess (NMRS record sheet RCR/1/1).

Newmore [Fig. 8.21] is virtually the only early house of the Munros that has remained intact, but only just. It survives as an ivy-clad ruin, now reduced to a single storey. By 1543 the lands of Newmore were being held in *feu ferme* by descendants of the Munros of Milton, and the first reference to a house of Newmore occurs in 1560 (Munro 1980). What survives, however, appears to be of later sixteenth- or early seventeenth-century date, but probably not as late as 1625, the date commemorated on a lost datestone that is said to have come from this site (RCAHMS 1979a. no. 262, and ref. cited). The internal arrangements comprise

Fig. 8.22   Burial vault, Rosskeen churchyard; view from south-west, 1966.

vaulted ground-floor cellarage and kitchens linked by a corridor, and a newel stair in an extruded stair-turret gives access to what was formerly a first-floor hall. The entrance is rebated to receive an inner-wrought-iron yett, and is further protected by a small battery of redented gun-ports (NMRS record sheet).

The Munros of Newmore and Culrain were intimately associated with the parish of Rosskeen and east of the derelict parish church of 1832, but possibly close to the site of the medieval church, there is a seventeenth-century burial vault [Fig. 8.22]; a burial enclosure dated 1675 lies to the east. The mortuary chapel, restored in 1908, is a neat and well-detailed little building whose construction has been ascribed to 1664 on the questionable grounds that a casual payment was made to masons working here in that year (MacGill 1909, no. 531; NMRS record sheet RCR/7/1).

The castle of the Munros of Milton was built only with great difficulty in the face of stiff opposition from the neighbouring Rosses of Balnagown (above). It was then superseded by the more grandiose works of the MacKenzies and no visible remains of the Munro castle now survive (Fraser 1876. II. 429–31, 432; RCAHMS 1979a. no. 261).[5] This branch of the Munros was probably responsible, however, for the eye-catching turreted burial-aisle at the eastern end of Kilmuir Easter Church which is dated 1616 in the differently constructed upperworks. Given that the church occupies a position close to the shore facing the narrows of the Cromarty Firth, the tower could have been used, possibly even designed, as a sea-mark.

Meikle Daan [Fig. 8.23] in the uplands of Edderton parish is a later house of the Munros of Foulis, standing on property acquired from the Rosses of Balnagown (McInnes 1940. no. 72, 123, 129 and passim). This two-storeyed house, which is associated with a walled enclosure and ruinous outbuildings, appears at first glance to be of conventional eighteenth-century appearance. Closer examination reveals an asymmetrical three-bay frontage, and a rear projection contains part of an old stair. The door-lintel is inscribed with the initials A.M., M.F. and the date 1680; the same initials and date are on an elaborately sculptured fireplace lintel which came from Daan and is now in Balnagown Castle (*NSA*. XIV. 449; MacRae 1910–11. 398–400). Alexander Munro, a minister of Edderton, and his wife, Margaret Forrester, are the persons in question, Alexander being son of Hector Munro, who acquired Daan, and his wife, Euphemia Ross. However, a house at Daan first comes on record in 1592 (Forbes 1892, xxviii; *Inverness Scientific Trans*. 1918–25. 151) and some of the remains on this site may antedate the Munro connection.

Similar problems of analysis surround the origins and building histories of two other lesser Munro houses, Ardullie Lodge and Fyrish, both of which incorporate displaced datestones from the latter half of the seventeenth century. Both appear to belong substantially to the eighteenth century, but there is reason to believe that the (?T-plan) nucleus of Ardullie Lodge could correspond with either of the surviving 1669 or 1688 datestones.

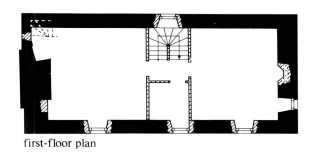

first-floor plan

ground plan

■ c.1680   ▨ 18th century   ⬚ 19th century

m |_____5_____10_____15
ft.|____10____20____30____40____50

MEIKLE DAAN

Fig. 8.23   Meikle Daan; plans.

ARCHITECTURAL PATRONAGE AND LOCAL COMMUNITIES

In some areas such as Tarbat parish a relatively dense pattern of sites and monuments commands attention collectively as a group, not just in terms of their individual family backgrounds. In the late eighteenth century it was reported that this parish 'produces much more corn than is sufficient for the support of its inhabitants' (*OSA.* VI. 422), and Tarbat has always had particular importance as a centre of seaborne communications and fishing. There were about nine sub-medieval lordships in Tarbat parish before Fearn was detached in 1628; some (e.g. Meikle Allan, Little Allan, Meikle Tarrel, Arboll, Easter Ard) had a complex divided pattern of ownership and few of these relate to any surviving remains. The castles appear to correspond with unitary or undivided properties such as Cadboll, Easter Tarbat, Little Tarrel and Lochslin (*OPS.* II. 2. 441–53; Macfarlane *Geographical Coll.* I. 215).

The patronage of this relatively numerous group of local lairds and seafaring communities found common expression in the fabric of the local parish church of Tarbat at Portmahomack which was dedicated to St Colman (above) [Fig. 8.15]. Although partly rebuilt in 1756 and now mostly remembered for its exotic pyramidal belfry, the main block of this T-plan church retains its medieval east–west orientation, and underneath the eastern end of the church is a vaulted crypt, first described in the early eighteenth century (Macfarlane *Geographical Coll.* I. 215). The numerous early cross-slabs and symbol stones that have come to light around this churchyard clearly testify to the long-established importance of the site (e.g. Allen and Anderson 1903. III. 73–75, 88–95; Higgitt 1982). Apart from the chapel at Hilton of Cadboll (RCAHMS 1979a. no. 224), however, there are now few visible remains to mark the comparatively large number of sacred sites, about eight altogether, that lay in the outlying areas of the parish in the Middle Ages (Macfarlane *Geographical Coll.* I. 215; RCAHMS 1979a. nos 208, 210, 224, 227, 243–45).

With the exception of a few survivors in Fortrose (and possibly Rosemarkie), there are now no readily identifiable burgh houses of seventeenth century or earlier date in Easter Ross. The building known as 'The Ark' in Tain was alleged to have accommodated the Marquis of Montrose on his last journey in 1650, but pictures of the building taken before its demolition in 1940 would seem to indicate that the house dated from the first half of the eighteenth century (Munro 1966. 61 and n; photographs in NMRS). Corporate civic patronage in Dingwall and Tain is, however, clearly reflected in the architecture of their tolbooths which formerly housed their municipal offices, courts and prisons. Dingwall Tolbooth is a symmetrical two-storeyed horizontal block with a centrally-placed tower and forestair; it is of seventeenth-century origin, but was substantially remodelled in 1732–33, altered in 1782 and its gaol was finally declared unfit to receive criminal prisoners in 1830 (Stell 1981. 450 and refs cited). Tain possesses a renowned tolbooth which has a dominant and strong-looking tower topped with a conical spire and angle bartizans. Despite its archaic appearance and the claim that it is one of the earliest surviving tolbooths, this building was in fact erected mainly between 1706 and 1708 and was not finally completed until 1733. It incorporates a bell (dated 1630) and an inscribed fragment of 1631, both of which were inherited from its predecessor which was demolished after serious storm damage in 1703 (Munro 1966. 74, and n; Stell 1981. 453 and refs cited). The conservative style of the existing early eighteenth-century structure does, however, serve as a final and splendid testament to the fine tower-building and masoncraft traditions prevalent in Easter Ross during the preceeding three centuries.

But beyond the more impersonal aspects of style, quality and function, architectural history provides a looking-glass through which we ought to see reflected, however imperfectly, the social life of earlier times. It is the medieval and later inhabitants of Easter Ross that we observe through the medium of their buildings, although our view is perforce distorted and restricted mainly to the architecture of landownership. As in many other parts of Scotland, we have not yet learnt to identify clearly the buildings associated with the medieval peasant-farmer, the urban 'indweller' and those below them in the social hierarchy. There are also aspects of human behaviour and the quality of life-style to which the architectural evidence can serve only as a limited or uncertain guide. As Sir George MacKenzie remarked of the lesser gentry houses of Ross-shire in the later Georgian period, whatever the merits or defects of their architecture, 'there are many mansions, where uncontrouled hospitality reigns, and in which an abundance of comfort, though not much elegance, is to be found' (MacKenzie 1813. 73).

Notes

[1] The term Easter Ross is defined here in its widest geographical sense, corresponding to the area dealt with by Mowat (Mowat 1981. 1–2, 166n.1, map on 240), but comprehending also the parishes of Edderton and Kincardine. The Act of Union in 1707 has been chosen as a terminal date purely as a matter of convenience.

[2] On the question of law and order Hugh Miller (Miller 1835. 350) reported on 'the change which began to take place in the northern counties about the year 1730, when the law of Edinburgh, as it was termed by a Strathcarron freebooter, arrived at the ancient burgh of Tain, and took up its seat there, much to the terror and annoyance of the neighbouring districts'.

[3] In *The Gentleman's Magazine* (1742. XII. 545) it was reported that on Sunday 10 October 'In the time of Worship the Roof of the Church of Fearn in Ross-shire, Scotland, fell suddenly in, and 60 People were killed, besides the wounded. The Gentry whose seats were in the Niches, and the Preacher falling under the Sounding board, were preserved'. NLS. Adv. MS 29.4.2(xi), f.263r, states that 17 were killed on the spot, but others (number unspecified) died later.

[4] One of the earliest recorded members of this branch of the family appeared in 1457 and was brother of Robert Vass of Barnbarroch, an estate in Wigtownshire situated a short distance from Whithorn. The link with the south-west emerged again in 1554 when Mr Patrick Vass, parson of Wigtown and later laird of Barnbarroch, received a royal grant of the marriage of the three daughters of John Vass of Lochslin and of any other heirs likely to succeed to Lochslin and Newton (Reid. R. C. ed. *Wigtownshire Charters*. Scottish History Society, 3rd ser. 1960. LI. 166, no. 144 and note; see also Munro 1971). The Vasses of Lochslin also seem to have enjoyed kinship with a merchant-burgess family of the name in Inverness.

[5] In the course of altering Tarbat House in 1728 George, 3rd Earl of Cromartie reportedly issued instructions to 'throw down that part of it called Monro's Old Work, being two sides and one gable, to clear and rid the foundation, and then to build up and erect the walls and gable, being the wester mid-gable of the house, to the same height and thickness as before . . .' (Fraser 1876. II. 432, citing Cromartie Papers. I. no. 64).

Site References

Alness Old Church	NH 644690
Ardullie Lodge	NH 586623
Ballone Castle	NH 928837
Balnagown Castle	NH 762752
Brahan Castle	NH 511545
Cadboll Castle	NH 878776
Caroline Park, Edinburgh, *see* Royston House	
Castle Leod	NH 486593
Craig Castle	NH 631638

Acknowledgement

The author wishes to record his thanks to all his colleagues who have been involved in the work of surveying Ross-shire buildings for the National Monuments Record of Scotland, and to those who prepared the Lists of Archaeological Sites and Monuments for Easter Ross (February 1979) and The Black Isle (October 1979). He gratefully acknowledges the cooperation of all owners, agents and tenants, and the considerable interest and support given to all aspects of this work by Mrs Jane Durham of Scotsburn, Kildary.

For permission to use and reproduce Figures 8.1, 8.2 grateful thanks are due to Mr Bruce Urquhart of Craigston; to the Trustees of the National Library of Scotland, for Figures 8.5, 8.6; to the Historic Buildings and Monuments Division (Scottish Development Department) for Figure 8.7 which is Crown Copyright; to Mrs H. Ross of Lochslin for Figures 8.12, 8.13; and to Mr and Mrs R. W. Munro for Figure 8.14. Of the remainder, Figures 8.8–8.10, 8.15–8.23 are Crown Copyright, Royal Commission on the Ancient and Historical Monuments of Scotland.

References

Allen, J. R. & Anderson, J. *The Early Christian Monuments of Scotland. 1903.*

Anderson. A. O. ed. *Early Sources of Scottish History to 1286.* 1922.

Anderson, M. L. *A History of Scottish Forestry.* 1967.

Bain, R. *History of the Ancient Province of Ross.* 1899.

Barrow, G. W. S. ed. *Regesta Regum Scottorum II, The Acts of William I, King of Scots 1165–1214.* 1971.

Beaton, A. J. Notes on Ormond or Avoch Castle, in the Black Isle, Ross-shire . . ., in *PSAS.* 1884–85. XIX: 400–05.

Bond, F. *An Introduction to English Church Architecture.* 1913.

Chron. Wyntoun (Laing). Laing, D. ed. *Androw of Wyntoun's Orygynale Cronykil of Scotland.* 1872–79.

Clough, M. Making the most of one's resources: Lord Tarbat's development of Cromarty Firth, in *Country Life.* 1977. vol. 162: 856–58.

Colvin, H. M. *The White Canons in England.* 1951.

Cowan, I. B. & Easson, D. E. *Medieval Religious Houses in Scotland.* 1976.

DNB, *Dictionary of National Biography*, From the Earliest times to 1900. 22 vols. 1921–27 edition.

Dunbar, J. G. The medieval architecture of the Scottish Highlands, in MacLean, L. ed. *The Middle Ages in the Highlands.* 1981: 38–70.

Dunlop, J. *The Clan MacKenzie: Independence in the North.* 1953.

Durkan, J. The Sanctuary and College of Tain, in *The Innes Review.* 1962. XIII: 147–56.

Exch. Rolls. Stuart, J. et al. edd. *The Exchequer Rolls of Scotland.* 1878–1908.

Forbes, A. P. *Kalendars of Scottish Saints.* 1872.

Fraser, H. A. Investigation of the artificial island in Loch Kinellan, Strathpeffer, in *PSAS.* 1916–17. LI: 48–99.

Fraser, W. *The Earls of Cromartie: their kindred, country and correspondence.* 1876.

Gordon, R. *A Genealogical History of the Earldom of Sutherland.* 1813.

Hay, G. *The Architecture of Scottish Post-Reformation Churches.* 1957.

Higgitt, J. C. The Pictish Latin inscription at Tarbat in Ross-shire, in *PSAS.* 1982. CXII: 300–21.

Hist. MSS Comm. Royal Commission on Historical Manuscripts, Series I, II Second Report 1871, Appendix, Duke of Sutherland (Dunrobin MSS).

Inverness Scientific Trans. Transactions of the Inverness Scientific Society and Field Club.

Kalendar of Fearn. See Forbes 1872. xxv–xxix: 67–78; *Hist. MSS Comm.* 1871: 179–80; *Inverness Scientific Trans.* 1918–25. IX: 141–53. The manuscript is now lodged in the National Library of Scotland, Deposit 314.18.

Laing, G. *Kinkell, the reconstruction of a Scottish castle.* 1974.

Lesley, J. *De Origine, Moribus et Rebus Gestis Scotorum Libri Decem.* 1578.

MacDonald, A. & MacDonald, A. *The Clan Donald.* 1896–1904.

MacDonald, W. R. The heraldry in some of the old churchyards between Tain and Inverness, in *PSAS.* 1901–02. XXXVI: 688–732.

Macfarlane, *Genealogical Coll.* Clark, J. T. ed. *Genealogical Collections concerning Families in Scotland made by Walter Macfarlane* (Scottish History Society, 1st series) 1900. XXXIII–XXXIV.

Macfarlane, *Geographical Coll.* Mitchell, A. ed. *Geographical Collections relating to Scotland made by Walter Macfarlane* (Scottish History Society, 1st series) 1906–08. LI–LIII.

MacGibbon, D. & Ross, T. *The Castellated and Domestic Architecture of Scotland.* 1887–92.

MacGibbon, D. & Ross, T. *The Ecclesiastical Architecture of Scotland.* 1896–97.

MacGill, W. *Old Ross-shire and Scotland.* 1909.

MacGill, W. The 'Breve Cronicle of the Erllis of Ross', in *Glasgow Archaeol. Trans.* (new series). 1924. VII pt 3: 313–29.

McInnes, C. T. *Calendar of Writs of Munro of Foulis 1299–1823* (Scottish Record Society). 1940. LXXII.

MacKenzie, A. *History of the MacKenzies.* 2nd edn. 1899.

MacKenzie, G. S. *A General View of the Agriculture of the Counties of Ross and Cromarty.* 1813.

MacKenzie, W. M. *The Old Sheriffdom of Cromarty* (Reprinted extract from the 'Northern Chronicle', Inverness). 1922.

MacKenzie, W. M. *The Medieval Castle in Scotland.* 1927.

MacKenzie, W. M. Old Cromarty Castle, in *PSAS.* 1947–48. LXXXII: 60–68.

Mackinlay, J. M. *Ancient Church Dedications in Scotland: Non-Scriptural Dedications.* 1914.

MacRae, D. Notice of some unrecorded sculptured stones at Edderton, Ross-shire, and at Foss, Perthshire, in *PSAS.* 1910–11. XLV: 398–402.

Macrae N. *The Romance of a Royal Burgh. Dingwall's story of a thousand years.* 1923.

Major, *History.* Constable, A. ed. *John Major's History of Greater Britain (1521),* (Scottish History Society, 1st series). 1892. x.

Miller, H. *Scenes and Legends of the North of Scotland,* 1835.

Miller, H. *My Schools and Schoolmasters.* 1854.

Mowat, I. R. M. *Easter Ross 1750–1850: the Double Frontier.* 1981.

Munro, J. & R. W. *Tain through the Centuries.* 1966.

Munro, R. W. [1971]. The Vasses of Lochslin: A Genealogy, in *Clan Munro Magazine.* 1971. XII: 35–39.

Munro R. W. [1971a]. MacCullochs of Plaids: A Genealogy, in *Clan Munro Magazine.* 1971. XII: 40–44.

Munro, R. W. *Notes on the ownership of Newmore* (typescript). 1980.

NLS. National Library of Scotland, Hutton MSS=Advocates' MSS, 30.5: 22–23 (plans and drawings), and 29.4.2(i)–(xii) (correspondence); 29.4.2(xi), ff.225–300, relate to Ross-shire.

NMRS. National Monuments Record of Scotland, record sheets (typescript MSS), photographs and drawings.

NSA. The New Statistical Account of Scotland. 1845.

Omand, D. *The Ross and Cromarty Book.* 1984: chapter by Stell and Beaton on 'Local Building Traditions'.

OPS. Origines Parochiales Scotiae. 1850–55.

OSA. The Statistical Account of Scotland. 1791–99.

Paul, J. B. Royal Pilgrimages in Scotland, in *Trans Scot. Ecclesiol. Soc.* 1904–05. I. pt 2: 147–55.

Phemister, J. *Scotland: The Northern Highlands* (British Regional Geology) 3rd edn. 1960.

RCAHMS. *Inventory of Midlothian and West Lothian.* 1929.

RCAHMS. *Archaeological Sites and Monuments Series* No. 6, Easter Ross (February 1979) [1979a]; No. 9, The Black Isle (October 1979) [1979b].

Reg. Sec. Sig. Livingstone, M. et al. eds. *Registrum Secreti Sigilli Regum Scottorum.* 1908–.

Reid, F. N. *The Earls of Ross and their Descendants.* 1894.

Ross, A. Three Antiquaries: General Hutton, Bishop Geddes and the Earl of Buchan, in *The Innes Review.* 1964. XV: 122–39.

Scots Peerage. Paul, J. B. ed. *The Scots Peerage.* 1904–14.

Scott, A. R. *Illustrations of Fortrose Cathedral.* 1873.

Sinclair, J. *General View of the Agriculture of the Northern Counties and Highlands of Scotland.* 1795.

Stell, G. The earliest tolbooths: a preliminary account, in *PSAS.* 1981. CXI: 445–53.

LATE SEVENTEENTH AND EIGHTEENTH CENTURY ESTATE GIRNALS IN EASTER ROSS AND SOUTH-EAST SUTHERLAND

Elizabeth Beaton

The fertile coastal plains of Easter Ross and the eastern parts of Sutherland were good corn growing land in the eighteenth century and earlier, with the added advantage that any surplus could be exported by sea from the various small harbours and beaches, particularly from the Cromarty Firth which afforded shelter for shipping. Sea transport was all important; roads were not well developed nor were wheeled vehicles common until the early nineteenth century, when Thomas Telford and the Commissioners for Highland Roads and Bridges constructed roads north of Inverness, bridging the Conon River at Conon Bridge and the Kyle of Sutherland at Bonar Bridge. Maritime transport for bulk goods was not usurped, however, by these new roads, but rather by the railways, established between Inverness and Sutherland in the 1860s and 1870s. Until then a surprising number of craft plied between local and national coastal ports, and further overseas.

THE NEED FOR GRAIN STORAGE

Until the end of the eighteenth century, and even into the nineteenth, agricultural rents were paid in service and in kind, and of all the commodities grain, bere barley and oats, with some wheat, was the most important and the most common. In turn, farm servants received barley and oatmeal as a recognised portion of their wages; public servants such as schoolmasters and ministers were also paid some of their salary or stipend in this form by their Parish Heritors. Such bulky wealth obviously required storage, a requirement which increased as agricultural improvements gained momentum during the latter half of the eighteenth century. Improved seed, better drainage, more effective land management, all combined to create a surplus for landlords on the larger estates. The estate girnal or storehouse was constructed to house this wealth, pending its reissue as wages or its sale to realize cash. A number of these fine and functional storehouses survive around the coasts of Easter Ross and southeast Sutherland, at Alness Point (NH656679), Ankerville Corner (NH818744), Foulis Ferry Point (NH599636), Invergordon (NH709685), Little Ferry (NH801957), Nigg (NH796687) and Portmahomack (NH915846), a remarkable grouping in Scottish as well as in local terms [Fig. 9.1].

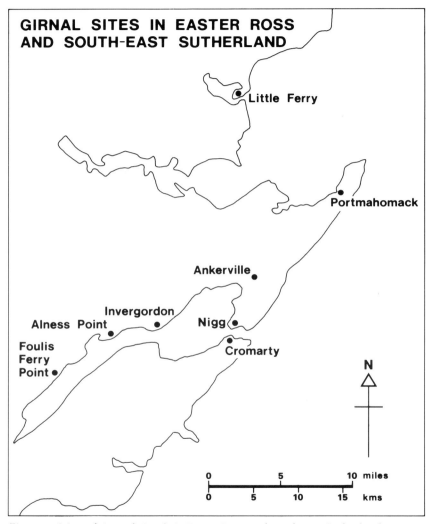

Fig. 9.1　Map of sites of girnals in Easter Ross and south-east Sutherland.

Accounts survive for 'Barley received at the Store-House of Foulis' in 1784 (being the crop of 1783), and vary in quantities from the tenant at the Mains of Foulis who paid ninety-eight bolls one firlot, down to John Ross, slater at Lemlair, two bolls, and David Mackay, one boll one firlot, adding up for the year to one hundred and sixty-nine bolls two firlots. Further accounts for 1795 show 'Note of Barley and Oat Meal given into the Store House of Fowlis by Tennants on the Estate of Fowlis, the crop of 1794'. Items include various recipients who, 'on Munro's Orders', were given meal or barley, including the Minister, Mr Harry Robertson, who received thirty-eight bolls and the schoolmaster at Drummond (the township preceeding Evanton, not laid out until c.1800) whose portion was eleven bolls one firlot three pounds of barley.[1]

Ian Mowat (1981. 24) cites examples of mid-eighteenth century annual rentals, such as Mains of New Tarbat valued at sixty-two bolls, while a tacksman on the same estate rented land valued at ninety-three bolls.

Even as late as 1810, when most rents were being paid in money and long leases of nineteen years were becoming established practice, Sir George Steuart Mackenzie of Coul swithered as to whether rentals in kind or in cash were the most profitable. 'Rents are now chiefly paid in money, but there are leases still subsisting which direct the rents to be paid in kind ... if prices were sufficiently variable the rent in kind might probably render the balance pretty equall during a lease (of nineteen years) for both parties' (Mackenzie 1810. 142).

THE GIRNALS

The storehouse was therefore a necessity on the prosperous eighteenth century agricultural estate. The design requirements for these girnals was simple and functional: they had to be strong, secure, well ventilated, provide maximum storage and facilities for handling and loading. They were best sited on the coast, close beside a beach which boats could use with reasonable ease and safety, and with a level area or yard at the rear where packhorses could assemble, goods be gathered, and people work and check material. The girnals were plain rectangular buildings, similar to the large estate threshing barns such as the very fine eighteenth century barn at Balnagown, but with no need of internal flooring set high enough to accommodate the arm stretch and the flail of the threshers, nor to be orientated to take advantage of the prevailing winds to make a draught pass through opposing winnowing doors. They were sited in exposed coastal positions and were therefore subject to considerable weathering, so lime harling protected the rubble masonry which was bonded with a lime mortar (the use of valuable lime itself indicating wealth). Further finish was obtained by ashlar margins, architraves and other dressings and the well slated roofs steeply pitched to throw off water, the gable apices sometimes graced with stone ball finials. Through-ventilation was essential to keep stock aired and dry, and was furnished by slit vents or small, shuttered and barred rectangular windows, or a combination of both as at

Alness Point storehouse, usually with splayed ingoes to increase the internal light. Single end chimney stacks on some girnals indicate that the buildings were occasionally heated, probably for the comfort of a custodian, for unless the hearth were tended, there would always be risk of fire in a store housing such combustible contents.

The earlier girnals can be identified by their steeply pitched crowstepped gables with square apex finials; the later ones by flat skews, shallower rooflines and ball finials for decoration. Consistently measuring around 6.2 m (20 ft) deep, but with a varying overall length of up to 30.5 m (100 ft) or more, these girnals were sometimes larger than the neighbouring parish churches and many times finer than the homes from which the tenants came with their weighty rents — cottages that were of field rubble bonded with mud or clay mortar, and with turf and straw thatched roofs through which the smoke from the central hearth seeped its slow passage, 'houses which provided accommodation for neither man nor beast' (*NSA* 1840, XIV. 464). No doubt, too, a fine girnal impressed the neighbouring lairds, for a good store, and even more a full store with attendant activity, was a sure indication of prosperity and success.

Some landlords combined the roles of improving agriculturalist and trader with that of lawyer or public servant in the wider sphere of national life, bringing home to their acres the latest farming treatise or technique, but requiring those acres to realize cash to finance their social and public life in Edinburgh and elsewhere. As Monica Clough has so lucidly described (1977 and this volume), George Mackenzie, Lord Tarbat and first earl of Cromartie, was a pioneer practitioner of this dual role. He had served six sovereigns by the time of his death in 1714, in various legal capacities such as Lord Justice and as Secretary for Scotland; but with official salaries up to seven years in arrears he had to find income from other sources, and from 1670 onwards developed his lands in Easter Ross — farming, the grain trade and the salmon fishings on the Conon River. At Cromarty there was a 'Girnall House for my Lord's use' (Clough 1977. 857) while at 'Portmahobuagg . . . ane handsome little peer was built there by George, late Erle of Cromartie' (Macfarlane *Collections* 1906. I. 215), and almost certainly the smaller of the two storehouses. Not for nothing did Lord Tarbat build his Edinburgh mansion, Royston House, conveniently near the port of Leith which would have received the produce exported from his northern estates, the house that bears the Latin inscription beginning 'Riches unemployed are of no use; but being made to circulate they are productive of much good . . .' (Clough 1977. 857).

Portmahomack

In 1798 Portmahomack consisted of 'two storehouses for the reception of rents in kind and three houses' (*NSA* 1840. XIV. 463), together with the 'handsome little peer' which probably forms the core of the present harbour improved by Thomas Telford, 1811–16 (Hume 1977. 296). The two girnals [Fig. 9.2] form the back-drop to the harbour with their long

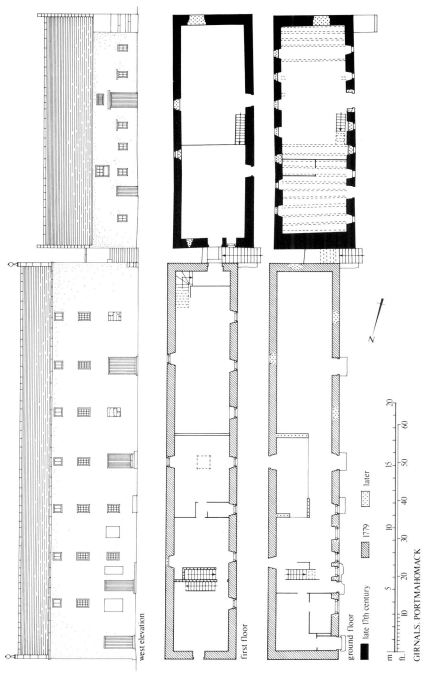

west elevation

first floor

ground floor

GIRNALS. PORTMAHOMACK

■ late 17th century   ▨ 1779   ⬚ later

m
ft.

5   10   15   20

10   20   30   40   50   60

Fig. 9.2   Plans and elevation, Portmahomack storehouses, 1983.

elevations facing west to the sea and linked by a forestair at the north gable of the smaller, the older of the two, which dates from the late seventeenth century. This is a simple rectangular building with harled rubble walls on reddish boulder footings, measuring overall 19 m by 6.4 m (62 ft by 21 ft). The two doors in the long west elevation are of unequal height, their chamfered sandstone dressings having a worn rounded appearance. Six small windows light the ground floor; two loft vents survive, one enlarged. A broad buttress shores up the end of the building, close to the south gable, projecting out into the road, and a similar loading door to that in the north gable is now blocked in the south. The steeply pitched West Highland slate roof has a stone ridge, crowstepped gables with square apex terminals and cavetto skewputts.

The ground has been built up to the rear, blocking the back entrances, but a small horizontal vent, cut out of a single slab, lies off-centre under the eaves.

Internally the girnal has a half loft at the north end reached by the north gable forestair. It retains its late seventeenth century open timber roof, which is basically of oak, is of collar rafter construction strengthened at the wallhead by stub (or sole) and ashlar pieces and tied by upper and lower collars. All joints are pinned by wooden pegs, with Roman numeral assembly marks roughly scored on the rafter faces. These 'carpenters' marks' were cut into the wood off-site, in the carpenters' yard, and indicate the order in which the timbers were to be erected [Fig. 9.3].

The later storehouse stands to the north, dated 1779 on its north-west skewputt. This is considerably larger than its neighbour, measuring 31.8 m by 5.5 m (104.75 ft by 18 ft) on plan, is of two storeys and loft and has seven wide bays, somewhat irregular in the ground floor but retaining their symmetrical fenestration in the first and second (loft) floors. The masonry is of coursed and pinned squared rubble with some harling to the gables and the seaward front, but the rear (east) is left exposed. The slate roof is of a shallower pitch than the earlier building, has a heavy stone ridge, flat skews and apex ball finials raised on slender bases. Internally it is gutted and most of the original features have disappeared, though some evidence of seating for iron bars in the ground floor windows and shuttering in those in the upper floors has been identified.

To the rear of these storehouses is a roughly walled yard, running back to the sloping hillside and the road winding down from the farmland above. Doors in the rear of the buildings (some now blocked) gave onto this area which was an integral part of the complex.

Little Ferry

To the north, not too far across the sea from Tarbat Ness and Portmahomack as the seagull flies, is Little Ferry or Little Unes, on Loch Fleet. The Unes (or Fleet) is one of the three rivers (other two, Brora and Helmsdale) that 'have good harbours for the ships that do traffique in that country to transport from thence their Corns, Salt, Coal, Salmon, Beef,

Fig. 9.3 Roof timbers, late seventeenth-century storehouse,
Portmahomack, 1983.

Fig. 9.4 Detail, Taylor and Skinner's *Survey and Maps of the Roads of North Britain*, 1776, showing Little Ferry girnal to far left of road on north side of channel.

Fig. 9.5 South front, Little Ferry Girnal House, 1983.

Fig. 9.6 Rear, Little Ferry Girnal House, 1983.

Hides, Wool, Linen, Tallow, Butter, Cheese, Plaids and other Commodities (Macfarlane *Collections* 1908. II. 100). The Sutherland coastal plain as far north as Helmsdale is sheltered by hills to landward, and the well-drained fields slope down to the shores, east and south. Thomas Pennant recorded in August 1769, that 'The Demesne (of Dunrobin) is kept in excellent order, and I saw there a very fine field of wheat, which would be ripe about the middle of next month. This is the most northern wheat which had been sown this year in North Britain'; while the Rev. Alexander Pope, who a few years later added an appendix to this travelogue, opens his description of Golspie Parish with the words 'This is fine corn country' (Pennant (1769) 1790. 190, 360).

At Little Ferry the early eighteenth century Sutherland Estate girnal stands a little to the west of the present ferry pier [Fig. 9.4]. Estate factors' accounts show that it was regularly used for grain and meal shipments during the eighteenth century (Adam 1960. xxvii–xxviii). The long harled building, 24.4 m by 6.7 m (80 ft by 22 ft), with steeply pitched roof and crowstepped gables stands close to the shore, south-facing on a crescent shaped shingle beach [Figs. 9.5; 9.6]. The girnal was converted by the Sutherland Estate in 1859 to five dwellings, ground and first floor flats at both ends and a single two storey dwelling in the centre, a sympathetic adaptation in Arts and Crafts Movement style reminiscent of some other Estate cottages of this period in Golspie [Fig. 9.7]. The east and west gables retain their original first floor centre entrances with simply chamfered architraves, and are served by forestairs with similarly treated ashlar parapets. The main south frontage dates entirely from 1859 in appearance, with three entrances, various asymmetrical tripartites (three–light windows) and a projecting rectangular bay window. Four gabled dormers break the roof at wallhead, the outer with inscribed stone panels, one with the date and the other with the double SS monogram of the Sutherland/Stafford family. Pronounced skewputts, painted timber facing and a diminutive swept light ring the changes in detail for the remaining dormers; all windows are multi-pane casements. Tall paired coped stacks crown the ridge and even taller shaped chimneys rise from the rear wallhead, combining to give the impression of extra height. All original stone facings are of grey ashlar, some replaced or re-tooled, while those of the 1859 conversion are in stugged red sandstone, contrasting well with the white-grey harling.

The adaptation of the Little Ferry girnal was undoubtedly influenced by a similar conversion the previous year, when the English architect George Devey (1820–86) was commissioned by the Duchess of Sutherland to turn an old estate barn into four cottages. This early exponent of the Vernacular Revival created a picturesque composition from the simple rectangular building on a hillside not far from Dunrobin Castle (NLS 313/1285, 313/1291: Mr John Gifford, Buildings of Scotland Research Unit, *pers. comm.*).

The house is now a single holiday home. Inside, the original low ceiling height is retained with original joists left visible in the ground floor. The

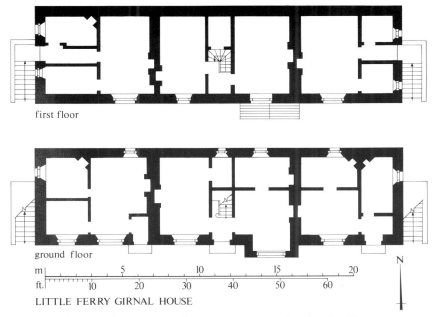

first floor

ground floor

m |————————5————————10————————15————————20

ft. |——10——20——30——40——50——60

LITTLE FERRY GIRNAL HOUSE

N

Fig. 9.7   Plans, Little Ferry Girnal House as converted to five dwellings, 1859.

various small rooms that comprised the three ground floor dwellings are all now linked one into the other, and separate communication to each upstairs room has been achieved by the insertion of a long, narrow rear corridor. Plain tooled ashlar chimney pieces frame the fireplace, some with original cast-iron grates.

Ankerville Corner, Nigg and Cromarty

Another conversion of a girnal to dwellings, said to have taken place in the early 1900s, is the Old Storehouse, Ankerville Corner, in Nigg Parish [Fig. 9.8]. Measuring 24.4 m by 6.4 m (80 ft by 21 ft), only the crow-stepped gables and worn, cavetto skewputts indicate the early eighteenth century date of an otherwise totally undistinguished terrace of three, two-bay cottages, each with entrance door flanked by a window and each with paired gabletted dormers. The site of this girnal is unusual within this group of storehouses, for it is the only one that is some distance from the shore, and that the tidal, muddy waters of Nigg Bay. In the mid-eighteenth century, Ankerville was the richest portion of the Inverchassley Estates belonging to David Ross, Lord Ankerville, who successfully combined the career of an agricultural innovator with that of Senator of the College of Justice, one of the group of lawyers whose lands were concentrated near Tain (Mowat. 1981. 29, 65).

Fig. 9.8 Former storehouse, Ankerville; now three cottages, 1983.

Further south in this parish, close by Nigg pier and facing Cromarty town and the narrow channel linking the Moray and the Cromarty Firths, another girnal stands close by the shore. Its present role as an hotel bar, with modern horizontal metal-framed windows, is a deceptive disguise, but the rectangular form, 21.94 m by 6.4 m (72 ft by 21 ft), the crow-stepped east gable and the long elevation facing the shore and the sea, all indicate the original use of the building, its early date confirmed by the simple chamfered door lintel inscribed 1712.

Nigg Parish was 'noted a few years ago for the abundance and beauty of its barley; now little barley is raised … wheat is the farmer's mainstay' (*NSA* 1836. XIV. 34).

Opposite, on the other side of the channel, is Cromarty, until early in the nineteenth century the most important Ross-shire harbour. Fragments of the first Earl of Cromartie's 'Girnall House' (Monica Clough, *pers. comm.*; see also this volume) can be traced between the harbour and the lighthouse.

Invergordon

Three girnals survive, in whole or in part, on the north shores of the Cromarty Firth. Between Shore Road and Mill Street, Invergordon, steeply pitched crowstepped gables with square apex finials and the long rear wall with three unusually long centre windows (1.83 m by 46 cm: 6 ft by 1.6 ft) are incorporated in the present garage complex. Measuring 38.8 m by 6.4 m (127 ft by 21 ft) it is the longest building in the group, appears to date from early eighteenth century, and might be the 'Store-house' illustrated on a map of *c.*1750 of the estates of Sir John Gordon of Invergordon (RHP 37985) [Fig. 9.9]. If so, artistic licence has given the sketch an end chimney stack, of which there is no evidence in the present

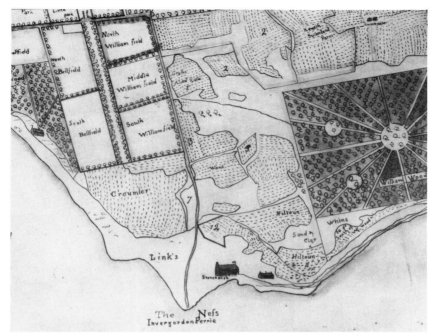

Fig. 9.9   Detail from Plan of lands belonging to Sir John Gordon of Invergordon, *c*.1750, showing storehouse at Invergordon (RHP 37985).

building. Sir John intended, amongst other ambitious building projects, to establish a village at 'Ness of Invergordon'. Here he envisaged a settlement for fishermen and ferrymen, which developed (on paper at least) to a sizeable community with a market place, stocks, a public house and a new granary decorated with cupola, weathervane, a crane, ventilators and an enclosure. How much was completed by the energetic Sir John is doubtful, though a century later Invergordon had superseded Cromarty as the principal harbour on the Cromarty Firth (Mowat 1981. 68).

Alness Point

Further west, standing isolated by the shore at Alness Point, gaunt against the skyline and now surrounded by flotsam and garbage, is a tall four-storey, three-bay storehouse measuring 11.8 m by 6 m (38 ft by 20 ft), with the south-east elevation to seaward and the north-east gable giving onto a tidal basin, now virtually obliterated [Fig. 9.10]. The left skewputt in the north-east gable is initialled and dated, enough surviving to decipher McK and (?)74. Captain James Munro inherited Teaninich, Alness, in 1766, married Margaret MacKenzie of Ardross in 1768, and died in 1788, so the datestone could be reconstructed as '17 JM MMcK 74' (Mackenzie 1898. 423). Though smaller on plan than other local storehouses, the

Fig. 9.10 Alness Point
Storehouse, 1983.

builders must have been too ambitious about its height, for constructed
with walls only 61 cm (2 ft) thick, it had subsequently to be heavily
buttressed, the north-east gable and the long south-east elevation having
respectively two and three substantial triangular buttresses projecting
2.4 m (8 ft). These partially block two low entrances in the seaward
elevation and are irregularly placed in the principal gable in order to
accommodate a forestair leading to a first floor doorway. Two loading
doors are in the second and third floors of the north-east gable, the upper
having a stout iron hoist bar with hooked end projecting from the lintel.
The seaward side has three symmetrical rectangular openings to each
floor, some with their paired horizontal bars still in place; the rear
elevation has three long vertical slit vents in each floor, with extra paired
vents and small (blocked) window very low at ground level. The finial has
disappeared from the south-west apex, though the iron seating survives;
there is a long crack in the rear wall and the slated roof is badly holed.

Internally the building is gutted, but joist seatings in the walls indicate
the four floors, a very low ground floor served by low seaward doors, an
equally low first floor served by the entrance reached by the forestair, and
two more generous upper floors with loading doors.

Foulis Ferry Point

Finally, west again from Alness along the coast at Foulis Ferry Point, the
finest girnal of the group stands on a spit of land projecting into the
Cromarty Firth. Known as the Old Rent House [Figs. 9.11; 9.12], it is a
landmark from land and sea. It appears to date from around 1740,
measures 28.8 m by 6.4 m (96 ft by 21 ft) on plan, is of two storeys and
attic in height, and its wide near symmetrical five-bay east elevation gives
onto a curved shingle beach where boats could easily pull up. Though
there have been some later alterations, including the addition of the

146

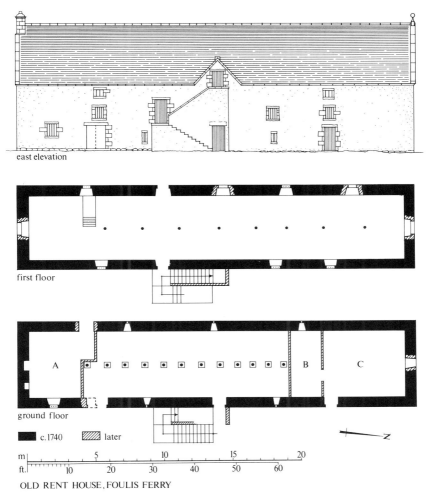

east elevation

first floor

ground floor

■ c.1740   ▨ later

m | 5 | 10 | 15 | 20
ft. | 10 | 20 | 30 | 40 | 50 | 60

OLD RENT HOUSE, FOULIS FERRY

Fig. 9.11   Plans and elevation, Foulis Ferry Old Rent House, 1983.

massive forestair in the centre of the east (seaward) elevation, these are of considerable age, and do not detract from the mid-eighteenth century character of the building. There are three ground floor entrances in the seaward side, that to the south has been widened. The later forestair leads to a first floor off-centre entrance and to a centre loft door under a gablet which breaks the wallhead. Small first floor windows echo the symmetry of the east front with smaller loft windows above. To the rear [Fig. 9.13] there is a single ground floor entrance, and at off-centre a loading door in the first floor. Through draught is provided by a series of slit vents and further loft windows. Original openings have plain chamfers, the later

Fig. 9.12 Foulis Ferry Old Rent House, 1983.

Fig. 9.13 Rear, Foulis Ferry Old Rent House, 1983.

ones, such as the single windows in the north and south gables, have plain tooled ashlar margins. There is a simple chamfered eaves cornice, the chamfer detailing returning up the gables under the flat skews. A ball finial terminates the north gable, while at the south there is a chimney stack with nicely moulded corniced cope, the decoration of which is similar to that serving the Sutherland aisle at St Andrew's Church, Golspie, dated 1738. The West Highland slate roof was restored *c.*1960.

Internally there is a blocked grate in the south gable wall, and the loft floor is missing. The first floor is supported by a row of posts down the centre, which are slotted into pad stones; similar posts survive at first floor which supported the former attic flooring. Most window and vent openings have splayed ingoes, slots for former window bars, and the

Fig. 9.14 Key, Foulis Ferry Old Rent House, 1983.

internal walls are neatly and smoothly finished with cherry cocking and vestiges of the plaster with which they were previously covered.

The north end of the ground floor of the granary is partitioned off as a separate room, with its own door in the outer bay of the east elevation, and with a small window in the north gable [Fig. 9.11(c)]. There is some evidence that girnals or bins were fitted around the outer edges of the room, and another small wood-lined store opens off it [Fig. 9.11(b)], closed by a door on which various early nineteenth-century graffiti record details of loadings and disbursement of grain. The window is, like some of the other openings, a later insertion, and this room was probably made after the rentals in kind had ceased, to store the meal which farm servants customarily received as part of their wages, referred to in parts of Ross-shire as 'perquisites'.

The granary key is of interest [Fig. 9.14]. It is a substantial handmade article, with a small ringed head through which passes a metal loop. This key was intended to be slung on the custodian's belt, and is worn and polished through contact with clothing.

The west (rear) elevation is now fronted by a lawn, which appears to have been the former yard or assembly area with direct access from the road to accommodate the arrivals of grain and meal.

THE DECLINE OF THE GIRNALS

Grain exported from these coastal storehouses found a ready market during the eighteenth century in the nearby military garrison at Fort George, in Inverness and in the expanding urban centres in the south.

In general, seaborne trade flourished despite the agricultural slump that followed immediately after the end of the war Napoleonic Wars in 1815, for the area had the local advantage of the market for barley provided by distilleries. Traffic, however, mainly became centred on harbours and piers which facilitated lading and enabled boats of larger draught to load cargoes direct. Portmahomack harbour was re-built in the early nineteenth century. Invergordon developed as a port, and various piers were constructured around the coast, such as the one at Balintraid designed by Thomas Telford in 1817 (Hume 1977. 289). At Little Ferry the piers of 1808 (RHP 11/6/55), and W. Leslie's probable re-build of 1850 (NLS 313/3618), shifted the centre of maritime activity further east along the shore from the girnal.

The farm diaries of General John Munro of Teaninich, Alness, which survive for the years 1848–50,[2] frequently mention sending goods and livestock to Invergordon for export to Edinburgh; they also mention the distribution of meal to farm workers and the landing of coal for the distillery on the beach to save both cartage and pier dues at neighbouring Dalmore. But of the storehouse built on that same beach by his father, Captain James Munro, in 1774, there is no word. It had outlived its usefulness.

For as long as Portmahomack harbour remained a trading centre, the girnals there served as warehouses, and after that as fishing stores. Invergordon became 'a large village-town rising very fast into importance — as fast indeed as Cromarty is going down; it being the cause' (Mowat 1981. 72). The Invergordon granary continued as a barleystore, and then as a seed store, moving into the railway age when the branch line was built between it and the sea, but when that trade declined it eventually became incorporated into a garage. At Ankerville and Little Ferry the respective estates required accommodation for their workers rather than for the fruits of those workers' labours, and both storehouses were converted into dwellings, the latter subsequently becoming a single holiday home, still called 'The Little Ferry Girnal House'.

The Foulis Ferry storehouse achieved local historical notoriety when marched on by a meal mob from Dingwall, during food shortages in 1796 (Logue 1979. 43).[3] It continued to serve the estate as a store after rents in kind had ceased; and for many years coal was brought by sea to Ferry Point and off-loaded on the shore into carts on log pontoons. A small cart remains in the store with single central shaft and small wide wheels for use on the shingle, and it was possibly to accommodate this vehicle that the door in the east elevation was widened. The south end of the building was separated for use as a byre [Fig. 9.11(a)], with a portion of the ceiling removed and with direct access to the first floor (useful for fodder storage) by a wooden stair. The crofter-ferryman in the neighbouring cottage (now a restaurant) plied the ferry between Foulis and Findon on the other side of the Firth, paying his rent in kind until the middle of this century by collecting gravel from the shore and wheeling it around the Foulis Castle policies to surface the paths and roads, earning the nickname 'The Wheeler'. The ferry ceased to operate in the 1930s and the last ferryman died in the 1940s, leaving his daughter to be known as 'Jessie the Wheeler' (Mr Hector Munro, *pers. comm.*).

These girnals span a period of a hundred years from the late seventeenth to late eighteenth century; both ends of this building spectrum, the earliest and latest buildings of the group, being represented at Portmahomack. As trade expanded, as the cultivated land produced better grain harvests and as the estates grew in size, in productivity and in wealth, so the girnals were built longer or higher, as at Invergordon and Alness Point respectively. They survive as physical evidence of certain economic, social and agricultural patterns in eighteenth century Easter Ross and Sutherland.

Notes

[1] Information by courtesy of Mr Hector Munro of Foulis from accounts relating to The Old Renthouse held at Foulis Castle. A boll is a dry measure, varying in extent according to its locality and the article measured. A boll of oats or barley weighed around 160–170 lb, and of meal around 140 lb. A firlot is a quarter of a boll. The boll was also a measure of land, computed according to the quantity of bolls it could produce.

[2] Typescript copy in possession of Mrs Jane Durham.

[3] Grain, said to be Indian corn no longer required for the American war, was distributed from Cromarty Firth girnals during the famine of 1796 (Mr W. Munro, Clashnabuiac, Alness. *pers. comm.*).

Acknowledgement

I would like to thank the following: Mrs Jane Durham and Mr D. M. Walker for reading the draft of this paper; Mrs Durham for material loaned and comments on Easter Ross farming history; Mr Hector Munro of Foulis for time spent at Foulis Ferry Old Rent House and information about the building; Miss Helen Hoare for permission to reproduce her plans of the Little Ferry Girnal House and Miss Louise Beaton for re-drawing those plans; Messrs A. J. Leith and G. P. Stell for further help with plans. Figures 9.2, 9.3, 9.11 are reproduced by kind permission of The Royal Commission on the Ancient and Historical Monuments of Scotland and Figures 9.5, 9.6, 9.8, 9.10, 9.12, 9.13, 9.14 by the Historic Buildings and Monuments Division, SDD, all being Crown Copyright. Figure 9.4 is reproduced by permission of the Trustees of the National Library of Scotland and Figure 9.9 by permission of Mr John Forsyth, Balintraid, Ross-shire. Figure 9.1 has been redrawn by Douglas Lawson.

References

Manuscript:

Scottish Record Office (SRO)
 RHP 37985
 RHP 11/6/55

National Library of Scotland (NLS): Sutherland Papers
 Dep. 313/1285
 Dep. 313/1291
 Dep. 313/3618 W. Leslie's plan for pier at Little Ferry.

Printed:

Adam, R. J. ed. *Home's Survey of Assynt.* 1960.
Clough, M. Making the most of one's resources; Lord Tarbat's development of Cromarty Firth, in *Country Life.* 1977. vol. 162.
Hume, J. *The Industrial Archaeology of Scotland.* 1977. vol. II.
Logue, K. J. *Popular Disturbances in Scotland, 1780–1815.* 1979.
Macfarlane, W. *Geographical Collections relating to Scotland.* 3 vols. 1906–08.
Mackenzie, A. *History of the Munros of Fowlis.* 1898.
Mackenzie, Sir G. S. *A General View of the Agriculture of . . . Ross and Cromarty.* 1810.
Mowat, I. R. M. *Easter Ross 1750–1850: The Double Frontier.* 1981.
NSA. *The New Statistical Account.*
Pennant, T. *A Tour in Scotland, 1769. 5th. ed.* 1790.

LAND ASSESSMENTS AND SETTLEMENT HISTORY IN SUTHERLAND AND EASTER ROSS

Malcolm Bangor-Jones

There are those who would argue that land assessments are among the more arid, and certainly more obscure, topics in Scottish history! Yet land assessments are not only of great interest in themselves, but they possess considerable importance for the study of settlement history. This is particularly so when they are set alongside other sources of evidence, landholding, place-names, and archaeology, in what may be termed a retrospective approach — moving back in time from the more recent past. This paper comprises two parts: first, a consideration of the uses, nature, and origins of land assessments, in particular davochs and pennylands; secondly, a discussion of more specific aspects of settlement history and territorial organization.

THE USES OF LAND ASSESSMENTS

Davochs and Pennylands

The earliest references from Ross and Cromarty and Sutherland are to the twelve davochs of Skelbo, parish of Dornoch (in Bishop Gilbert's constitution of the diocese of Caithness, 1222 × 1245: Fraser 1892. III. 3–6), and to the two davochs of 'Clon' or Clyne, now Mountgerald, parish of Kiltearn (1224 × 1231) (Moray Reg. 333–34). Pennylands first appear in 1539 with the three pennylands of the island of 'Sanda' and the two pennylands of the island of 'Hoae', which were granted along with 'Davach Ereboll' and the lands of Hope, parish of Durness (*OPS*. II. pt. 2. 705; *RMS*. III. no. 2048). Subsequently, references to pennylands are mostly confined to estate papers of the seventeenth and eighteenth centuries, while davochs continue to be found in a variety of sources well into the nineteenth century.

Davochs and pennylands survived, not through the formal recitation of terms fossilized and long-forgotten, but because they still possessed meaning. They were used for assessments related to areas of known extent whose bounds included not only a range of land usages — arable, meadow, and pasture — but also the pattern of settlement (in particular, major settlements and their dependencies or 'pendicles').

Assessments effectively defined a territorial framework which could serve for many purposes, the most obvious of which was the ownership or conveyance of land. This is clearly demonstrated by an agreement of 1275 between Bishop Archibald and the Earl of Sutherland, which lists lands by their assessments in the parishes of Dornoch, Creich, and Rogart (*Bannatyne Misc.* III. 21–4). Land ownership, however, was burdened with various obligations and it is no surprise that assessments had important fiscal functions: the fourteenth century charter of the davoch of Pitmaduthy, parish of Logie Easter, for example, requiring the grantee to render 'forensic service to the King such as pertains to a davoch land' (*Munro Writs*, no. 2). Assessments feature also in the records of ecclesiastical administration, such as when the presbyteries of Tain and Dornoch met in 1649 to discuss the accommodation of Kincardine and Creich with 'ane trid stipend', and discovered that there were 'betwixt Achinduich and Pulrossie . . . nyne miles . . . sexteine davach lands having also 500 yat may be able to communicate' (McGill 1909–11. I. no. 67).

As might be expected, land assessments were used in the management of landed estates, both for general administration and the letting of land. In the absence of absolute measures, assessments gave an indication of arable capability which provided an idea of the comparative extent of farms and holdings. On a broad scale, for instance, there are abstract rentals of the earldom of Sutherland (1620s) mainly calculated in pennylands (NLS 175/85), and of the barony of Ferrintosh in the Black Isle drawn up under the heads of the 'daughs' of Mid Kinkell, Muckle Kinkell, Mulchaich, Dunvornie, and the half davoch of Alcaig (NLS 2971, f. 7–9). Yet individual holdings, essentially of arable but with proportional rights to pasture grounds, could also be reckoned in davochs and pennylands. This was so especially where shareholding tenure associated with the runrig system of intermixed arable strips was practised. Thus a rental of the Crown lands in Ross, as let in 1504, gives the tenants' possessions in quarters and bovates, being fractions of davochs (*ER.* XII. 660–65). And on the Sutherland estate in 1724 (NLS 313/2133), the farm of Mellaig, parish of Golspie, extending to 6 pennylands, was possessed by:

James Sutherland	with	2¼ pennylands
Donald Sutherland	with	1¼ pennylands
Hugh Macpherson	with	1¾ pennylands
Hector Munro	with	¾ pennylands

Rents and services were further dues that could be calculated on the basis of assessments. In 1637 the Balnagown baron court ordered 'the oxgang sett lands in Invercharron cutt and cary to ye toune as support to the laird twelff cupil' of timber (McGill 1909–11. II. nos. 1073, 1074). And during the eighteenth century it was still the custom on the Skelbo estate for each pennyland, no matter how possessed, to pay 10s. for peats and 3s. for conversion of other services. Additionally, until 1775, 'each Penny Land is bound to shear an Acre of Corn', which in practice meant providing seven hands for the laird's harvest (SRO CS 235/G/30/1).

Other Land Assessments

There were other, later types of land assessment, however, apart from davochs and pennylands. A number of valuations for the purposes of apportioning national taxation were made in pounds, shillings, and pence; also in merks, equivalent to 13s. 4d. These gave rise to poundlands, merklands, shillinglands and pennylands. These pennylands are quite different from the pennylands already mentioned; fortunately they are very rare.

The earliest such valuation, the *Old Extent*, an assessment restricted to lands holding directly of the Crown, is usually dated to the reign of Alexander III (1249–86). Thereafter, tax burdens were revised, ostensibly on account of the effects of war and devastation, and a major revaluation associated with the payment of David II's ransom was made in 1366. It revealed a fall in land values, which has been attributed both to wholesale deflation and, more plausibly, to a decline in population. The establishment of an entirely new assessment, which became known as the *New Extent*, is thought to date from 1474. The *Old Extent*, however, continued to be used as a basis for taxation up to 1667; and until 1832 one qualification for the vote was the possession of freehold land to the value of forty shillings old extent. These extents were based on the same land units as the davoch and pennyland assessments, and there are references to lands which combine different assessments such as the 4 merkland half davoch of Garve in Kintail (1509) (*RMS*. II. no. 3313). Church lands, on the other hand, were assessed according to valuations carried out by ecclesiastical authority, the most important being that known as *Bagimond's Roll* (1275) which, with modifications, continued to be the basis for the taxation of ecclesiastical revenues until the Reformation.

Another method, common in some east coast areas, was to reckon land according to the amount of grain required for sowing, thus 'a piece of land extending to 8 bolls' sowing of bere or thereby . . . lying in the south or west part of the town of Tayne' (1571) (McGill 1909–11. I. no. 406). Bolls' sowing was the usual measure, but smaller units, firlots and pecks, were used where necessary. The grain was always bere, rather than oats; the sowing of a boll of bere being 'something more than a Scotsh acre' (Creich 1791: *OSA*). Land could also be reckoned by its rental value, however, especially in eastern districts, where a high proportion of rent was paid in victual rather than in money. A portion of the Mains of Braelangwell, parish of Resolis, was described as 'yt part Lying betuixt yet two Burns called Aldacharmich [Ballycherry?] and Duach [Allt Dubhach] which extends to ye yearly pay of Four Chalders farm victuall' (1728) (SRO RS 38/8, f. 379). Elsewhere, a land conveyance from the parish of Dornoch included an old pennyland assessment, a tenant's name, and the rental value — 'that pennyland of the Lands of Breamorton then possest by Marion Baxter Extending to Six Bolls of Rent yearly of Bear' (1728) (SRO RS 38/8, f. 368).

Such rentals are not necessarily the current value of the land. The valuations give no indication of other forms of rent payment and moreover the bolls' pay may represent a level of accounting which had been in use for a considerable period and achieved an almost customary status.

The measurement of land by area was mainly restricted to burghal properties, both plots and holdings of burgh lands. In some instances only the length was specified, in others both length and breadth. Thus a piece of ground in Fortrose was described as extending to '13 Scots ells from north to south and 5 ells from west to east' (1728) (SRO RS 38/8, f. 377). From there it was only a short step to measurement by the Scots acre, equivalent to 1.26 Statute acres, and consisting of 4 roods, each rood being of 40 falls, and a fall containing 36 square ells. A grant of lands in the territory of Dingwall included a rood of land in Thombane and an acre in the field of Acris-Scotte (1526) (*RMS*. III. no. 38), while the countess of Seaforth's lands in Fortrose, 'bewest the Cross', extended to 4 roods, 'twixt Lands & Tenements' (1686) (SRO B 28/7/2, p. 109a). On occasion the acre was used as a loose term for a piece of land, in other words a superficial measure which in such instances should be regarded in the same light as riggs and butts — butts being truncated riggs. As ever, different measures may be found in combination, so that a possession in and about the burgh of Cromarty included 'Thre acres of land in the field called the Goosedeals ... Five bols pay in the Shortbutts and pepperdeals ... and The easter one half of the Ormandsheirs' (1710) (SRO RS 38/7, f. 384).

The demise of the davoch, the pennyland and other assessments, was linked to the agrarian changes which, though begun in the seventeenth century, were to culminate in the era of 'improvement'. These changes included reorganization of holdings, developments in land tenure, and the rise of the land surveyor.

DAVOCHS AND PENNYLANDS: DISTRIBUTION AND ORIGINS

The distribution of davochs has been mapped for the northern mainland [Fig. 10.1]. It is simply a map of all the references to davochs, and takes no account of the value of individual assessments. Although the evidence for some areas is very patchy, and the distribution therefore far from complete, it is reasonable to conclude that davochs extended over the whole of Ross and Cromarty, Sutherland and probably Caithness. The complementary distribution of pennylands [Fig. 10.2, for which the same considerations apply] consists of three main areas: Caithness and eastern Sutherland, where there is an almost complete cover, with the odd gap such as Freswick; north Sutherland, where there is extensive evidence for the existence of pennylands, but as the documentary sources are less satisfactory, it is difficult to discuss the pattern in detail; and lastly the west and central parts of Sutherland where there appears to be a genuine absence of pennylands. The overall distribution of pennylands is in accord with the mainland Scottish possessions of the earls of Orkney. It covers the ancient Pictish province of Cat, which included both Sutherland and Caithness. Norse settlement and political control extended south into Easter Ross and though the Norse frontier in this region was essentially a fluctuating one, the pennylands do suggest that the Dornoch Firth and the River Oykel may have been a boundary of more then temporary significance (see Crawford, in this volume).

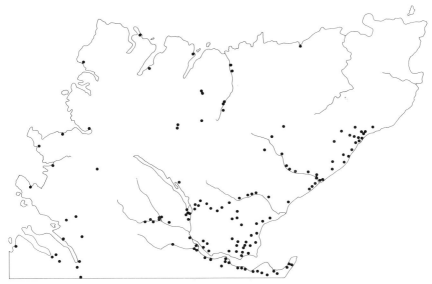

Fig. 10.1   Distribution of davochs: north mainland.

The pennylands of Sutherland and Caithness were not only based on the same land units as the davoch, but there is an exact relationship between the two assessments: a davoch being equivalent to 6 pennylands. There is direct evidence for this in a reference of 1575 to the davochs of 6 pennylands of Swordal, Migdale, Little Creich and Cuthil, in the parishes of Creich and Dornoch (*RMS.* v. no. 112). Furthermore there are numerous instances of other, independent evidence relating to the same lands. Lairg, for instance, was assessed at 18 pennylands (1623) (NLS 175/85), Wester and Easter Lairg each containing 9 pennylands. But Lairg was also known as the 3 davoch lands of Lairg (1611) (NLS 313/477, p. 284), 'Westir Larg' and 'Largester' each being 1½ davoch lands (1510) (*ER*. xiii. p. 264). The two assessments were interchangeable, therefore, and are found in use side by side, though there was a tendency for them to be used separately in differing circumstances. So the Barony of Gruids, parish of Lairg, was known as 'the six daaches of Gruid' (1682), but the tenants' possessions were calculated in pennylands (NLS 175/85).

The pennyland system had no inherent advantages for the designation of small tenants' possessions, however, for the davoch could also be split up into small subdivisions. In the northern mainland, the davoch was composed of half davochs and quarters or quarterlands, in turn containing two oxgangs or oxganglands, also referred to as oxgates or bovates, which were further divided into four pecks. A davoch thus contained thirty-two pecks. In Culkenzie and Guillies, parish of Rosskeen, however, the peck was replaced by the sheaf, 'Compting twelve sheaves . . . in a quarter of the Davoch' (1721) (SRO RS 38/8, f. 62).

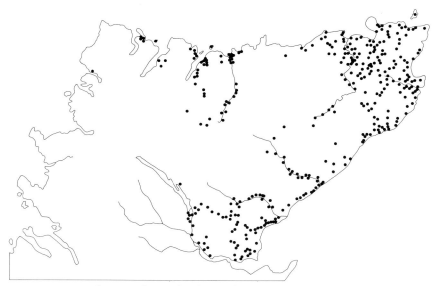

Fig. 10.2   Distribution of pennylands: north mainland.

Pennylands, by contrast, were subdivided into halfpennylands, farthinglands or fourths, and octos or eighths. Other, more awkward fractions, are to be found in sources such as estate rentals, but there were no two-pennyland units similar to the 'great' or 'double' pennylands of the Western Isles; nor has any evidence been found for the use of Gaelic terminology.

The term davoch is derived from *dabhach*, an Old Irish word meaning a large tub or vat. As a land assessment it was a measure of arable land, an application which may have originated in its use as a measure of tribute corn, or less probably of seed corn. The emphasis on arable land is confirmed by the overall distribution of davochs in the northern Highlands, with the contrast between the low assessments of the west and central areas where the cultivable ground is both poor and limited in extent, and the much higher assessments of the more fertile eastern straths and coastal areas.

Davochs and pennylands were measures of the productive capacity of the land so that there can be no basis for assuming precise and standard sizes. At the same time, it is reasonable to expect a range of acreages around which these assessments might vary. There are suggestions from a number of areas for a pennyland of 8 Scots acres, although there is also evidence for pennylands of around 12 acres, or ranging from 12 to 18 acres. Pennylands of 8 or 12 acres, therefore, would give davochs of from 48 to 72 acres. The oxgang, however, of which there were 8 in a davoch, is generally assumed to be 13 acres, which would produce a davoch of 104 acres, equivalent to a lowland carucate or ploughgate. Some davochs,

158

though, appear to have been considerably larger than this, and should be seen perhaps in the light of evidence from north-east Scotland, where land coloniz-ation in the late medieval period doubled their size (see e.g. the *Scottish National Dictionary* for different sizes and sub-divisions of davochs: Ed.).

Questions of size lead to problems of origins, and it is here that one is on very difficult ground. The pennyland, from its areas of occurrence in the Northern Isles, northern mainland, Hebrides and western mainland and south-west Scotland, is generally assumed to be a fiscal assessment of Norse origin. The davoch, on the other hand, has been given a Pictish association, which would make it the earlier assessment, and the basis for the pennyland assessment. In areas such as much of Caithness, however, davochs have been completely replaced by Norse pennylands.

No ouncelands (ON. *eyrisland*, the assessment associated with the Norse naval defence system) have been found for Sutherland, but the few from Caithness appear to be the same as the Orkney ouncelands of 18 penny-lands. On the strength of this, and given that 1 davoch equals 6 pennylands in the north mainland, it must be asked whether the Orkney ouncelands are not in fact equivalent to 3 davochs, rather than to single davochs, as is usually stated.

The 20 pennyland ouncelands of the Western Isles are a further compli-cation, apparently equivalent to davochs, but owing their structure, it has been argued, if not their origin, to the Dalriadan 20 house unit. Full elucidation of these early land assessments is still a long way off.

LAND ASSESSMENTS AND SETTLEMENT HISTORY

Reconstructing the pattern of assessments

The study of land assessments and settlement history must begin with a consideration of the problems involved in reconstructing the original pattern of assessments. Some assessments are clearly missing; they have not found their way into the documentary record and are now lost. Errors have also crept into the record, which once acquired have tended to remain; and many references to assessments are difficult to interpret. Early charters, for instance, frequently relate to quite extensive areas, com-prising what must have been a number of different land units. The converse, where land had been divided up, perhaps through inheritance, can also be a problem, for the assessments have to be reconstituted. Some settlements have disappeared entirely: land has been eroded by the sea, inundated by blowing sands, devastated by spating rivers, or left un-cultivated. On the other hand there has been a considerable amount of colonisation, by the breaking in of new land. But in none of these cases have assessments been materially affected. Expansion of the arable area was not marked by higher assessments; rather was such land incorporated into existing assessments so that in the long term the acreages corre-sponding to particular assessments tended to rise. There is though, no evidence to support the idea that the infield/outfield system originally corresponded to assessed/non-assessed land. Where infield/outfield existed in the northern Highlands, and that was only in the more fertile 'lowland' areas, the outfield was considered a part of the assessed land.

There were, however, areas which, while they cannot strictly be considered as non-assessed land, were often treated apart from the assessed land. 'Crofts', as small discrete patches of land held individually, being often associated with mills, alehouses or specialist craftsmen were sometimes excluded as they did not form part of the common arable. Lothbeg, for instance, consisted of 'Fifteen penny land, a miln and two crofts' (NLS 213/2113). Of course crofts did not necessarily have a permanent identity; in time they might become part of the general arable, and perhaps be commemorated in a field-name. 'Wards' and 'loans' were also sometimes considered as non-assessed land. In the 'Bischopis-warde' in Dornoch (1627) (*RMS*. VIII. no. 1045), the term ward probably referred to a piece of enclosed ground; more frequently it was interchangeable with loan, in the sense that both referred to land which, while maybe enclosed, was essentially 'improved', either for pasture or for cultivation. Loans were generally on the wetter ground, a meaning derived from the Gaelic *lòn*, a marsh or bog. Wards and loans are mostly confined to the historical record, as for instance the 'Lands of Craggan & Inver ... with the new ward of the samen', parish of Alness (1728) (SRO RS 38/8, f. 388), but some have survived as place-names. The Loans of Rarichie, parish of Nigg, and the Loans of Tullich, parish of Fearn, are both on low-lying ground which has been well-drained. Occasionally such reclamation is well-documented, as for the 'loan called Loanmore' of Ospisdale, parish of Creich. Between 1755 and 1775, Robert Gray of Airdens reduced some 25 acres of what had been 'an useless spot partly a Bog or Ougmire and partly a useless Moss and partly covered with bushes' to arable and grass grounds for hay and pasture, in what must have been a 'very expensive and laborious work twixt rooting of wood, ditching & sunk drains' (SRO CS 235/G/30/1).

A very important point is that the relationship between assessments and their actual layout on the ground was not always straightforward. Where land was held in consolidated units assessments generally refer to compact blocks of land; but under runrig or shareholding an assessment might well be made up of intermixed strips, whether held by a landlord (proprietary runrig) or, more commonly, by a multiple tenant (tenant runrig). An example of proprietary runrig is provided by a disposition by Alexander Ross of Pitkerrie (1712) of the 'Just and equall half of the toune and lands of Leachclovag Salachie and Clashnamuck & Kinletter', comprising the davoch of Gledfield, parish of Kincardine, possessed by him and his 'tenants and Servants in Comune with William Ross of Aldie heritable proprietor of the other half' (SRO GD 274/7/7/22).

Land Units and Settlement History

With these considerations in mind, it is now possible to proceed to an examination of the internal structure of land assessments.

Some subdivisions are referred to without any indication of their status, so much so that they appear to be the whole land unit rather than merely a subdivision. Frequently, however, subdivisions are identified by designations, as for instance the 'laich' and the 'over' or 'upper' quarters of Rogie, parish of Fodderty (1695) (SRO RS 38/6, f. 43), or the 'easter' and 'wester' quarters of the half davoch of Pelaig, parish of Kiltearn (1719) (SRO RS 38/8, f. 2). It is also common for quarters and like subdivisions to have actual names: Nigg contained a quarter called Culnald and an oxgate called 'The Torran', otherwise to be referred to by the names of their present possessor or past occupier (SRO RS 38/8, f. 333); the davoch of 'Mid Cunlich', parish of Rosskeen, included 'three half oxgang lands called Clanhendricks Lands' (1684) (SRO RS 38/6, f. 105).

There is considerable evidence to suggest a distinction between the 'highland' areas, where arable tended to be limited to small isolated patches and assessments frequently comprised a number of quite separate parts, and the more fertile areas where large blocks of arable land gave rise to more compact assessments. All assessments, however, appear to have possessed some form of internal structure, sometimes quite complex. 'Lowland' assessments comprised several separate though perhaps contiguous units; it is merely that in the 'highland' areas, especially where landholdings were smaller, such structure is more evident. Knockarthur, parish of Rogart, was described in 1787 as 'twelve pennys land which go under the several separate names and possessions of' Achork 1 pennyland, Tanachy 1, Rhilochan 1, Dalreoch 1, Shunvail 2, Inchomry 3, Achuvoan ½, Achogeil ½, and Breakacky 2 — an example of a 12 pennyland, or 2 davoch, land unit subdivided into four 3-pennylands, or half davochs (NLS 313/81, *Decreet of Sale ... Skelbo ... 1787*). A more 'lowland' example is provided by Meikle Clyne which in 1712 comprehended 2 quarterlands called 'Calleachdu' and 'Rinmore', 3 oxgangs *tuo viis* otherwise called 'Lie Droman', 'Laite and Belnagvie', the 2 half oxgangs of 'Paapanoch and Badenags' and the pendicle of 'Leadnacarn' (SRO RS 38/8, f. 109).

Where it is possible to discover the full internal structure of assessments, it is clear that they are closely adjusted to the physical capability of the ground and the pattern of landholding. Yet the relationship between land assessments and actual settlement is not so straightforward, and just how complicated is well demonstrated by estate plans which survive from the pre-improvement era. Most importantly, the settlement pattern derives from the structure of landholdings. At the extremes, there is a great contrast between the large farm, held by an individual and comprising farmhouse and perhaps labourers' cottages, set against the multitude of small tenants who might live in several townships with associated cottar settlements.

A further consideration is that the limits to settlement have not remained constant. It is probable that there was a significant amount of colonization during the medieval period, but evidence from elsewhere suggests that rather than a continuous upward trend, there have been marked phases of colonization. Indeed the margins of settlement may have fluctuated. Even in the late eighteenth century the taking-in of new land could be a risk, as witness the fate of some fields on the farm of Morvich in Strathfleet, 'Formerly improved now waste' (NLS 313/3616). The fact that land does not appear to have been reassessed in response to colonization, means that assessments can account for neither the enlargement of existing settlements nor for when part of the assessed land of one settlement becomes the focus of a new settlement. Moreover, settlements frequently 'split' into two, or sometimes three or more subdivisions, reflecting the need for smaller, more manageable runrig units. One cannot ignore, therefore, the variability and dynamism of past settlement. Individual settlements might expand, divide, contract, disappear or even shift about. Land assessments can only give a broad impression of actual settlement.

The internal structure of assessments nonetheless supports the view that settlement was much more extensive than the charter evidence, for instance, suggests. The names which occur in many charters are not, as the assessments remind us, those of settlements, but rather of land units which include both major and minor settlements. The latter, being dependent or satellite settlements, often referred to as 'pendicles', only attained independent status at a comparatively late date. As for Domesday England, the fact that such settlements do not feature in the documentary record is not evidence for their non-existence at such an early period, but rather that they were 'hidden' within larger land units. This is confirmed by those assessments, mainly from the more upland areas, which are not named after any settlement, being instead the names of land units or territories containing a number of settlements. Just how early such settlements are is a different question, to be explored jointly with archaeology. It may be concluded, however, that the evidence of land assessments points to a well-developed and extensive settlement pattern in the northern Highlands, certainly by the early medieval period, if not considerably earlier.

Broadscale fluctuations in the margins of settlement appear, then, to have taken place within the framework provided by the pre-existing pattern of land units, as identified by the land assessments. More profound changes in the settlement pattern on the other hand, came with the integration of the northern Highlands into the national economy between the seventeenth and nineteenth centuries. The introduction of commercial agriculture brought a certain amount of settlement contraction. But while sheep farming was associated with the clearance of whole areas, the creation of large arable farms, as in Easter Ross and on the eastern coast of Sutherland, was accompanied by a much greater degree of settlement continuity. For, although many of the smaller settlements disappeared, the new farmsteads tended to be situated on the older and more favoured sites. At the same time, the availability both of non-agricultural sources of income and of areas for colonization such as the Dornoch Moors and on the Black Isle, encouraged landlords to retain their small tenant population on the more marginal land (see Houston, in this volume).

Territorial Organization

A particularly interesting aspect to emerge from the study of land assessments is the evidence for early territorial organization — in essence the defining of large land units by the grouping together of a number of assessments, perhaps two to six or more davochs or an equivalent number of pennylands. So there are the four davochs of Rarichies, parish of Nigg (1333) (SRO GD 297/165), or the six davochs of Rovie in Strathfleet (1364) (*RRS*, vi, no. 320). There is no apparent regularity in the size of such units, but there is no doubting their cohesion, evidenced not only by the ties between central settlements and their dependencies, but also by the links between settlements and grazings. Strathoykel, with its pattern of major settlements in the lower strath and smaller dependent settlements and grazings in the upper reaches, identifiable in the sixteenth and seventeenth centuries, is particularly illuminating. These territories were not only the basis for settlement organization, of course; they were also the units of lordship, from which the inhabitants rendered rents and services to the landlord at his castle or hall.

Discounting a certain amount of fragmentation and re-arrangement, there is no doubt that such territories are quite ancient. Indeed the pattern of land units (although not necessarily of land ownership) may well show a much greater degree of continuity than actual settlement, many of the earlier parishes appearing to have been based on the pre-existing territorial organization. But just how ancient this organization is in the northern Highlands is highly speculative. The appearance of defensive structures during the first millennium BC, suggesting a markedly stratified society with a largely service population, may not be irrelevant!

A Case Study: Golspie

The pennyland assessment for the parish of Golspie, in Sutherland [Fig. 10.3] has been derived from estate rentals, particularly that of 1623 (NLS 175/85); with the possible exception of Little Ferry it gives a complete cover. The very regular pattern of pennylands is clearly demonstrated, with such references to 'a davach of Bakys' (1471) (*OPS*. II pt. 2. p. 673) and the two davochs of 'Cragtoun' (1509) (*ER*. XIII. p. 264) providing an exact match with the davoch assessment.

The map gives a good picture of the layout of the various lands. Hints as to the existence of larger units are provided by Culmaily and by Golspie itself, both interestingly associated with the name of the parish, known formerly as Culmaily. The lands of Culmaily, while 'extending to thrie davach of land' (1577) (NLS 313/213/166), are known to have included the six pennylands of 'Sallach' or 'Sallichtown', possibly Rhiorn, as well as the nine pennylands of Culmaily itself. Golspie comprised the Tower, Golspie Mor, Kirkton, and possibly other lands (NLS 313/2101, 2111, *Plans of Golspie*). The three pennylands of Golspie Kirkton (Clynekirkton was also three pennylands) were probably a late subdivision in much the

Fig. 10.3 Land assessments from estate rentals, parish of Golspie. Unit size is given in pennylands.

same way that, of the twelve pennylands of Kildonan, 'thair are thrie pennie land assignit to the minister for his gleib' (NLS 313/85).

A number of other important settlement features occur. Inverboll, referred to as 'Innerbo Heiche and Laiche' in 1563, indicating a split settlement, is found later as a single township (*RSS*. v. no. 1463). There is also the usual development of small crofts, which were considered as non-assessed land; the inevitable alehouse crofts, but appropriately a gun-smith's croft near to Dunrobin (NLS 313/2101). Farlary, a pendicle of Uppat, was a small settlement which only achieved a separate tenurial existence at a quite late date, but was probably first colonized at a much earlier period (NLS 313/225/242; 313/2101). By contrast, a number of settlements disappeared in the expansion of the Dunrobin policies. In 1735 a part of Orletown, or Allertown, was 'inclosed in the park under my Lords cows', and another part was 'now laboured by my Lord being enclosed in the new parks' (NLS 313/2133). By 1750 Orletown was effectively within the Mains and by the end of the century Mellaig, Clayside, and Inverboll had all been absorbed. Finally there are the changes associated with the major period of estate improvement which were to make an even stronger break with the pattern of land units associated with the early assessments; the small tenant settlement behind Backies, the establishment of Golspie village, and the creation of the large arable farms at Rhives, Drummuie, Culmaily, and Kirkton (NLS 313/2111, 2133; Adam 1972).

A Case Study: Meikle Allan

The davoch of Meikle Allan, parish of Fearn, was broadly coincident with the present-day farms of Allan and Clays of Allan: all that has taken place is some straightening of marches in the eighteenth and nineteenth centuries (SRO RHP 219, 239, 20000/247). In the more distant past, however, Meikle Allan and Little Allan formed a single unit of the two davochs of Allan (*OPS.* II pt. 2. 445–46; *RMS.* XI. no. 97). Meikle Allan comprised the west quarter of Wester Allan or Balinroich and the eastern three-quarters of Knocks or the Hill quarter (*Kerrownaknock*); also the south or Summerwell quarter (*Kerrow-tobber-hawrie*) and the Clay quarter (GD 71/79, 80, 95, 100(1), 101, 132, 143(6), 267; GD 128/16/5/7). The disposition of the quarters is in part a reflection of the local topography. The Hill quarter is presumably named after the rising ground on which Allan is situated, the Summerwell appears to be a well to the east, while the Clay quarter occupied the lower ground. However, the particular landholding history of Allan is also an essential factor, for while Balinroich does lie on the west of Allan, it was also for some considerable period of time under separate ownership and a settlement in its own right (SRO RHP 239; Watson 1924. 43). It may be noted in passing just how many *baile-* names, being actual settlements and the subdivisions of land units, had quite small assessments.

A mid-eighteenth century survey of Allan indicates the manner in which the arable fields were allocated between the various quarters (SRO GD 71/82). Not surprisingly Balinroich formed a single unit; but the Hill and Summerwell quarters, while generally comprising fields of their own, also shared a number of fields in runrig. At the same time the Clay quarter was divided into two halves, the oxgate of the Clay (or half Clay) and Feagolich (SRO GD 71/76, 95, 119, 182). These two halves also shared a few fields between them. Thus although the 'easter three oxgangs' (1623) (SRO GD 71/34) or the 'just and equal half, of the three easter quarters' (1737) (SRO GD 71/156) may well have comprised three compact blocks of arable, there may have been an element of runrig in their disposition.

The quarters did not necessarily include, however, all the arable land of Meikle Allan, as a reference to the 'quarter of Knocks and Tailyore Croft' confirms (1671) (SRO GD 71/75). The croft was probably at one time an individual holding, but by the mid-eighteenth century it had become a part of the general arable. More important were the areas on the lower ground, prone to wetness and known as the wards or loans; they were evidently considered to be distinct appendages. Thus 'the Clay quarter with the wards of the same' (1692) (SRO GD 71/101).

The field-names that have survived present a fascinating mixture of Gaelic and Scots: 'Knockmeidan', 'Bardinordish', 'Achnacoill'; 'The Hen Croft', 'Thistle Field', 'The Clay Riggs'. Sometimes both forms are given, as 'Crooked Riggs or Cromghales'. Some are plain descriptions of natural features; others incorporating terms such as 'rigg', 'field' or 'croft' — the latter frequently associated with a former possessor, for instance 'Andrew Roys Croft' (SRO GD 71/182).

Of the actual settlements, Allan, Balinroich and Feagolich occupied the higher ground formed by a tongue of glacial drift. The lower ground was probably settled later; indeed some of it at a comparatively late date. Much is underlain by raised beach deposits whose present productivity is largely the result of artificial drainage, a process which had begun by the mid-eighteenth century with the cutting of the new canal and a number of major drains. The other settlements (1756) appear more as individual houses, reflecting what was probably piecemeal colonization; later (1786) they were grouped together under place-names such as Groam, Bardcroich and Bard Fearn. These names, which were clearly former field-names, eventually disappeared with farm amalgamation (SRO GD 71/217; RHP 239).

Acknowledgement

I would like to thank John Baldwin who has done much to improve this paper, Alan Small (Dundee) for his comments on a first draft, and Barbara Crawford (St Andrews) and Ian Fraser (Edinburgh) for further advice and encouragement; Nancy Ferrier for typing; Carolyn Bain for cartography. I take full responsibility for the final version.

References

Manuscript:

Scottish Record Office (SRO)
    B28
    CS 235
    GD 71
    GD 128
    GD 274
    GD 297
    RHP 219
    RHP 239
    RHP 20000
    RS 38

National Library of Scotland (NLS)
    Dep. 175
    Dep. 313
    MS. 2971

Printed:

Adam, R. J. ed. *Papers on Sutherland Estate Management 1802–1816.* 2 vols. 1972.
Bannatyne Misc. The Bannatyne Miscellany. 1827–55.
ER. The Exchequer Rolls of Scotland. 1878–1908.
Fraser, W. *The Sutherland Book.* 3 vols. 1892.
McGill, W. *Old Ross-shire and Scotland.* 2 vols. 1909–11.
Moray Reg. Registrum Episcopatus Moraviensis. 1837.
Munro Writs. Calendar of Writs of Munro of Foulis 1299–1823. 1940.
OPS. Origines Parochiales Scotiae. 1851–55.
OSA. The Old Statistical Account.
RMS. Registrum Magni Sigilii Regum Scotorum. 1882–1914.
RRS. Regesta Regum Scottorum. 1960–.
RSS. Registrum Secreti Sigilli Regum Scotorum. 1908–.
Watson, W. J. *Place Name of Ross and Cromarty.* 1924.

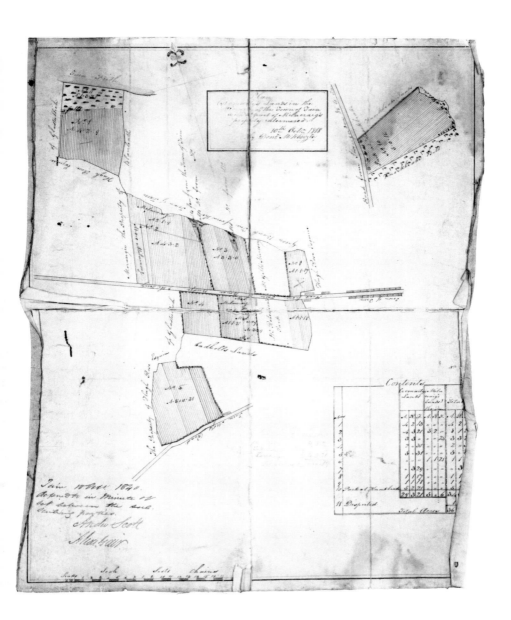

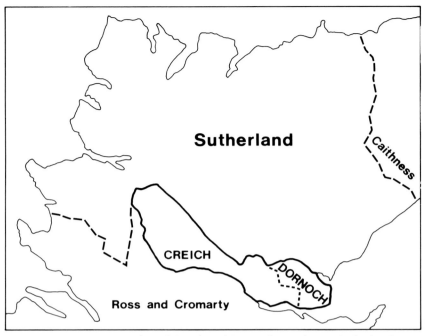

Fig. 11.1   Location: parishes of Creich and Dornoch, south-east Sutherland.

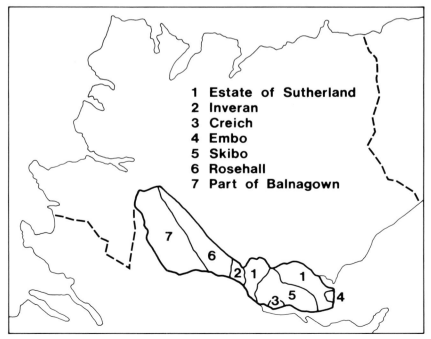

1 Estate of Sutherland
2 Inveran
3 Creich
4 Embo
5 Skibo
6 Rosehall
7 Part of Balnagown

Fig. 11.2   Estates in the parishes of Creich and Dornoch.

THE CLEARANCES IN
SOUTH-EAST SUTHERLAND

Rod Houston

For the purposes of this paper, south-east Sutherland consists of the civil parishes of Creich and Dornoch [Fig. 11.1]; the events are those spanning roughly one hundred years from about the middle of the eighteenth century to about the middle of the nineteenth century.

What, however, of the term 'Clearances'? This is a term which tends to cover two distinct, though not necessarily unrelated processes: the removal of people from traditionally occupied townships as a result of the change of leasehold of an area, and the trend in the Scottish Highlands at that time towards migration out of the area to destinations either within Great Britain or abroad. For such a dual definition to be valid there would have to be a clear and universal causal link between removal and out-migration, a link whose provenance, however, is varied and nebulous. By way of definition, Adams (1976. 188) deems the 'Clearances' as: 'The general term given to the destruction of townships and eviction of people to make room for sheep which occurred in the Scottish Highlands in the 19th Century.' Though certainly precise, specific use of the word 'sheep' may be problematic, as also the restriction to the nineteenth century.

Within these defined parameters, there are two possible approaches to setting an overall context for events in south-east Sutherland. First, there is the thread of widespread agrarian change, commented on by Richards (1982. 18, 25) when writing that 'The Scottish Highlands was part of the net of time and circumstance which extended across Europe ... The Highland Clearances were a substantial regional variant of the enclosure movement and the associated changes in British Agriculture'. The crux of this line of argument is that agrarian reform constituted a continental movement and that the Scottish Highlands were simply due their turn in the process of time. The problem lies in the presupposition of an inevitable diffusionary process of agricultural reform, for that in turn begs the question which forms the second thread of approach, that of historical timing. A general survey of Britain during the period centred on 1800 suggests the pertinence of the chronological coincidence of events in the Highlands with the broader sweep of the Industrial Revolution, particularly given Smout's assertion (1970. 247) that the Industrial Revolution should be 'compared with the Reformation as an event that stopped and turned the current of man's ... life'. Such profound change can but entail the Highlands as part, even though they form a peripheral part of the country.

Finally by way of introduction, it can be argued that one fundamental aspect of change associated with the Industrial Revolution was the adoption of a 'new' mode of economic thinking. This might be summarized by stating that man's attitude to the 'Factors of Production', land, labour and capital, changed with the onset and development of the Industrial Revolution. How, then, does all this apply to Sutherland?

LAND: COMMON INHERITANCE OR ECONOMIC ASSET

Writing of rent, Adam Smith in *The Wealth of Nations* (1974. 247) deemed it 'the price paid for the use of land ... the highest the tenant can afford to pay in the actual circumstances of the land'. This seems particularly appropriate to Sutherland where the basic unit of land holding was the estate [Fig. 11.2], and the prime form of estate revenue was rent. The simple fact that land was now being considered as an economic asset in terms of monetary rent was evidence itself of change.

Hobsbawm (1973. 184) viewed this change in attitude as an important aspect of post-Culloden Highland life, the discouragement of clan life giving rise to the possibility of viewing land in this way rather than as an item of assumed common inheritance held by the clan chief. Hobsbawm's analysis carried two further key points. First, for change to occur the mass of population had to become mobile wage earners, another direct effect of post-Culloden attitudes as traditional rights to land in return for goods and services declined. Second, change only occurred after the ownership of land was transferred to the hands of people who were prepared to enact such change. This was largely effected through the appointment of estate managers. In the case of the Estate of Sutherland, managers such as William Young, Patrick Sellar and James Loch were well-versed in the art of advocating radical reorganization of estates, as a result of successful enterprises elsewhere.

A combination, therefore, of the attitudes of *The Wealth of Nations* and of the desire for enclosure came to bear on Sutherland as the late eighteenth century gave way to the dawn of the nineteenth, with the net result that plans for the 'improvement' of estates proliferated. Dempster, for example, attempted to introduce change on the Estate of Skibo in the 1790s with the opening of a textile mill at Spinningdale. Its destruction by fire in 1806 meant an end to its short life and the ruinous remains are still to be seen (Sinclair 1795. 131). What the ill-fated Spinningdale venture did evidence nonetheless was the advent of change on a radical scale in Sutherland, where locally-based factory employment had previously been unheard of.

Not that factory employment became the principal manifestation of change. This was to be found, rather, on the land: a massive reorganization in the overall distribution of settlement with the onset of large-scale farm leasing; and a notable change in the more particular laying out of settlements after enclosure.

OVERALL DISTRIBUTION OF SETTLEMENT

Figures 11.3 and 11.4 illustrate the distribution of settlement before and after the main era of reorganization in south-east Sutherland, in 1755 and 1841 respectively. Each map draws on a source which attempted to provide a comprehensive survey of the area. Major General William Roy had been commissioned to produce a military survey of the Highlands. His several years' labour ended in 1755 and his map sheets provide a source of information on the distribution of settlement. The 1841 Census, by contrast, is the first for which Enumeration Rolls survive, thus providing a later source. More detailed discussion on the nature of each as a source is available elsewhere (Houston 1980. 78–82).

In 1755 [Fig. 11.3], settlement in the western part of the area was distributed into three broad groups. The Estate of Skibo housed a distinct number of townships along the shores of the Kyle of Sutherland and up the valley of the River Shin, along with a few around Migdale and a further few in the upper parts of the valley of the River Evelix to the north. Strath Oykell, the march between Sutherland and Ross and Cromarty, was part of Balnagown Estate and its northern bank was occupied by a string of settlements well up into the heights of the strath. The northern boundary of Balnagown Estate, the River Cassely, separated it from the Estate of Rosehall, and on either side of the river a line of settlements marks out this particular strath. The eastern part of the area is dominated by the Royal Burgh of Dornoch. Some townships existed along the links to the north of the Burgh, while settlements were also located on Skelbo Estate along the southern shore of Loch Fleet. Strath Carnach, running west from the head of Loch Fleet, also housed its group of townships. The general pattern suggested by the map is that in 1755 there was comprehensive occupation of the available low-lying ground by a substantial number of townships.

By 1841, however [Fig. 11.4], the pattern shows substantial change. The whole of the western sector of the area was devoid of settlement, whilst a substantial concentration had developed both around Bonar Bridge, by then a major village at the head of the Kyle of Sutherland, and inland around Migdale. Lower Strath Oykell continued to house settlements, albeit more densely crowded than had been the case in 1755, and the legacy of the Spinningdale mill is apparent from the larger township to be found there in 1841. Further east, there was a marked clustering of townships in the Skibo area, centred on Clashmore and reflecting its role as a reception area for displaced tenants. This, indeed, is the case for much of the parish of Dornoch, and by 1841 there had been a substantial thickening of settlement on the moors of Achvandra, Balvraid, Rearquhar and Birichen.

The means by which these changes occurred have become the focus of much controversial debate. In terms of the management of an estate, plans for its reorganization would be drawn up. The subsequent adoption of such a plan was probably followed by a series of leasehold arrangements aimed at creating a given area over which there was simultaneous renewal

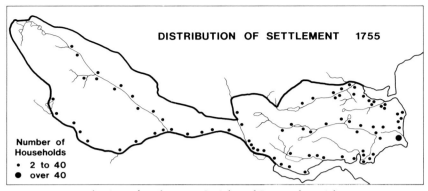

Fig. 11.3   Distribution of settlement, Creich and Dornoch parishes, 1755.

of leases. The potential leasehold of the given area was then advertised and granted to the highest bidder, and in this manner, land became the marketable commodity alluded to by Adam Smith.

In south-east Sutherland the resultant sequence of events can be plotted to some degree, although the evidence is patchy and insufficient to account fully for the marked differences in settlement pattern between 1755 and 1841. What has survived shows that the first set of removals occurred in 1790 when Balnagown Estate was converted to a series of sheep farms (Richards 1982. 287), whilst Sage's references to removals in Strath Oykell in 1800 (1899. 185n), may relate to the same event or to subsequent activities in the area. Napier evidence (para 40077) carries reports of the removal of 194 families on Skibo Estate, and although dating that reorganization is problematic it may account for the thickening of settlement in the east of the estate, where the area around Clashmore received displaced tenants and the village of that name was established [Fig. 11.5]. In addition, several families were removed from Balchraggan, Reenare and

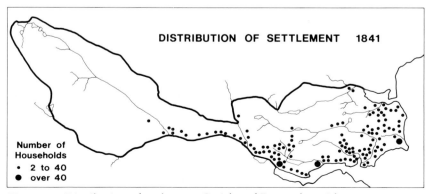

Fig. 11.4   Distribution of settlement, Creich and Dornoch parishes, 1841.

Acharrie in about 1833, while seven families were evicted from Coiloag to make way for a deer forest (Napier: para 39998). In the east, Strath Carnach was cleared in 1813 on the establishment of Torboll Sheep Farm (Adam 1972. I. lii–liii), and some thirteen years later the lots of Torboll saw four tenants have their holdings subdivided into seven (Napier: para 39636). Adam also refers to the creation of a number of arable farms in the Parish of Dornoch in 1809–10, and this must have created displaced tenants. Explanation of the patchwork of townships to the north and west of Dornoch however, as we have seen, also lies in that area's primary role as a reception area for tenants from other parts of the Estate of Sutherland, especially the parishes of Lairg, Rogart and Golspie.

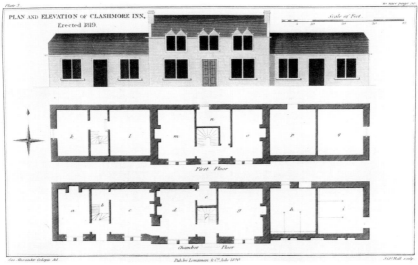

Fig. 11.5   Clashmore Inn, 1819. Clashmore was established to receive displaced tenants from nearby estates. From James Loch, *An Account of the Improvements on the Estates of the Marquess of Stafford*, 1820.

So the evidence from different sources is patchy, but the impression is one of massive change. The other point raised by the dearth of evidence is that, other than the outline plans and organization of lease-timing noted above, the whole process hardly provides a classic example of detailed planning. Displaced tenants, for example, often turned out forcibly by over-zealous estate agents, seem to have drifted to any reception area, reflecting the lack of evidence suggestive of an allocation of new holdings to them. The broad sweep of change seems to reflect the broad sweep of the plans for change.

LAYOUT OF SETTLEMENTS ON THE ESTATES

The second key element of change was in the manner in which land was occupied. Maps survive covering the Skelbo–Achvandra area in the Parish of Dornoch before and after reorganisation. It lies on the southern shore of Loch Fleet, on the north-eastern fringe of south-east Sutherland [Figs. 11.6–11.8].

Aitken's plan of 1788 [Fig. 11.7] shows that it can be subdivided into three parts. In the north-west of the plan lies the Mains of Skelbo which, judging by its grouping of small rectangular fields, had by that time experienced a degree of enclosure. To the south of the Water of Skelbo there is an irregular series of open fields which vary in size but appear to be part of Skelbo itself. The remainder of the area is occupied by three farming townships: Achvandra, Cubecmore and Cubecbeg. All three illustrate the open field pattern of farming, accompanied by a scatter of buildings: Achvandra in particular was fairly sizeable, judging by both the size of the arable fields and the number of buildings which lie within its bounds.

Comparison of Figures 11.7 and 11.8 needs a little background. Three features help with this. Skelbo Castle and the Water of Skelbo are relatively consistent features. Thirdly, the boundary of Figure 11.7 encloses an area of about 1.1 km (0.7 ml) north–south by about 1.9 km (1.2 ml) east–west, while the boundary of Figure 11.8 is about 1.5 km

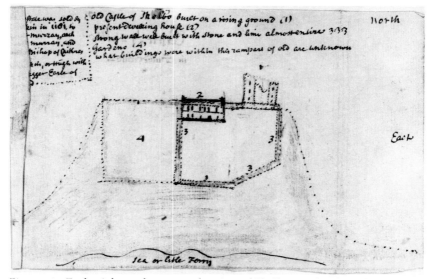

Fig. 11.6 Early eighteenth century drawing of Skelbo Castle; the old Castle (1), the present dwelling house (2), almost entire, strong, stone and lime wall (3), gardens (4).

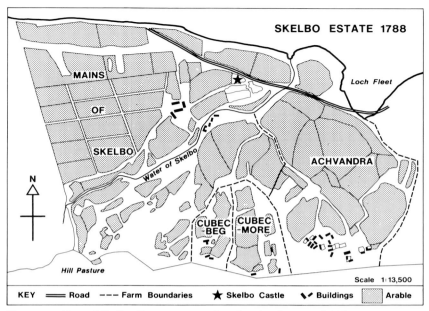

Fig. 11.7 Part of Skelbo Estate, 1788; after the plan by David Aitken.

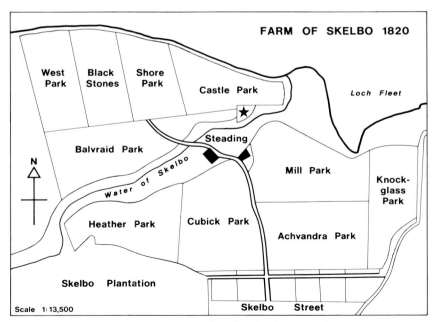

Fig. 11.8 The farm of Skelbo, 1820; after the plan by W. Forbes.

175

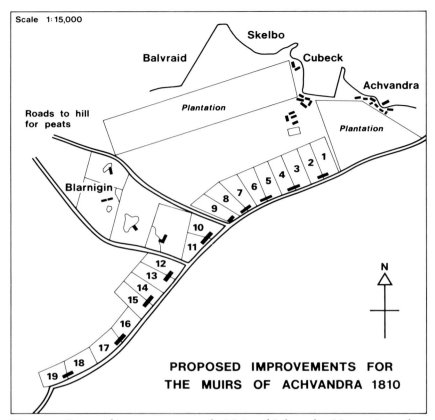

Scale 1:15,000

Skelbo

Balvraid   Cubeck

Achvandra

Roads to hill
for peats

Plantation

Plantation

Blarnigin

1 2 3 4 5 6 7 8
9
10
11
12
13
14
15
16
17
18
19

N

PROPOSED IMPROVEMENTS FOR
THE MUIRS OF ACHVANDRA 1810

Fig. 11.9   Proposed improvements on the Muirs of Achvandra, No. 2, 1810; after
the plan by Benjamin Meredith.

(0.9 ml) north–south and about 2 km (1.25 ml) east–west. The plans,
therefore, cover an approximately equivalent area; clearly there has been a
transformation of the landscape.

Skelbo Farm in 1820 consisted of 104 ha (257 acres) of arable ground
and 17 ha (42 acres) of pasture. The arable was made up of ten large
named fields plus the Stallions' Park immediately to the west of Skelbo
Castle. The names of the fields themselves are indicators of change.
Achvandra Park and Cubick Park cover areas which were part of the
arable ground of these townships in the 1788 plan. Knockglass Park is
adjacent to where the lands of Knockglass were in 1788, when Knockglass
was the immediate neighbour to the east of Achvandra and just outwith
the area represented by Aitken. The amalgamation of the smaller fields
which formerly comprised the Mains of Skelbo is brought out by the Plan
of 1820, as is the move to create as rectilineal a pattern as possible in the
landscape.

Taken together, the two diagrams (re-drawn from the originals) show that the pattern of 1788 was completely supplanted by one large arable farm and a group of six smallholdings, Skelbo Street. The removal of the tenants who held leases in the former townships was an integral component of this change. Mackay stated that this transformation happened between 1810 and 1814, along with the establishment of twenty-four other large farms on the Estate of Sutherland (1889. 190–91).

The portrayal of Skelbo Street indicates the type of smallholding to which displaced tenants could move; Meredith's plan of 1810 for a series of such holdings on the Muirs of Achvandra [Fig. 11.9], extends the point. The hill ground lay immediately to the south of the Skelbo area; it is dominated by the line of nineteen numbered holdings strung out along the roadside. The work on Achvandra was one of the earlier of the resettlement schemes organized by the Estate of Sutherland, and was very much tied up with the early visit to Sutherland by William Young and Patrick Sellar in 1809–10. The sequence of events around that time has already been well documented by Adam; however, an interesting point arises from a letter dated 12 April 1811, written by William Young to the Marchioness of Stafford. In that letter, Young writes:

> The Achvandra people are taking Lotts, indeed battling about the Moor, and I will in every parish lay off places of the same sort with which the people will I think be perfectly satisfied and ten times more comfortable, for such a mass of confusion as these Lands are in at present I never witnessed. (Adam 1972. II. 140)

The use of the word 'confusion' seems pertinent. It suggests that the patterns of land holding and land use which had existed prior to change were made orderly by the introduction of a system dominated by geometrical lines. That attitude, along with the wholesale effect of change on the mass of people in the area, was to be the focus for vitriolic criticism from a wide variety of sources, attracting the attention even of Karl Marx. The nub of the debate, almost irrespective of the origin of a particular point of view, was whether or not the mass of tenantry was, in the words of Young, 'more comfortable'.

EFFECTS OF LAND REORGANIZATION ON THE PEOPLE

Various sources highlight the manner in which the mass of people in southeast Sutherland were affected by reorganization, notably the *Old Statistical Account* for the 1790s and the *New Statistical Account* for the 1830s.

According to Webster, the total population of Creich was 1,705 in 1755, and Dornoch had 2,780 inhabitants. By 1841, the totals were 2,582 for Creich and 2,714 for Dornoch. In the case of Creich there was an increase in the parish total at each Census; for Dornoch the pattern of totals was more variable, though within that variation perhaps the most important figure for our purposes was that of 1831: 3,380. In general terms, therefore, this was a period of steady overall growth in population in the area; there was also a change in the density of population as a result of organization. If we estimate the area of settlement on the maps [Figs. 11.1; 11.2], we find that in Dornoch at both periods the total was some 67 sq. km (26 sq. ml). In Creich, however, the total of 120 sq. km (46 sq. ml) in 1755 was reduced to 96 sq. km (37 sq. ml) in 1841. In the context of population growth, this represents a marked increase in the density of population in the area as a whole.

The pattern of life depicted by the *Old Statistical Account* might broadly be summarised as one in which most people were subsistence small-holders, cultivating crops for domestic supply and rearing black cattle towards payment of rent. Crop supply was, according to the report for Dornoch, 'Not much more than is sufficient' in ordinary season. In Creich, it was noted that 'in tolerably good years' the crop supply was able to provide 'rather more victual than would be sufficient for supplying itself'. Both reports illustrate the variable nature of this food supply from smallholdings by inclusion of reference to famine. In the case of Dornoch, 1782 was cited as one in which 'a severe dearth was experienced here', whereas the summers of 1783 and 1784 were times of 'great distress' in Creich. Indeed, this pattern of occasional catastrophe seemed to strike about once a decade, with 1766, 1782 and 1793 being other disastrous seasons.

The question of food supply became paramount for most people at that time, other essentials such as shelter and clothing receiving scant attention in the Accounts, and fuel apparently being available. In Creich people were 'well supplied' with peat, and this seems to have been the case in Dornoch, although the Account asserts that the means of collection was 'peculiarily injurious to health'. If the 'improvements' were to assist people beyond the level of subsistence, however, as argued by the more fervent protagonists of change such as James Loch, then perhaps the question of food supply offers a measure for drawing judgement.

The *New Statistical Account* of Dornoch contains no direct reference to the adequacy of food supply, the reporter addressing himself to other matters from a standpoint which clearly supports the changes which occurred. This is also the case for Creich. There is a possible explanation for the omission, however, other than approval of change. Famines did occur in Sutherland as a whole in 1807–08 and 1816–17, but not in the 1820s. Both these Accounts were written in 1834, almost a generation after the last notable famine, and this may have led the reporters to feel that the spectre of famine had passed, no doubt as a result of reorganiza-tion. This was not to last, however, as famine returned to parts of the County in 1836–37, and Sutherland suffered in common with many areas during the cataclysm of potato blight in the second half of the 1840s. It seems fair, therefore, to suggest that the 'improvements' led only to a short term alleviation of the incidence of famine.

Another means of judging the effect of change is by looking at the migration of people out of Sutherland, particularly overseas emigration. In 1773, for example, before the main phase of reorganization, the brig 'Nancy' left Dornoch for New York. Estimates of the number of emigrants on board vary from Meyer's 200 to Graham's 280, but it can be assumed that both totals included people from south-east Sutherland. After reorganization, the *New Statistical Account* for Dornoch noted that some 300 people had recently emigrated to 'British America'; the sharp drop in population in Dornoch between 1831 and 1841 is also suggestive of outmigration; and Duncan Ross, the General Assembly's teacher in Creich, gave evidence to the Poor Law Inquiry in 1843 that there was 'a great willingness in the people to emigrate . . .'. In addition to emigration overseas, there was also movement to destinations within Great Britain. Unfortunately data in terms of permanent movement is lacking, although the *Old Statistical Account* for Dornoch refers to seasonal movement to the south in search of work, and both the *New Statistical Account* and the *Minutes of Evidence to the Poor Law Inquiry* indicate a similar seasonal migration.

PLUS ÇA CHANGE?

While such instances are by no means fully comprehensive, they serve as important indicators: the 'improvements' seem not to have led to a change in the pattern of people leaving the area; and there is nothing to suggest that 'improvement' stemmed the flow. On the contrary, many critics argue that the effect of change was to increase the rate of out-migration. There is simply insufficient reliable data for that assertion to be fully tested, however, with recent work by Bumstead (1982) illustrating the problems. What is relevant to the present review is that, as with famine, there was no lasting alteration to the patterns of migration which seemed to have held sway prior to reorganization.

The link which can be drawn between the two is apparent. The continued risk of famine might be viewed as a force pushing people from the area, while the perceived advantages of such possible destinations as the factories of central Scotland or the available lands of North America serve as forces of attraction. But explanation of the link extends beyond Hobsbawm's mobile labour force. If a wage economy had adequately accompanied reorganization, then food could have been bought in by people. However, other than short-term employment on road building projects (see Haldane 1973), there was a singular lack of lasting non-agricultural employment in south-east Sutherland throughout the period. Those who did not migrate as a result of being displaced from their old holdings, therefore, were thrown back to dependence on their new holdings for survival. In the context of a rising population, pressure on these holdings increased, and their relative ability to provide diminished as population densities thickened. This culminated in the potato famine of 1846 and its aftermath.

So for the mass of the population, the chief impact of reorganization was not primarily on a near-subsistence lifestyle which motivated some to migrate in search of a better future; it was more in the dislocation of settlement, resulting from evictions and re-allocation.

CONCLUSION

What conclusions can be drawn from this review of the Clearances in south-east Sutherland? First, and importantly, much research hitherto for this period has focused on events in other parts of Sutherland. Strathnaver and the Strath of Kildonan have attracted much attention, probably reflecting Loch's publication and the notorious trial of Patrick Sellar, but the price of this emphasis has been a tendency to overlook the all-pervasive nature of these changes. The case of south-east Sutherland, an area in which there were a number of estates other than the Estate of Sutherland, serves as illustration. Second, the connection between the Clearances and sheep, while popular, is not entirely accurate. The case of the Skelbo area indicates that the impact of the creation of large arable farms was no less important. Perhaps a definition in terms of the replacement of open field farming by large scale commercial farming is appropriate. Third, the changes of which the Clearances were an integral part did not solve the basic human problem of periodic famine which bedevilled the area in the second half of the eighteenth century. The case of south-east Sutherland is but another example of the inability of economic change to take account of human circumstances.

Acknowledgement

Photographs were kindly provided by the Scottish Tourist Board (Fig. 11.5), the Scottish Ethnological Archive, Royal Museum of Scotland (Fig. 11.6) and the Royal Commission on the Ancient and Historical Monuments of Scotland (Fig. 11.7). Figure 11.7 is reproduced with the permission of Dr J. Close-Brookes; maps and plans have been redrawn by Douglas Lawson.

References

Plans:

Dunrobin Castle, Golspie
    Plans of Skelbo, 1788, by David Aitken.
    Plans of the Proposed Improvement on the Muire [*sic*] of Achvandra, No. 2, 1810, by
      Benjamin Meredith
    Plan of the Farm of Skelbo, 1820, by W. Forbes.

Printed:

Adam, R. J. *Sutherland Estate Management*. 2 vols. 1972.
Adams, I. H. *Agrarian Landscape Terms*. 1976.
Bumstead, J. M. *The People's Clearance: Highland Emigration to British North America, 1770–1815*. 1982.
Graham, I. C. C. *Colonists from Scotland: Emigration to British North America 1707–1783*. 1956.
Haldane, A. R. B., *New Ways Through the Glens*. (1962) 1973.
Hobsbawm, E. J. *The Age of Revolution*. 1973.
Houston, R. *The Impact of Economic Change on Sutherland, 1755–1851*. Unpublished Ph.D. thesis, University of Edinburgh. 1980.
Loch, J. *An Account of the Improvements on the Estates of the Marquess of Stafford*. 1820.
Mackay, A. *Sketches of Sutherland Characters*. 1899.

Marx, K. Sutherland and Slavery, or the Duchess at Home, in *People's Paper*. 12 March 1853.

Meyer, D. *The Highland Scots of North Carolina*. 1961.

Minutes of Evidence to the Poor Law Inquiry Commission for Scotland. 1843.

Minutes of Evidence to the Commission of Enquiry into the Condition of the Crofters and Cottars in the Highlands and Islands of Scotland. 1884.

NSA. New Statistical Account of Scotland. IV.

OSA. Old Statistical Account of Scotland. 1793. VIII.

Richards, E. *A History of the Highland Clearances*. 1982.

Sage, D. *Memorabilia Domestica*. 1899.

Smith, A. *The Wealth of Nations*. Skinner, A. ed. 1974.

Smout, T. C. *A History of the Scottish People*. 1970.

Fig. 12.1 Glen Torridon, Wester Ross — grazing country.

THE LONG TREK:
AGRICULTURAL CHANGE AND THE
GREAT NORTHERN DROVE

John R. Baldwin

INTRODUCTION

The Highlands were for long considered a wild and remote place, virtually inaccessible from the rest of Scotland. The (?)thirteenth-century Bodleian Map designated that area of the far north-west facing the outer isles with the words *hic habundant lupi*, wolves are plentiful hereabouts, whilst at much the same period the entire western coastal fringe of the Highlands north from the Clyde was described by Matthew Paris as 'A country marshy and impassable, fit for cattle and shepherds'. Inland was 'A mountainous and woody region, producing a people rude and pastoral, by reason of marshes and fens...'. In the fourteenth century, Fordoun continues: 'the upland districts and along the Highlands [were] full of pasturage grass for cattle and comely with verdure in the glens along the water courses', and flesh may be said to have been put on the bones towards the end of the sixteenth century by Bishop Leslie (in Hume Brown 1893. II. 132): 'in the mountanis of Aargyl and Rosse lykewise and sindrie utheris places ar fed ky, nocht tame, as in utheris partes, bot lyke wylde hartes, wandiring out of ordour and quhilkes, throuch a certane wyldnes of nature, flie the cumpanie on syght of men' — beasts of like temperament perhaps to those wild British bulls hunted and caught 1,000 years earlier by means of strong nets (Gildas, in Logan 1876. II, 36–37)!

More than three-fifths of Scotland consists of mountains, hills and moorland, the bulk of it in what we know as the Highlands and Islands. Through time, the climate has contributed a blanket of peat bog over much of the moorland, and marshland in many a wider river valley. And the mountain areas, especially in the north and west with their heavy rainfall, have never been anything other than regions of natural poverty — a poverty reinforced by warring and feuding, and by agricultural practices that may be described as basic, though not necessarily or invariably inappropriate to the geographical conditions.

Climatic improvement from time to time may have ameliorated the lot of the inhabitants, and undoubtedly a number of locations were better favoured — island machairs, parts of certain broad and fertile, sheltered straths, and the attractive coastal fringe of such areas as Easter Ross and south-east Sutherland. In general, however, vast areas of Scotland were, and are, relatively ill-suited to an arable economy and over much of the Highlands what little cultivation there was, was restricted to narrow glens and coastal pockets.

13

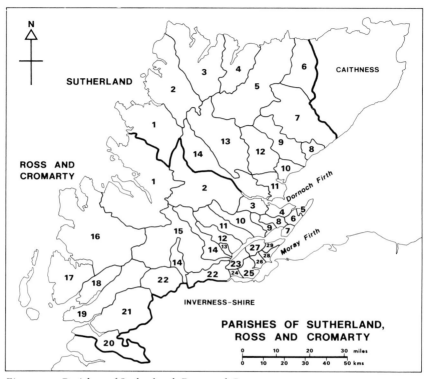

Fig. 12.2 Parishes of Sutherland, Ross and Cromarty.

SUTHERLAND	ROSS AND CROMARTY	
1. Assynt	1. Lochbroom	16. Gairloch
2. Eddrachillis	2. Kincardine	17. Applecross
3. Durness	3. Edderton	18. Lochcarron
4. Tongue	4. Tain	19. Lochalsh
5. Farr	5. Tarbat	20. Glenshiel
6. Reay (part of)	6. Fearn	21. Kintail
7. Kildonan	7. Nigg	22. Urray
8. Loth	8. Logie Easter	23. Urquhart and Logie Wester
9. Clyne	9. Kilmuir Easter	24. Killearnan
10. Golspie	10. Rosskeen	25. Kilmuir Wester (Knockbain)
11. Dornoch	11. Alness	26. Avoch
12. Rogart	12. Kiltearn	27. Kirkmichael (Resolis)
13. Lairg	13. Dingwall	28. Rosemarkie
14. Creich	14. Fodderty	29. Cromarty
	15. Contin	

Like much of northern England, Ireland, Norway and the North Atlantic islands, therefore, survival depended upon a primarily pastoral economy. The grazing potential was enormous as later landowners and flock-masters well appreciated, though without controlled and responsible exploitation the land eventually became sour as well as denuded of trees and woodland. But in spite of the increasing pre-dominance of sheep-farming from the third quarter of the eighteenth century, it was cattle that had long provided a focus for the economy; and though sheep came to be driven in large numbers during the nineteenth century, both cattle and sheep continued to be moved 'on the hoof' to and from the less accessible parts of the north and north-west well into the present century.

This paper seeks to concentrate on droving in the north of Scotland and on the pivotal role of the eastern firthlands in the later eighteenth and nineteenth centuries. Some indication of contemporary agricultural and pastoral practice will help provide a context.

LIVESTOCK HUSBANDRY AND PATTERNS OF AGRICULTURE

Across Ross and Cromarty and Sutherland there was no single agricultural model. Very broadly speaking, by the late eighteenth century there appear to have been three somewhat overlapping patterns, geographically-based and reflecting differing environmental factors.

The 'western districts' [Fig. 12.1] consisted of mainly rough, wild and uncultivated mountains and moorland, and numerous woods (until they were burnt). They were very well suited for grazing, had numerous bays

Fig. 12.3   Valley of the River Shin, south-east Sutherland — restricted but good arable, plentiful hill grazings and diversified resources.

Fig. 12.4 Tarbat Ness, lighthouse and Ballone Castle — the fertile, eastern plain.

for fishing, and stretched from Kintail and Lochalsh, northwards by the parishes of Gairloch, Lochbroom, Assynt and Edderachillis as far round the northern coast as Strathnaver [Fig. 12.2]. The 'central districts', to include parts of Strathnaver, Kildonan and Clyne, and parishes such as Rogart, Lairg, Creich and Kincardine, contained extensive and attractive straths, often well-wooded and stretching inland amongst large tracts of high and inhospitable mountains [Fig. 12.3]. They too were well-suited to a pastoral economy whilst having the advantage of a wider, more plentiful range of natural resources, cornland, deer, game, salmon, timber, as well as greater accessibility to the higher-populated eastern districts. This 'eastern seaboard', by contrast, was low-lying, fertile and very much agricultural, taking in all or much of Contin and Dingwall parishes, the Black Isle, the north shore of the Cromarty Firth, the Tarbat peninsula [Fig. 12.4] and the coastal fringe of the Dornoch Firth, creeping north-wards along the east coast of Sutherland. In terms of land-use it would also include the north-eastern parts of Caithness as well as the southern shores of the Beauly and Moray Firths, though these are outwith the present study.

In short, most inhabitants of the western and central districts were necessarily pastoralists; whilst the inhabitants of the eastern seaboard, also heirs in considerable part to the Gaelic language and culture, were primarily farmers.

The North-West Coasts and Hinterland

The life-style of the north and west was based on a dual system of winter-toun and summer shielings [Fig. 12.5], on the most careful exploitation of natural grazing. At its simplest, once the lower pastures had been grazed bare, stock were taken to the higher pastures and shielings to let the lower grazings recover for further use during the later part of the year. In practice it was rarely that simple, for a good herd had to make the best use of all his available fodder. He was particularly fortunate, for instance, if he had low-lying meadow land too wet to till; he would also have infield pasture very good for fattening cattle, but very little of it. He might well have tracts

Fig. 12.5   Milking cattle outside the dyke, Uist (Cathcart Collection).

of good natural grass on the lower slopes of the hill not far distant from the township dyke; and he would have the mountain pastures, moors and commons generally sited between 250 m and 915 m (800 ft–3,000 ft). The herd had to know the potential of all his land: some pastures yielded only early grasses, little use for providing winter feed; on the other hand, most Highland pasture being high, it provided good grazing in summer but not early in the season, so there was little point in trying to use it too soon (Walker 1812. 1. 311–18).

To aid optimum exploitation, distinctions were made between the grazing of milking cows and of the yeld, barren or non-milking cattle, young cattle, horses and other stock. In Assynt, for instance, in western Sutherland, the narrow glens and valleys and the small plains or local woodlands amongst the hills were kept for pasturing milk cows, goats and sheep in summer and harvest-time [Fig. 12.6], leaving the higher parts for the yeld cattle. At the same time, certain grazings within the area known as *Me-in-Assint*, the middle of Assynt — tracts of heath, moss, heathery hills, small rocks and freshwater lochans bordering on the outskirts of the coastal farms — were preserved during the three harvest months, and used as outwintering for cattle from the end of the harvest or early November until the beginning of February or thereabouts, when the animals would be taken in, housed and fed. Certain small islands within the same parish, like Oldany and Soay, were similarly exploited (Mackenzie 1794. 274–87); and the Summer Isles in Coigach.

At one time, the Highlanders' stock comprised as many goats and native sheep, small horses as well, as it did cattle [Fig. 12.7]. By the late eighteenth century however, 'Every farmer rears a few sheep and goats, but their number is very inconsiderable; and they are chiefly intended to reach at that pasture which, by its very steepness, is inaccessible to black-cattle' (Morrison 1792. 524). For cattle now formed the mainstay of the

Fig. 12.6   Grazing goats, Diabeg, Loch Torridon, 1972.

economy, and most were sold before winter — partly to pay the rent, partly because of the shortage of winter fodder, partly to buy in extra supplies of oats, barley and other human necessities. Traditionally it was the corn crop that failed, bere and sma' oats; but even in the best years of the later eighteenth century, Wester Ross was importing oatmeal from Ireland, the Clyde or Caithness (Sinclair 1795. 118–19).

As for the overwintered stock, they would frequently die in their thousands. Milk cows apart, there was no preferential treatment, so that in Sutherland: 'During Summer they procured a scanty sustenance with much toil and labour by roaming over the mountains; while in winter they died in numbers for the want of support; notwithstanding a practice which they universally adopted of killing every second calf on account of the want of winter keep.' (Loch 1820. 64–65). Loch continued by stating that in Kildonan parish alone in the spring of 1807, 200 cows, 500 head of cattle and more than 200 small horses died. As for those that did not die, the writer of an article on Perthshire Husbandry in 1808 commented:

> I well remember to have seen the poor wives during the nipping cold winds in May, provincially called the *Cowquake*, tending their cows, reduced to a skeleton and covered with a blanket, while they picked up any spires of grass which had begun to rise in the kailyard or at the bottom of walls and banks. And to such extremities were they reduced at times that I have heard of their taking the half-rotten thatch from the roofs of their houses and giving it to the half-dead animal as the means of prolonging its miserable existence. (Anon. 1808. 436).

Fig. 12.7 Milking the goat indoors. Painting by William Simson, *Goatherd's Cottage*, 1832.

Fig. 12.8   At Duncansby, Caithness, 1969.

Those that survived the winter emerged from the byre dizzy with weakness. They were often so weak that they had to be carried outside; and then, when seeking shoots of new vegetation in bogs and marshes, they had to be dragged clear, too weak to extricate themselves. Far from disappearing last century, similar, if not so dire scenes survived in Wester Ross (Coigach) and Caithness (Duncansby), for example, into the 1960s and 1970s [Fig. 12.8].

At the very least, these examples underline the need that there was for plentiful and well-managed hill-grazings: survival itself required a summer shieling system for milking stock, along with freer, less supervised, upland grazing for other stock. They also help explain the close association of special rites, instance Beltane fires and rowan sprigs, with the protection of animals. And it was no accident that the key dates in the seasonal calendar, Bealltuinn, Lùnasdal, Samhuinn, were closely associated with the movement of livestock (MacDonald 1978. 80). The men of the north and the west were almost totally dependent upon their stock.

The Eastern Lowlands

Across on the eastern firthlands, the local farmers also kept considerable numbers of cattle, small horses and sheep. The proportions, however, were somewhat different. In the 1780s and 1790s, according to the *Statistical Accounts*, northern and western parishes might have four, eight, even fifteen times as many cattle as horses; east coast parishes just about twice the number:

	Dingwall 1790–91	Tarbat 1792	Lochalsh 1793	Edderachillis 1791–92	Tongue 1791
Black Cattle (inc. cows, calves)	600+	1176	3115	2573	2142
Horses	374	573	275	351	538
Sheep	?	2080	2475	2624	2846
Goats	?	?	1011	1307	714

This may be explained partly by the growing importance of cattle-breeding in the harsher non-agricultural areas, set against a drop in horse-breeding; partly by the fact that, a few milking cows apart, east coast stock were primarily working animals [Figs. 12.9; 12.10]. For whilst he did on occasion breed and rear a few of his own black cattle, the east-coaster was a farmer not a cattle-breeder; rather would he buy in as required most of his animals, cattle and horses, at the different local fairs held each October and November in Ross and Cromarty and Sutherland. After a few years' labouring, the animals were again sold, either to the drover or to the butcher, and often at a price higher than that first paid (Balfour 1792. 640). If they had survived, that is. For these animals still required feeding throughout most of the year and such was the system of pre-improvement agriculture that, as in less hospitable areas, this was far from assured. On a farm on the Shandwick estate round about 1800, there were 30–40 'shelties' (probably garrons) and 40 small oxen. The farmer had not one acre of fallow or turnips, and his straw stubble, never very long, was quite insufficient to keep the animals alive during seven months of the year

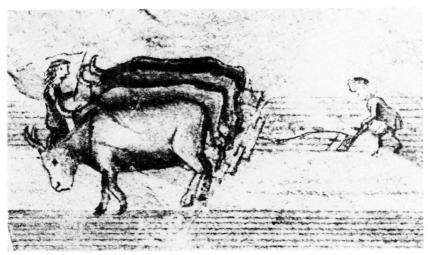

Fig. 12.9 The Lighter version of the old Scots plough still pulled by four oxen yoked abreast. From W. Aberdeen's plan of Castlehill, Caithness, 1772.

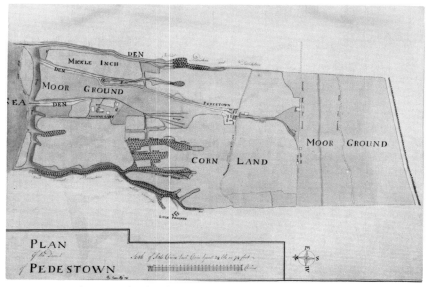

Fig. 12.10 The Davoch of Pedestown, south-west of Cromarty, Black Isle. Plan by James May, 1748 (Craigston Castle Drawings).

(Mackenzie 1810. 83, 97–99). Many perished each winter and spring through absolute want.

And on a farm with just ten horses and six head of cattle (besides young cattle) Mackenzie (1810. 82) further observed that one spring:

> The land was remarkably full of weeds of all sorts. After the cattle had done ploughing, they were turned upon the field on which they had been working in order that they might feed upon the weeds which had been turned up. I never observed that they got any other sort of food during the day, except a small quantity of oats just before they went to work. At night the horses and cattle were turned to some patches of waste ground to pick up a miserable pittance of grass.

This was the farm where two farmers, jointly, were following what would by then appear to have been the decidedly uncommon practice of common ownership of the land:

> Thirty acres were occupied by two men who had large families. They possessed the land, not in runrig, but in common. Both exerted themselves in cultivating the fields and they agreed respecting a particular but very irregular rotation of crops, and divided the produce equally between them.

During the summer months they sent their animals

> to graze on some bare hills; the horses being brought down when the peats were ready for storing, and sent back as soon as the fuel was got home. When the corn was ready to be taken from the fields, the whole stock was brought home and allowed to range on the stubbles.

Thus it becomes clear that, traditionally, the native firthlands farmers had access both to modest grazings close-by and to wider hill grazings some considerable distance away: 65–80 km (40–50 ml) distant for some Cromarty farms (Sinclair 1795. 10–11). From the parish of Urray both horses and black cattle were sent to the western hills from May until Michaelmas; from Nigg, and from Kirkmichael and Cullicudden in the Black Isle where over-stocking was equally common, the animals were dispatched in summer to the 'cold Highland grazings' (Downie 1791–92. 672; Arthur 179?. 537; Macadam 1793. 590).

The Inland Uplands

Mountainous like the west coast hinterland, the central, inland districts of Ross and Cromarty and Sutherland also held considerable breeding stocks of black cattle and hill horses, some sheep and some goats. At the same time their more varied resources allowed Strathnaver, for instance, to buy corn from Caithness in the mid-seventeenth century, in exchange for timber; and 'particularly tall firs' from Strathcarron were exported near and far (Gordon ?1640, in MacFarlane. II, 447–48, 453–54).

But in addition, and to a much greater extent than the western districts, the central mountains played host to those summertime herds of lowland animals requiring pasture. Whilst the inland pastoralists often over-stocked with their own animals, in relation to the number they could keep alive during the winter, nonetheless the hills were still apparently under-grazed — initially at least. To allow them to buy in essential foodstuffs and to retain more of their own 'surplus' stock during winter and spring, they were induced to lease out grazing. This practice led eventually to real overstocking, so that the low country cattle and horses never fully lost the generally poor-looking, stunted appearance engendered by overstocking in the low country (Mackenzie 1810. 133–35). Put a little differently, an upland tenant in Creich parish would overwinter as many of his own black cattle as feed would allow. But if circumstances were particularly straightened: 'In that case, he takes cattle from others, who may have more than they can feed, at the rate of 2s., 6d., or 3s., through the winter and spring, as provender is plentiful or scarce.' (Rainy 1791. 338). Such winter leasing suggests cash-crop grazing taken to an extreme; it reflects the pressures that were growing upon both native Highlander and firthland Lowlander.

Nevertheless, demand for these more distant grazings, leased from Highland occupiers, grew as more localised grazings were swallowed up in lowland improvements; at the same time their rent increased as the hills were turned over to beef cattle and sheep. From 1s. a head per season, creeping up eventually to 5s. and 6s per head, it was simply a matter of time before the native lowlander would be outpriced, or, indeed, excluded. So that of farmers in Nigg parish in 1793 it was said (Macadam 1793. 590): 'it is supposed that they shall soon be obliged to adopt a different method; because great part of the Highlands, where their cattle were wont to be grazed in the summer season, are now converted into sheep farms, the number of which is still increasing'.

The New Farmers and Farming Practice

This old firthland farmer, however, was of a dying breed regardless. By the later eighteenth century, eastern seaboard farms were being amalgamated, re-divided, enclosed and re-let to improving farmers, many of them from the south, so that by the time of the *New Statistical Account* in the 1830s and 1840s, very little seems to have remained of the old system based on large numbers of labouring animals [Figs. 12.11; 12.12]. By 1837 in Contin parish for example (Downie 1837. 240–41): 'The few black cattle reared for sale are the remains of the old Highland breed, which seems to have degenerated in the same ratio in which the circumstances of the people declined.'

The Shandwick estate already referred to was taken over by a Mr Cockburn Ross from Row Chester in Berwickshire. He reckoned that four good horses (presumably Clydesdales) would do the work of 70–80 small horses and oxen; and always intent on reaping considerable profits through improved techniques and efficiency, it was generally felt that one substantial farmer could easily occupy and cultivate the 400 acres of lowland Easter Ross that represented the holdings of 20 native families. According to Mackenzie, such a farm would require seven pair of good horses each with a horseman whose family might average five persons — a total of 35 persons rather than 100 formerly supported by the same land; and in a very different, dependent, situation socially (Mackenzie 1810. 85).

Another such improver was MacLeod of Geanies, who had both lowland and upland estates. By the early 1780s he had introduced Norfolk husbandry and plantations in Easter Ross, and by 1784 was 'presently building a family seat' (Wight 1784. IV. i, 268–70) [Fig. 12.13]. About this same time he was also leasing Cromartie land in Lochbroom from the annexed estate commissioners (ibid.; Mackenzie 1810. 130):

> At Coigach, on the west coast, Mr. MacLeod possessed a large farm, which maintains about 300 horned cattle and 60 horses during the summer months. They run out summer and winter, by which they are hardy and healthy. The horned cattle continue unmixed with any other kind. The management of them is good. Every winter the one half are brought down to Geanies, where they have plenty of food. Both parcels are thereby improved, plenty of pasture being left for the half that remain in the high lands.

Though his stock was clearly of a superior breed, MacLeod was not initiating anything totally new. Nearly 20 years earlier in 1766, a professional drover, Charles Gordon of Skelpick in lower Strathnaver, had taken a tack of remote mainly inland Rientraid in Assynt, a little to the north; and there are clear indications of a healthy commercial cattle trade in Coigach a full century earlier. References in the Cromartie papers refer to

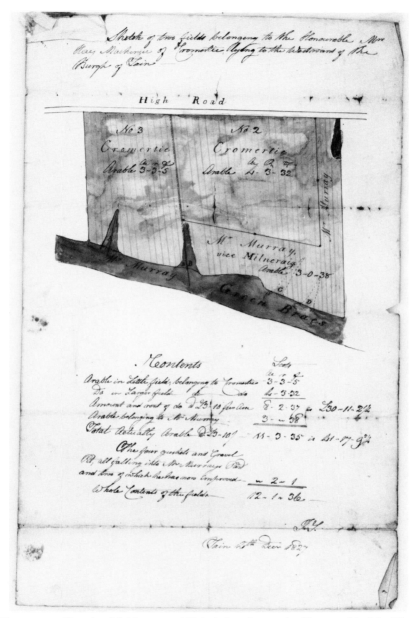

Fig. 12.11 Sketch of fields west of Tain belonging to the Honourable Mrs Hay Mackenzie of Cromartie. Plan by T. Shand, 1827.

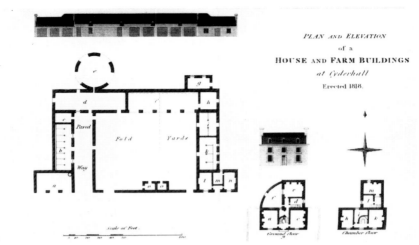

Fig. 12.12 The new farm and steading at Cyderhall, 1818. From James Loch, *An Account of the Improvements on the Estate of the Marquess of Stafford*, 1820.

Fig. 12.13 Geanies House, parish of Tarbat, from the south, by C. C. Petley.

rents in silver rather than in kind from Coigach in the mid-seventeenth century (Monica Clough: *pers. comm.*) — silver almost inevitably realized from the sale of cattle; whilst around the same time Gordon of Straloch says more generally of Wester Ross '... every year many herds of oxen raised here are driven far and wide for sale' (in MacFarlane 1907. II. 445).

Whilst this trend towards the large-scale commercial hill-grazing of cattle, which had long gone on alongside smaller-scale shieling practice, was to continue into the nineteenth century, further change had already begun. Around 1790, for instance, the same MacLeod of Geanies was looking to replace his Coigach/Lochbroom cattle with sheep. But yet again he was not the first.

Sheep-farming reputedly began in the highland areas of Ross-shire with Sir John Lockhart Ross of Balnagown. A Mr Geddes of Tummel Bridge in Perthshire, to whom farms were let on the Sutherland–Ross-shire border in 1781 or 1782, was maybe the first sheep-farmer (certainly amongst the first) to settle in the north; soon after, Ross's forest of Freevater and the highland parts of Munro of Culcairn's Ross-shire estate were let to a Mr Cameron of Fort William. It was all wedder sheep at this time, for fear that a breeding stock would not survive the climate (Mackenzie 1810. 126–30), but even so, 'For every pound of beef, that a Highlander can send to market, a shepherd can at least bring three pounds of mutton' (Sinclair 1795. 110).

It would be erroneous to assume that cattle now all but disappeared from lowland or highland landscapes. Numbers declined in favour of sheep, but they were still considerable (Henderson 1812. 189):

	Assynt		Creich		Golspie	
	1790–98	1808	1790–98	1808	1790–98	1808
Black Cattle	3840	2000	1300	906	1100	1100
Horses	384	90	1531	965	350	260
Sheep	3840	8000	4000	13000	1000	1000
Goats	1024	60	?	20	?	100

Actual ownership of the cattle, however, had largely passed into the hands of the new farmers and estate owners.

On the one hand, the lowland improvers looked to cattle as a cash crop. MacLeod of Geanies, for instance, had seen the wisdom of bringing half his stock across from mountainous Coigach to Tarbat each winter, where his improved system of arable husbandry provided plenty of winter feed. And increasingly what became known as a *flying stock* appeared. The new improving farmers of Easter Ross, being so far from the markets, found breeding itself uneconomic. Instead, along such seaboard parishes as Tarbat, Nigg and Killearnan farmers like George Mackenzie of Muckle Tarrel bought young Highland stock from the hill country, maybe three and four year old stots, fed them on surplus straw and turnips during the winter and spring, and sold them off to drovers at good prices in the summer (Henderson 1812. 116; Rose 1836. 33; Campbell 1840. 465; Kennedy 18?. 69). In this they were echoing, albeit rather differently, the annual buying and selling of their 'unimproved' predecessors and paving the way for their twentieth-century descendants. It made sound, economic sense.

At the same time the new sheep farmers also retained a strong interest in cattle, for in this early period of sheep farming considerable numbers of black cattle were kept on those parts of the new upland farms that were not, or thought not to be, well-adapted for sheep. Today we would consider a mix to be ecologically sound; in the early nineteenth century when the demand for Highland cattle (like corn) for export to England remained particularly high, fuelled by the French Wars of 1792–1815, the retention of cattle certainly proved profitable, even if the 'Highland bones to be covered with Scottish and English beef' (MacCulloch 1824. III, 103) were no longer the primary focus of the northern economy. They might be sold by the flock-masters either direct to the drovers or indirectly as flying stock, through the lowland improvers.

It is of little surprise, then, that under such pressures, the newly-dispossessed native farmers of the eastern seaboard, the 'lower classes' as Mackenzie terms them, should have made common cause with the dispossessed Highlanders turned off their traditional grazings and out of their long-established townships to make way for sheep. In the 1780s, hostilities had followed Geddes's newly-introduced flocks — 'numbers were shot and droves were collected, surrounded and forced into lakes and drowned'. And in the summer of 1792 'at the unfortunate time when the spirit of revolution and revolt was fast gaining ground over the whole kingdom', open insurrection broke out in Ross-shire. All the sheep that had been brought to the various farms were gathered and upward of 10,000 driven down from the high ground to be taken to Inverness and there left to stray or to be driven further south by those living in Inverness-shire (Mackenzie 1810. 129–32).

In general terms and sentiment, the words of John Robertson, writing in the *Glasgow National* in 1844 on the evictions of the Rosses from the Glens of Strathcarron [Fig. 12.14], applied as aptly to their coastal cousins:

> For a century, their privileges have been lessening; they dare not now hunt the deer, or shoot the grouse or the blackcock; they have no longer the range of the hills for their cattle and their sheep; they must not catch a salmon in the stream; in earth, air and water, the rights of the laird are greater, and the rights of the people are smaller than they were in the days of their forefathers. (in Mackenzie 1883. 140).

In spite of what might and should be seen therefore as revolutionary evictions in the north, in favour of improved agricultural estates along the firthland lowlands and massive sheep farms amongst the hills and glens of Ross and Sutherland, change in the actual use of highland grazings by livestock and in the movement of stock was essentially evolutionary. It had begun well in advance of these eighteenth- and nineteenth-century clearances and was due in no small part to the demand for cattle for the droving trade — a demand evident as early as the fourteenth century, maybe the thirteenth century, and which grew during the sixteenth, seventeenth and eighteenth centuries, to peak in the first half of the nineteenth century. The

Fig. 12.14 In the church and burying ground at Croik, Strathcarron, the inhabitants of Glencalvie sought refuge after their eviction in 1845. Their names are scratched on small, diamond-shaped window panes in the church.

rest of this chapter focuses directly on droving in the north, and particularly on the droving of cattle. For when sheep, power symbol of the new 'Highlander', came to be driven to the southern markets, they simply followed in the tracks of the old Highlander's principal symbol of personal wealth and status.

STOCK FOR DROVING

Perhaps the greatest trading asset of livestock in remote and inaccessible parts of the country was their ability to walk and even swim to market! They did not need to be transported except from more distant islands. This was as true over long distances as it was locally, and in the northern counties there had been a not insignificant local trade — a trade that embraced horses, as well as cattle and later sheep.

Native Garrons

Throughout the seventeenth century, as earlier, horses were bred widely across the rough and mountainous north-west Highlands. Gordon of Straloch, for instance (?1640, in MacFarlane 1906–08. II. 444–56) refers to 'herds of deer, cattle, and horses' in Assynt and Eddrachillis, to 'herds of cattle and many droves of horses' in Strathcarron, to 'countless numbers of cattle, horses, goats and other tame animals' in Strathnaver where 'The violence and numbers of most rapacious wolves ... prowling about wooded and pathless tracts, cause great loss of beasts and sometimes of men'. These horses, black, brown and grey garrons standing some 118–127 cm (44–50 in) high, were well-suited to the pastures and climate. They were grazed on the high hills in summer and autumn, on the 'benty grass of the mountains' well away from the milking cows (Morrison 1792, 524); and nearer to the township during winter and spring. 'There being little need for them in the country' (Sinclair 1795. pt III. 149), the small but hardy animals were generally bred for sale.

Some were sold at the Dornoch market, for instance, to the natives of the parish of Loth for the pack transport of seaware, manure and peats (McCulloch 1791–92. 464); others were bought locally at £3–£4 each by the tenant farmers and cottagers of Urray and elsewhere for ploughing and other labouring (Downie 1791–92. 671–72). For the pre-improvement agriculture of the firthlands required large numbers of labouring stock, cattle and horses.

But there was an equally strong and long-established trade with Orkney whose native horses, though larger, were reckoned less hardy than those from the northern mainland counties (Sinclair 1795. pt V. 225). Some of the sales came from the east coast of Ross where, around 1795, animals bought in their first year from the west were kept at little or no expense and sold to Orkney at a year old for £3 to £5, an increase of some 15s. to 20s. a head from c.1790. And if kept until three or four years old, they fetched from twelve to fifteen guineas 'for the saddle etc' (Falconer 1791–92. 383; Downie 1791–92. 672; Sinclair 1795. pt II. 96). Henderson, writing of the mid and western districts of Sutherland in 1807 (1812. 107) provides a little more detail:

> the farmers used to keep numbers of brood mares ... and in general their colts were sold when they were about 14 months old, to horse-dealers, who drove them to the Orkney isles and sold them to advantage, generally by bartering them for five and six year olds of the same species, which they brought to the Caithness markets in August and September, and had their profit return ... These horses were never shod; they travelled over the flinty rocks without any inconvenience.

The end of an era, however, was close. Commercial cattle had long been increasing in numbers on the hills in proportion to breeding horses and colts, and in addition 'the Cheviot sheep now occupy the former habitation of the hardy Highlander and his horses' (ibid.). In 1805, 'Irish horse-jockies' simply contributed to the clearance, whilst helping the Highlander pay off three years of rent arrears. They bought all the old garrons they could find, at a tolerably good price, 'with all the refuse of that species of animals, and in short, every sort they could procure...' (Sage, in Henderson 1812. app III. 175–76).

Black Cattle

Alongside the trade in live horses, there had also been a local butcher trade in cattle and sheep. In the mid-seventeenth century, for instance, in

Strathnaver and Caithness as well as in Orkney and Shetland, barrelled salted beef was being sold to sailors, fishermen and other voyagers; and sometimes it was sent down to Leith (Gordon ?1640, in MacFarlane 1906–08. II. 445; Brand 1701). To the coastal parishes of Easter Ross too, in the late eighteenth century, butchers came from such centres of population and commerce as Inverness and Dingwall, buying first off the native farmers and later from the improving farmers who replaced them (Balfour 1792. 640). George MacKenzie, an improver in Muckle Tarrel, did not sell every year to the butcher, but when he did the cattle were kept tied up indoors, well-bedded and given straw to eat at midday and all night. By contrast, beasts for droving were left loose in sheds, better to travel (MacKenzie 1810. 116).

No particular attention was paid to rearing of cattle expressly for the butcher trade, and in general it was the oxen and old cows, nearing the end of their days, that were fattened up to satisfy the troops of Fort George and the shipping out of Inverness and Cromarty. The best animals seem to have gone to the drovers, so that on occasion the butchers were obliged to go considerably further afield for their supplies. And they certainly travelled as far as Edderachillis in western Sutherland in search of wedder mutton, said to be much liked by seamen (MacKenzie 1810. 216; Rose 1790–91. 372; Falconer 1791–92. 388).

Most livestock, therefore, was sold to the drovers, and so important had the trade become, that cattle were bred specially for this market [Fig. 12.15]. Those with the best reputation were the *kyloes*, originally swimming across the narrows or kyles from Skye en route for the southern

Fig. 12.15 West Highland Cattle from Aros, Mull and Caolis, 1840. From D. Low *Breeds of Domesticated Animals in the British Isles.*

trysts. Good stock was also reported from Kintail and Coigach (Sinclair 1795. pt II. 118–19), whilst Argyll stock was bred from the best of Kintail, Glenshiel and Skye (MacKenzie 1810. 247–48). From Ross and Cromarty, Sutherland and Caithness, on the other hand, came the *norlands*. Here, according to Sir John Sinclair (1814. III. 29), cattle-breeders had been neither very skilled nor successful before the 1790s:

> The stocks of these counties and parts adjacent were known in the markets of the low country, by their bad shapes and diminutive size. Their heads were coarse, backs high and narrow, ribs flat, bones large, and their legs long and feeble for the weight of the chest, and they were considered very slow feeders.

In 1795, Sinclair (1795. pt II. 95) had advocated the crossing of true Highland bulls, particularly from Skye, with carefully chosen, small and handsome, well-haired, hardy cattle bred 'in the country'. And he reported that their offspring, lean and weighing no more than 113 kg (250 lb), fetched more from the English dealers than would a 180 kg (400 lb) cross from an improved English bull. Such were the hardships endured on the hoof that these animals lasted best; they were also much the best and quickest improvers, and by experience were found to return the most profit to the grazier.

The drover, it was said, required three good qualities in a beast — 'a choice pile, weight and short legs' (Morrison 1792. 524); and it came to be that 'The taste of the Highlands is formed by that of the drovers who carry cattle to the south' (MacKenzie 1870. 217).

DROVING

Itinerant Dealers

It was said of Christopher MacRae of Inverinate in Kintail (MacPhail 1914. 219):

> if he was as frugal in keeping as he was industrious in acquiring, he had proven a very rich man in his own country, for he was the first man there who drove cows to the south country mercates and to that end bought cows yearly from MacKenzie's, MacDonald's and MacLeod's estates.

As the trade developed, therefore, dealers and drovers [Figs. 12.16; 12.17] may, on occasion, have been men from nearby parishes, or perhaps east coast men moving around the western districts; occasionally they could be local tacksmen or landowners; more generally they seem to have come from southern Scotland, often from Perthshire, Stirling, Dumbarton or Ayrshire; some came from as far away as Yorkshire (MacRae (1791–92) 1981. 408; MacKenzie 1810. 254; Henderson 1811, in 1812. 150; MacCulloch 1824. III. 103; McRae 1836. 209).

By all accounts, before the nineteenth century they preferred to scour the country acquiring stock directly from farmers and graziers, and gradually moving east and south across the northern counties towards the lowlands

Figs. 12.16; 12.17   Cattle droving. Pen and brown ink drawings by James Howe,
1830s.

of Easter Ross. This proved to be an unsatisfactory system from the seller's point-of-view, however, since he received payment only after the dealer returned from the great southern trysts. And that payment could be less than agreed. There were cases of default in parishes such as Clyne in the early 1790s (Ross 1793. 323); and further instances were recorded in the 1810s, 15–20 years later:

> ... [Sutherland] farmers are under necessity of selling their cattle to adven-turers, who take them on credit, and if they succeed in disposing of them in the southern markets to advantage, they return and pay the people: if otherwise, they demand so much per head, as discount, which is generally given. (Henderson 1812. (Suth.) 127–28)

On one occasion the creditors had to agree to a discount of 20s. per head, nearly 50% of an original price probably no more than 45s. (ibid.). Certainly some of the dealers were 'deluded adventurers' who themselves were ruined, but the principal sufferers were the country people who depended on the produce of their herds and flocks to pay their rents and support their families.

The Growth of Cattle Fairs

To Sir John Sinclair, the practice of driving the northern cattle as far as Crieff and Falkirk, 'nay into England, even as far as London or farther' was absurd, leastways without prepayment or some intermediate market which would allow of a system of guaranteed credit notes paid on time and without discounting (Sinclair 1795. 74–75). This led him to advocate a system, 'universally admitted', which would remedy the situation:

> by fixing upon a centrical station to comprehend the cattle of the whole North Highlands. Or if a sufficient collection could be formed, that there should be two such stations at proper distances of time and place, within reasonable reach of our own homes; where the English and South Country dealers would as certainly attend as they do now at Crief [sic] and Falkirk were they but assured of a sufficient choice and assortment of cattle.

The dealers' only alternative at that time, 'our limited trifling trysts', were those occasional local markets and fairs mentioned by other late-eighteenth century writers, to which the inhabitants of Assynt and Edder-achillis, for instance, repaired to sell their cattle and any surplus produce, and to buy food and other necessities (MacKenzie 1794. 319; Falconer 1791–92. 387). For however regular the markets may have been in Kintail and Glenshiel (MacRae 1791–92. 408; MacKenzie 1810. 254; McRae 1836. 209), further north they were less so and thinly-scattered.

In Caithness there were minor trysts at Georgemas and in the strath of Dunbeath; in Sutherland at Clashmore, Monibuie and Dornoch; in Easter Ross at Kincardine (Ardgay?) and at Kildary (Haldane 1952. 106). St Barr's Fair in Dornoch, however, was reported to be 'the only regular

Fig. 12.18 The Clach Eiteag, quartz stone, that marked the local Kincardine fairs. Now at Ardgay, 1983.

[cattle tryst] held within the county' (Henderson 1812. 115); whilst Kincardine's *Feille Edeichan*, market of the quartz stone [Fig. 12.18], although it offered a 'fine shew of Highland cows, fattened on the best heath' and said to be most flavoursome and tasty in their beef, could not possibly supply the increasing demands of the South Country drovers. The market was only once a year, moreover, held in the last week of November as at Dornoch, or in the first of December — far too late for the southern trysts (Gallie 1790. 517; Allan 1840. 432).

Certainly there had been plans much earlier, enshrined in an Act of the Scottish Parliament in 1686, to allow David Ross of Balnagown to raise 'the village of Ardgay to a barony to be called *Bonarness*, with burgesses, a tollbooth, baillies, courts of justice, a market cross, a weekly market and two annual fairs'. But this had never materialized (Allan 1840. 432 footnote). Nor by 1840, in the adjacent parish of Edderton to the east, was there yet a fair or market of any kind, '... and there is only one small inn, or rather alehouse, which is situated on the Struy road from Bonar Bridge to Sittenham' (Gordon 1840. 459). This alehouse, nonetheless, a forerunner presumably of the Aultnamain Inn, reflects the existence of a key drove route.

Rather was it in Sutherland, where there had been particularly strong complaints about earlier malpractices, that a series of new fairs was established in 1811 specifically for the sale of black cattle [Fig. 12.19]. They were sited on the main droving routes and timed to link with the

205

NEW FAIRS FOR BLACK CATTLE, EASTERN SUTHERLAND, 1811

A. Location	Dates	
DUILLISH (Kildonan, on the cattle road south from Caithness and Strathnaver)	14 August	12 September
↓		
PITENTRAIL (Rogart, Strathfleet, on the line of the same cattle road south, and near the junction with cattle roads from the west and north-west)	16 August	16 September
↓		
connecting with the great markets at:		
↓		
KYLE (of Sutherland)	19, 20, 21 August	18 September
↓		
and connecting with the great trysts at:		
↓		
FALKIRK	2nd Tuesday in September	2nd Tuesday in October

B. Location	Dates	
KNOCK-GLASS (parish of Clyne on the cattle road from Caithness)	9 October	
↓		
PITENTRAIL (Rogart, Strathfleet)	11 October	
↓		
connecting with the great tryst at:		
↓		
BEAULY	18 October	

Fig. 12.19 Details of new cattle fairs as listed in J. Henderson, *Additional Report of the More Recent Improvements in the County of Sutherland, 1811* (in Henderson 1812. 149–50).

principal trysts in the south. Their establishment was very much in line with Sir John Sinclair's proposals some sixteen years previously:

> Drovers from the south of Scotland may expect to find great numbers of Highland cattle at these newly established fairs or trysts, which will suit their views for the southern markets, and will prove of advantage to the Sutherland and Caithness farmers or cattle dealers, in getting fair prices, and ready money, for their cattle. (Henderson 1811, in 1812. 150).

Drove Routes in the North

The cattle from Caithness were brought down the east coast by Helmsdale and Brora where they met with stock from the glens of eastern Sutherland; also with stock from Strath Halladale and Strath Naver and from other hilly areas in the far north-west. They continued down to the Dornoch Firth. In general, however, the cattle from the north-west, from the Reay country in particular, were brought south-east by Loch Shin and Lairg to the Kyle of Sutherland where, crossing the narrows, they met with the east coast droves and also with droves from Assynt and Edderachillis brought down the Oykell [Fig. 12.20]. They went up over Struie (a drove stance is still marked on the map and visible on the ground beside the A836 south of Strathrory: NH 653752) or by routes further west to Strath Rusdale, before dropping down towards the Cromarty Firth, to Dingwall and the south.

South of Assynt on the west coast, and into Coigach, there was equally a degree of choice. Droves from Coigach could travel east by Loch Achall across to Kincardine; more usually, they would join the principal routes from Wester Ross by which mainland beasts (and beasts from Lewis and Harris landed at Ullapool, Gruinard or Aultbea) went east to Garve, Dingwall and Muir of Ord. Hebridean stock landed at Poolewe on the other hand travelled the north shore of Loch Maree, joining with the Lochcarron droves at Achnasheen before merging with the more northerly Wester Ross droves at Garve.

Many of these through-routes are of considerable antiquity, though documentary references are scanty. Defoe tells of droves from Caithness destined for East Anglia and Sussex in 1726, whilst in 1703 the Sutherland Estates were certainly exporting on the hoof (Defoe 1724 (1762 ed.). IV. 253; Sutherland Estate Papers, Bundle 19. nos. 619–44): 'Your Lordship will be pleased to order one of your drovers to give me [Charles Ross, in Edinburgh] two fatt cows to be my winter beef.' More specifically, litigation reaffirmed long-standing routes by the north shore of Loch Maree to Kinlochewe and beyond; also up the Gruinard River, past Loch-na-Shellag and on to either the Ullapool–Dingwall or Achnasheen–Garve tracks. Additionally, Roy's map confirms mid-eighteenth century routes from Loch Broom to Dingwall via Strathgarve, whilst some twenty or so years later Pennant remarked on the Craven-in-Yorkshire drovers coming up to Loch Broom. The same route by Strath Garve was the only practical one (Pennant 1772. I. 364: see also Haldane 1952. 103–09).

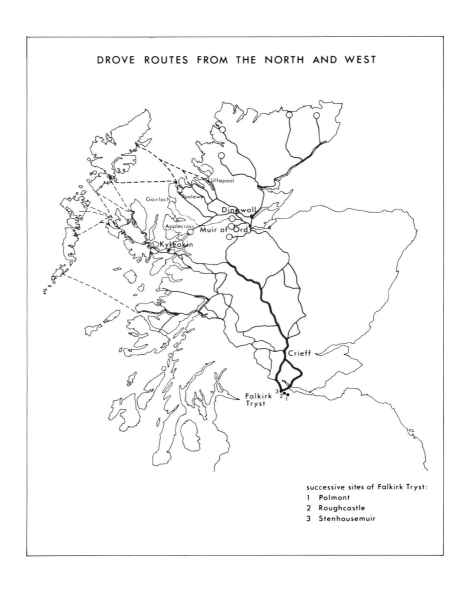

DROVE ROUTES FROM THE NORTH AND WEST

Ullapool
Gairloch Poolewe
Dingwall
Applecross Muir of Ord
Kyleakin

Crieff

Falkirk
Tryst

successive sites of Falkirk Tryst:
1   Polmont
2   Roughcastle
3   Stenhousemuir

Fig. 12.20   Drove routes from the north and west. After Haldane, *Drove Roads of Scotland*, 1952.

In so many cases the exact routes can no longer be determined. They were carried in the head and died with the last of the drovers. A sympathetic understanding of the shape of the land might suggest the reconstruction of routes; otherwise we are left with a few sparse records and with the lingering memories of those west coast crofters who were still taking sheep and a few cattle eastwards in the early decades of the present century.

In the 1940s, for instance, Haldane (1952. 108) noted not only that Lewis cattle had been landed at Ullapool within living memory, but that cattle from the Ullapool area were driven at times to Ardgay rather than to Dingwall. They took a route through Glen Achall and into the head of Glen Einig. Then, rather than continuing down into Strath Oykell, the track branched at Craggan over to Strath Cuileannach and down Strath Carron. This route seems to have been used regularly when taking beasts to the late autumn sale at Ardgay, and was used also perhaps by the tinkers who formerly bought horses at the Ardgay markets and sold them around the Coigach countryside (D. Fraser 1972).

Coigach informants are able equally to document the stances and routes used locally until the late 1920s and early 1930s. From Culnacraig, south-east of the main crofting settlements around Achiltibuie, there were three possible routes: an upper route following a shelf under the main ridge of Ben More Coigach, a middle route, and also a low and precipitous sea route, very dangerous for livestock. By the 1920s, however, these routes had fallen out of favour. Rather did the crofter first take his animals across the moor to Badagyle returning home for the night, then ford the Oscaig river the following morning and continue by the rough, untarred road to Drumrunie and Morefield, just outside Ullapool. Here, on a site belonging to the Cromartie Estates, a man was paid so much per 100 to look after the animals. There were further paid stances at Loch Droma and the Aultguish Inn, whence the way to Garve lay over the Corriemoillie Forest. They arrived at Garve 'in the darkling', where they left the animals inside a fence, without paying; thence to the Achilty Hotel (paid stance) and on to Dingwall. An alternative route from Aultguish lay through the Bealach Mór between Ben Wyvis and Little Wyvis, to Auchterneed and Dingwall (D. Fraser 1972).

All the drove roads from the far north and north-west, therefore, converged on Easter Ross, where they joined to form a mighty flood:

> We believe the great Northern Drove Road begins somewhere about the Kyle of Sutherland (at which place a number of important cattle markets are held throughout the year) and runs nearly parallel with one of the Parliamentary roads for a considerable distance, through the lands of Ardross, by Fowlis, and Dingwall to the Muir of Ord (another great market) — then branching away through the mountains towards Fort Augustus and from thence southwards — avoiding the public lines of road throughout the whole distance till it touches occasionally on the turnpike roads in Perthshire. There are other branch drove-roads leading from various parts of the country into this line, but this is unquestionably the principal one as proceeding direct from two of the greatest market stances in the North of Scotland. (*Inverness Courier* 26 September 1827).

Just as centuries before, because of its central, accessible position, Dingwall was selected as the *Thing-vellir* or assembly field of the Norse-speaking settlers whose legacy of place-names is so strong in much of Easter Ross and east Sutherland, so in the eighteenth and nineteenth centuries that narrow neck of low-lying land linking the heads of the Cromarty and Beauly Firths formed a natural assembly point for the droves from the north and west. The Kyle of Sutherland, at the head of the Dornoch Firth, was only the lesser because its hinterland was that much smaller; its key markets were also established in 1811, at the same time as those near Beauly, the *Feill-na-manachainn*. The site of the Beauly trysts was later moved about a mile further north, more accurately justifying the name 'Muir of Ord', though termed in Gaelic *Blair dubh*.

Southwards from Muir of Ord there were two major alternative routes [Fig. 12.20]. Although after 1817 Inverness became the great centre for sheep and wool in the north of Scotland, the cattle route via Inverness and Aviemore seems never to have been as attractive to drovers as that through Strathglass, by Guisachan and over to Glen Moriston, then to Fort Augustus and over the Corrieyairack Pass to Dalwhinnie where all the northern routes merged once again to travel through Drumochter and thence to the great trysts at Crieff or, shortly after 1750, at Falkirk (Haldane 1952. 112–14).

Roads, Ferries and Bridges

If the firthlands became a natural focus for the northern droves, they were equally so for the 'Parliamentary roads' referred to in the *Inverness Courier* (ibid.).

This was a time, around the late eighteenth and early nineteenth centuries, when improved communications became increasingly crucial to the new commercial development and economic success of the Highlands. Around 1790, for instance, the British Fisheries Society, on the recommendation of John Knox, undertook to make a road from Contin to Ullapool, where it had recently founded a new fishing station. The road was built between 1792 and 1797 by Kenneth MacKenzie of Torridon at a cost of £4,582, rather than for the original £8,000 which the Government had considered excessive. But so poor was its quality that within twelve years it was abandoned (MacRae 1792–93. 558; Ross 1835. 88–89; Haldane 1962. 12–13). It had, however, provided work for the poor and needy, and pointed the way both for future projects and future employment opportunities for some of those who had been dispossessed.

In 1803 a Commission for Highland Roads and Bridges was established; in 1814 it took over the improvement and maintenance of nearly 500 km (308 ml) of old military road; by 1828 it had constructed some 1,435 km (829 ml) of new road across the Highlands and created a major network north and west of Inverness — roads to Strathglass, Loch Carron, Tongue, Wick and Thurso, as well as that through Easter Ross to Tain and Bonar, and one through the Black Isle to Fortrose. It was all a long way

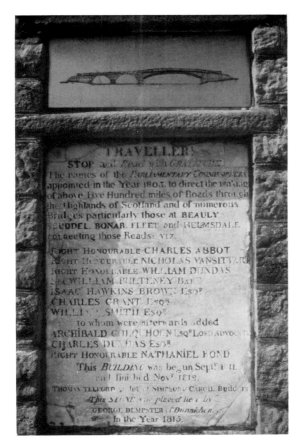

removed from Thomas Telford's report of 1803: 'Previous to the year 1742, the roads were merely the tracks of Black Cattle and Horses, intersected by numerous rapid streams, which being frequently swoln [*sic*] into torrents by heavy rains, rendered them dangerous or impassable.' (in Haldane 1962. 118).

It was the bridges, however, that were of even greater benefit to the drovers. For whilst the new trysts at Beauly, Muir of Ord and the Kyle of Sutherland were each a natural focus in the movement of stock west to east and north to south, their very locations underlined one of the main obstacles to droving — as to other developments in the north. The Kyle of Sutherland, that magnificent narrow stretch of tidal water fed by the rivers Shin, Cassley, Oykel and Carron had to be crossed; so did the major rivers Conan and Beauly.

In 1801, the solid and handsome five-arch Conon Bridge was built; in 1812, following the overturning of the infamous Meikle Ferry in 1809

Fig. 12.22   The iron Telford bridge at Bonar had a 150 ft (45.7 m) main span.
William Daniell aquatint, 1821.

Fig. 12.23   'Old' Bonar Bridge, destroyed by floods 1892.

when over 100 travellers drowned, Telford's Bonar Bridge was completed [Figs. 12.21–12.23], 'a spider's web in the air ... the finest thing that ever was made by God or man' (Southey (1819) 1929. 128–29; Holloway & Errington 1978. 102–03, 116). The iron bridge with its span of nearly 46 m (150 ft) was built by the Shropshire bridge-builders, Simpson and Cargil, and so successful was it in withstanding a frozen battering-ram of logs flooded down from the river Carron in the winter of 1813–14, that a similar bridge was commissioned for the Spey at Craigellachie. By 1813 the stone-built Lovat Bridge over the Beauly river was also complete, though during construction it too had been threatened periodically by timber floated downstream from Chisholm lands (ibid. 129; Allan 1840. 422; MacKenzie & MacDonald 1840. 378).

The last great stretch of water to be crossed was Loch Fleet, a problem solved in 1818 not by a bridge but rather by running a road over a 915 m (1,080 yd) long earthen mound or dam near the junction of the River Fleet and the upper end of the wide, shallow sea loch. Uni-directional flood-gates let fresh water pass outwards as the tide fell, but kept back salt water as the tide rose (Haldane 1962. 131), so that over 160 ha (400 acres) were reclaimed from the sea, part of which remains a wetland habitat to the present day.

It had taken nearly thirty years for initial suggestions and requests for the various crossings to be translated into reality. For it was back in 1791 (Rainy 1791. 341) that a bridge at government expense had been mooted for the Kyle at Culrain, presumably at or near the site of the later, present railway viaduct:

> Such a bridge would be particularly convenient for drovers; all the cattle driven to the south from Sutherland, Caithness, and Lord Reay's country, except the parish of Assint, having hitherto been obliged to cross the Kyle by swimming; which, when the weather is bad, and the Kyle much swelled by rains, hurts the cattle greatly, especially when the night following proves cold. Sometimes they refuse to swim, in which case they must be ferried over by the coble.

For good measure, the people claimed to foretell whether they would have a good market or not by the readiness of the cattle to swim (ibid.)!

Perhaps the best-known example of cattle swimming a kyle is that from Skye to the mainland [Fig. 12.24]. At the lowest ebb at Kyle Rhea (where the flood tide runs at over 11 km or 7 ml an hour), a 1 m (3 ft) length of rope with a noose at one end was put under the jaw of each cow in front, to a total of six or eight beasts, and a man standing in the stem of the four-oared boat held the rope of the foremost cow (Robertson 1808. xxxviii–xxxix). An earlier account of the same crossing, in 1787, described how:

> one is tied by the horn to a boat; a second is tied to the first; and a third to the second; and so on, to eight, ten or twelve ... [By contrast] ... When horses are to be taken over, they are pushed off the rock into the water. A small boat with five men attends, four of them holding halters of a pair on each side of the boat. (Knox 1787. 11–12).

The scene on a kindly day may well have resembled that from Port Askaig, from where cattle were transported from Islay to Jura, on their journey to the mainland (MacCulloch 1824. III. 103):

> The shore was covered with cattle; and while some were collected in groups under the trees and rocks, crowding to avoid the hot rays of a July evening, others were wading in the sea to shun the flies, some embarking, and another set swimming onshore from the ferry-boats; while the noise of the drovers and the boatmen, and all the hustle and vociferation which whiskey did not tend to diminish, were re-echoed from hill to hill, contrasting strangely with the silence and solitude of the surrounding mountains. The disembarkation formed a most extraordinary spectacle.

The Kyle of Sutherland, however, at or above Bonar, was more like a river, albeit tidal. In his *Letters from the North of Scotland* (1754. II. 133–34), Burt tells of an incident where such a river was in spate and where the only boat was to carry the drovers:

> The Cows were about fifty in Number, and took to the Water like Spaniels; and when they were in, their Drivers made a hideous Cry to urge them forwards ... to keep the Foremost of them from turning about; for, in that Case, the rest would do the like, and then they would be in Danger, especially the weakest of them, to be driven away and drowned by the Torrent.

Major rivers such as the Conon and the Beauly must have presented many such problems; smaller rivers in spate, too shallow to swim and too rapid to ford, would have been even more formidable, requiring on occasion considerable detours and delays.

If crossing rivers and the sea was time-consuming, so also was the process of walking the land. The main period of droving began in May, though stock was assembled from March or April until November. This allowed beasts to gain strength after a winter of near-starvation (in earlier times at least), as well as seeing past the worst of the weather; but if the animals were to reach the south of Scotland in good condition they could only move at a gentle pace [Fig. 12.25]. Although Coigach informants tell of 24 km (15 ml) a day for cattle (as compared to 16–19 km or 10–12 ml for sheep), this would hold good only over fairly short distances. For the two and three weeks it would take to move the droves to the southern trysts, four weeks from Caithness and northern Sutherland, a daily journey of 16–19 km (10–12 ml) was enough, particularly when the droves increased in size, numbering thousands of animals and stretching for miles along what for the most part were ill-defined tracks across and through the hills.

Increasingly well-made and metalled roads were a problem in later years, liable to injure the cattle's feet and to wear down their hooves. To counter such problems, Telford had insisted on the generous use of gravel in the north (Haldane 1962. 218) [Fig. 12.26], but shoeing became increasingly usual for those parts of journeys which had to follow the new roads. Trinafour, on the main drove route from Drumochter to Crieff was once such a shoeing stopover; Tyndrum south of Rannoch another. But

Fig. 12.24 Ferrying cattle at Kyleakin, Skye. Old postcard.

for the northern droves, shoeing took place around Muir of Ord and Dingwall. Perhaps seventy a day could be shod, perhaps on the outer edge only — but it must have been difficult work with half-wild cattle, fresh from Highland grazings and unused to handling (Haldane 1952. 34–35). Such, however, was the effect of metalled roads on unshod cattle bought at the sales in Dingwall and driven back to Coigach in the earlier part of this century, that they could travel only 6–8 km (4–5 ml) a day, and even then their hooves were badly worn down. Consequently they were left on a hill above Drumrunie for a week before the final stages to Achiltibuie. This let their hooves heal; it also allowed them to graze land they would not otherwise exploit.

The End of the Road

The flow and ebb of droving as a way-of-life must always be seen in the wider context of social and economic change. In the century between the Union of the Crowns and that of the Parliaments, 1603–1707, cattle had become Scotland's chief export, replacing fish, wool, hides and skins so that 'The country was little else than a mere grazing field for England' (Walker 1812. 1. 307–08). Cattle remained the principal export until the mid-eighteenth century, then fell to fifth or sixth by 1810–12. Yet in spite of the rapidly-growing sheep trade, actual numbers of black cattle sold continued to rise, encouraged by improved agriculture, communications and marketing, by growing urban appetites, and by the French Wars of 1792–1815. In 1723, therefore, Crieff had disposed of 25,000–30,000 head yearly; by the turn of the century some 50,000–60,000 were sold annually at the Falkirk Trysts (which had replaced those at Crieff); by 1827 annual sales are said to have numbered close on 150,000 cattle, together with rapidly increasing numbers of sheep (*Stirling Journal* Sept. & Oct. 1827).

Fig. 12.25   The beginning of a drove, Skye. Old postcard.

Fig. 12.26   Highland cattle in (?)Argyll. Old postcard.

But in the decades after 1860, and into the new century, though the trade in livestock continued to thrive, the means whereby they reached the markets entered a new phase. Railways spread their tentacles to Oban, Mallaig and Kyle, Wick and Thurso; steamships opened up the west coast; new marts run by auctioneers appeared at the new rail- and steamer-heads; cattle floats followed tortuous new roads into remote communities. And all the while, the increasing enclosure of wastes and commons made the overnight grazing of herds and flocks by drovers the more difficult, and physically fragmented the old routes, barring progress through the country.

As these obstacles to droving multiplied, a further factor contributed to its decline — the continuing disintegration of the old Highland economy which held cattle husbandry so highly. So today, it is in the knowledge and skills of the occasional ghillie, stalker and poacher, heirs to the cattle-raider, drover and herd, that lie the lineal but fragmentary echoes of a cultural and economic heritage that stretches back through Norse-spiked Celtic Scotland and Ireland to those pre-agricultural, pastoral societies of prehistoric Europe.

POSTSCRIPT

A Kincardineshire drover, Andrew Law, finally 'retired' in 1968. He never drove cattle, only sheep, but recalls a time in 1915 when he took a 'sma drove' of 540 sheep from Lairg to Perth. The route was termed 'the lang park'; he had two dogs; it took 28 days, 6.00 a.m. to 7.30 p.m.; he earned what he considered was good money, half in advance and half on delivery.

> But we took a lot o ... bye roads ... auld roads ... auld drove roads ye ken ... lot of auld drove roads we kent ...

> ... they fed on the road ... the front yins started eatin, an aye ... they had a good feed ... an then they landed at the tail ... well then they started walkin for'ard agin an we used tae continual circle roond ...

> ... ye were never harsh, ye ken ... ye juist let them stroll awa ... ye's juist like a drunk man ... the road was broader than it was lang, an ye strolled back an for'ard, back for'ard ... set up an fill'd yer pipe an carried on beside ...

> ... ye juist come near a corner o a hoos an ye juist walk up beside the sheep an ask the wifie if the teapot was aye het ...

> ... sometime ye caa'd an it was gettin pretty dark ... an if you've seen a nice gress field at the side o the road ... a bitty awa fae the ferm ... you juist caa's em doon there ... an that's you an the dugs lay doon at the back o the dyke ...

> ... cattle drovers' dugs was nae use on the sheep ... they were rauch ... they hed tae be ... some o yon cattle stuck a horn underneath a dug ... when he com up ... heaved him up in the air ... they hed to be tough, the cattle drovers' dugs, I'm tellin ye ...

... they didnae stand lang the cattle drovers ... an awfi speed cattle beside sheep, ye know ... ye hae an awfi job wi sheep tae get them ten mile oot doon the road in a day, ye ken ... generally only about seven, eicht mile a day, ye's ken ... knockin alang, nae bad ...

... the real, auld, auld drovers they used tae cairry a poke o meal an their cup, an their spoon ... then juist when they were hungry they juist put some meal in their cup, ye ken, a wooden cup ... an juist gaed tae the burn an put on water an ... what ye could call stir ... an that was a that they ate all the way doon ... maybe come doon fae Caithness richt doon tae Falkirk ... tae the trysts at Falkirk ... there was nae marts then ... they were all open sales ...

Acknowledgement

Much of the oral tradition relating to droving and livestock husbandry in Coigach was collected in the early 1970s from Mr D. Fraser (Achnahaird), Mr J. A. Campbell and the late Mr D. MacLeod (Culnacraig). My sincere thanks to them for their invaluable assistance. Material from Mr A. Law (Arbuthnot, Kincardineshire) was recorded by the National Museum of Antiquities of Scotland (now part of the Royal Museum of Scotland) in the late 1970s, and is housed in the archives of the Country Life Section. I am grateful for access to these recordings.

Illustrations are reproduced by kind permission of the Royal Commission on the Ancient and Historical Monuments of Scotland (Figs. 12.4, 12.9, 12.11, 12.12, 12.13, 12.14, 12.20), the Scottish Ethnological Archive in the Royal Museum of Scotland (Figs. 12.5, 12.6, 12.7, 12.8, 12.10, 12.15, 12.20, 12.23, 12.24, 12.25, 12.26), the National Gallery of Scotland (Figs. 12.16, 12.17, 12.22) and the Scottish Tourist Board (Figs. 12.1, 12.2). Mrs Jane Davidson of the Place-Name Survey in the School of Scottish Studies very kindly typed the manuscript; Figure 12.2, as well as the introductory map of the Firthlands, was drawn by Douglas Lawson.

References

Adam, R. J. (ed.), *John Home's Survey of Assynt.* (1775) 1960.
Aiton, W. *General View of the Agriculture of ... Ayr.* 1811.
Alexander, W. *Notes and Sketches, being Illustrations of Northern Rural Life in the Eighteenth Century.* 1876.
Allan, H. Parish of Kincardine, in *NSA.* 1840. XIV.
Anon. On Perthshire Husbandry, in *Farmer's Magazine.* 1808. 434.
Arthur, R. Parish of Kirkmichael & Cullicudden, in *OSA.* (179?) 1981. XVII.
Balfour, G. Parish of Tarbat, in *OSA.* (1792) 1981. XVII.
Bethune, H. Parish of Dingwall, in *NSA.* 1837. XIV.
Bethune, J. Parish of Dornoch, in *OSA.* (1791) 1979. XVIII.
Brown, P. H. *Early Travellers in Scotland.* (1891) 1973.
Brown, P. H. *Scotland before 1700 from Contemporary Documents.* 1893.
Burt, Capt. *Letters from the North of Scotland.* 2 vols. (1754) 1974.
Campbell, D. Parish of Tarbat, in *NSA.* 1840. XIV.
Defoe, D. *A Tour thro' the Whole Island of Great Britain in 1724.* 4 vols. 1762.
Dickson, W. K. *The Jacobite Attempt of 1719.* 1895.
Dingwall, J. Parish of Far [*sic*), in *OSA.* (1790–91) 1979. XVIII.
Downie, A. Parish of Lochalsh, in *OSA.* (1793) 1981. XVII.
Downie, C. Parish of Contin, in *NSA.* 1837. XIV.
Downie, J. Parish of Urray, in *OSA.* (1791–92) 1981. XVII.
Falconer, A. Parish of Edderachylis, in *OSA.* (1791–92) 1979. XVIII.
Fenton, A. *Scottish Country Life.* 1976.

Fraser, A. *Tayvallich and North Knapdale*. 1962.

Gallie, A. Parish of Kincardine, in *OSA*. (1790) 1981. XVII.

Gordon, D. Parish of Eddertoun, in *NSA*. 1840. XIV.

Gordon, R. Descriptions of Caithness, Strathnaver, Ross, Assynt, Moray, Sutherland (?1640:1608–61), in MacFarlane, W. (ed.), *Geographical Collections relating to Scotland*. 3 vols. 1906–08.

Grant, I. F. *Everyday Life on an old Highland Farm 1769–1782*. 1924.

Haldane, A. R. B. *The Drove Roads of Scotland*. (1952) 1973.

Haldane, A. R. B. *New Ways through the Glens*. 1962.

Handley, J. E. *Scottish Farming in the Eighteenth Century*. 1953.

Henderson, J. *General View of the Agriculture of . . . Sutherland*. (1807) 1812.

Henderson, J. *General View of the Agriculture of . . . Caithness*. 1812[a].

Holloway, J. & Errington, L. *The Discovery of Scotland*. 1978.

Inverness Courier. 26 September 1827.

Kennedy, J. Parish of Killearnan, in *NSA*. 18??, XIV.

Knox, J. *The Highlands and Hebrides in 1786*. (1787) 1975.

Loch, J. *An Account of the Improvements on the Estates of the Marquess of Stafford, in the Counties of Stafford and Salop, and in the Estate of Sutherland*. 1820.

Macadam, A. Parish of Nigg, in *OSA*. (1793) 1981. XVII.

McCulloch, G. Parish of Loth, in *OSA*. (1791–92) 1979. XVIII.

MacCulloch, J. *The Highlands and Western Isles of Scotland*. 4 vols. 1824.

Macdonald, D. *Lewis: A History of the Island*. 1978.

MacDonald, Mr. *Agriculture of the Hebrides*. 1811.

Mackay, W. *Records of the Presbyteries of Inverness and Dingwall*. 1896.

Mackie, Mr. A Journey through Scotland (1723), in *Scots Notes and Queries*. July 1964.

MacKenzie, A. *The History of the Highland Clearances*. (1883) 1966.

MacKenzie, D. & Macdonald, J. United Parishes of Urquhart and Logie Wester, in *NSA*. 1840. XIV.

MacKenzie, G. S. *General Survey of the Agriculture of . . . Ross and Cromarty*. 1810.

MacKenzie, J. Parish of Lochcarron, in *NSA*. 1836. XIV.

MacKenzie, W. Parish of Assynt, in *OSA*. (1794) 1979. XVIII.

McKenzie, W. & Ross, H. Parish of Tongue, in *OSA*. (1791) 1979. XVIII.

McLiesh, J. Parish of Kilchoma, Islay, in *OSA*. 1794. XI.

McLeod, A. Parish of Rogart, in *OSA*. (1791–92) 1979. XVIII.

MacPhail, J. R. N. (ed.), *Highland Papers I, 1337–1680*. 1914.

MacRae, J. Parish of Glenshiel, in *OSA*. (1791–92) 1981. XVII,

MacRae, J. Parish of Glenshiel, in *NSA*. 1836. XIV.

MacRae, R. Parish of Lochbroom, in *OSA*. (1792–93) 1981. XVII.

Marshall, Mr. *General View of the Agriculture of the Central Highlands of Scotland*. 1794.

Morrison, J. Parish of Kintail, in *NSA*. 1836. XIV.

Morrison, R. Parish of Kintail, in *OSA*. (1792) 1981. XVII.

Munro, T. Parish of Kiltearn, in *NSA*. 1839. XIV.

Murdoch, J. Parish of Killarrow & Kilmany, in *OSA*. 1794. XI.

Parry, M. L. & Slater, T. R. (eds.), *The Making of the Scottish Countryside*. 1980.

Pennant, T. *A Tour in Scotland and Voyage to the Hebrides, 1772*. 3 vols. 1790.

Rainy, G. Parish of Criech, in *OSA*. (1791) 1979. XVIII.

Robertson, J. in 'Glasgow National' (1844), in MacKenzie, A. *The History of the Highland Clearances*. (1883) 1966.

Robertson, J. *General View of the Agriculture of . . . Inverness*. 1813.

Rose, D. Parish of Dingwall, in *OSA*. (1790–91) 1981. XVII.

Rose, L. Parish of Nigg, in *NSA*. 1836. XIV.

Ross, A. Old Highland Roads, in *Trans. Gael. Soc. Inv.* 1887–88. XIV.

Ross, T. Parish of Lochbroom, in *NSA*. 1835. XIV.

Ross, W. Parish of Clyne, in *OSA*. (1793) 1979. XVIII.

Russell, J. Parish of Gairloch, in *NSA*. 1836. XIV.

Sage, Mr. Parish of Kildonan, in *OSA*. (1791) 1979. XVIII.

Sinclair, J. *General View of the Agriculture of the Northern Counties and Islands of Scotland.* 5 parts 1795.
Sinclair, J. *General Report on the Agricultural State and Political Circumstances of Scotland.* 4 vols. 1814.
Smith, C. L. *Journal.* 1835.
Southey, R. *Journal of a Tour in Scotland in 1819.* 1929.
Stewart, A. *A Highland Parish or the History of Fortingall.* 1928.
Stirling Journal. Sept. & Oct. 1827.
Symon, J. A. *Scottish Agriculture: Past and Present.* 1959.
Walker, J. *An Economical History of the Hebrides and Highlands of Scotland.* 2 vols. 1812.
Wight, A. *Present State of Husbandry in Scotland.* 4 vols. 1778–84.

CONTRIBUTORS

JOHN R. BALDWIN, Chief Executive of the Scottish Wildlife Trust in Edinburgh, is monographs editor for the Scottish Society for Northern Studies.

MALCOLM BANGOR-JONES is a postgraduate student in the Department of Geography, University of Dundee.

ELIZABETH BEATON, Hopeman, works part-time as an investigator for the Historic Buildings and Monuments Division, Scottish Development Department.

RONALD G. CANT is Honorary Research Fellow, University of St Andrews

MONICA CLOUGH, Drumnadrochit, has been carrying out considerable research on the Cromartie Papers.

BARBARA E. CRAWFORD lectures in Medieval History at the University of St Andrews.

IAN A. FRASER lectures in the School of Scottish Studies, University of Edinburgh, and heads the Place-Name Survey.

CON GILLEN lectures in the Department of Adult Education and Extra-Mural Studies, University of Aberdeen.

ROD HOUSTON is Principal Teacher of Geography, Golspie High School.

IAN R. M. MOWAT is Librarian, University of Hull and formerly Associate Librarian, University of Glasgow.

JEAN MUNRO, Edinburgh, is an historian who, with her husband, R. W. Munro, has made detailed studies of the Lordship of the Isles.

GEOFFREY STELL is an investigator with the Royal Commission on the Ancient and Historical Monuments of Scotland, Edinburgh.

Illustrations

Cover   : Bonar Bridge, Kyle of Sutherland. William Daniell aquatint, 1821 (N.G.S.).
Inside Cover: Inner Dornoch Firth towards Bonar Bridge and the Kyle of Sutherland (S.T.B.).
p. 153   : Farmland of the Black Isle (S.T.B.).
p. 167   : Cromartie lands near Tain. D. McKenzie, 1818 (Earl of Cromartie).
p. 221   : Timber bridge in Strathgarve, 1976 (R.C.A.H.M.S.).
Inside Cover: Falls of Rogie, Easter Ross (S.T.B.).